de Gruyter Studies in Organization 54
Labour and Industry in the Asia-Pacific

de Gruyter Studies in Organization

International Management, Organization and Policy Analysis

An international and interdisciplinary book series from de Gruyter presenting comprehensive research on aspects of international management, organization studies and comparative public policy.
It covers cross-cultural and cross-national studies of topics such as:
— management; organizations; public policy, and/or their inter-relation
— industry and regulatory policies
— business-government relations
— international organizations
— comparative institutional frameworks.

While each book in the series ideally has a comparative empirical focus, specific national studies of a general theoretical, substantive or regional interest which relate to the development of cross-cultural and comparative theory will also be encouraged.
The series is designed to stimulate and encourage the exchange of ideas across linguistic, national and cultural traditions of analysis, between academic researchers, practitioners and policy makers, and between disciplinary specialisms.
The volumes present theoretical work, empirical studies, translations and 'state-of-the-art' surveys. The *international* aspects of the series are uppermost: there is a strong commitment to work which crosses and opens boundaries.

Editor:
Prof. Stewart R. Clegg, Faculty of Business and Technology, University of Western Sydney, Macarthur, Campbelltown, Australia

Advisory Board:
Prof. Nancy J. Adler, McGill University, Dept. of Management, Montreal, Quebec, Canada
Prof. Richard Hall, State University of New York at Albany, Dept. of Sociology, Albany, New York, USA
Prof. Gary Hamilton, University of California, Dept. of Sociology, Davis, California, USA
Prof. Geert Hofstede, University of Limburg, Maastricht, The Netherlands
Prof. Pradip N. Khandwalla, Indian Institute of Management, Vastrapur, Ahmedabad, India
Prof. Surendra Munshi, Sociology Group, Indian Institute of Management, Calcutta, India
Prof. Gordon Redding, University of Hong Kong. Dept. of Management Studies, Hong Kong

Barry Wilkinson

Labour and Industry
in the Asia-Pacific

Lessons from the Newly-Industrialized Countries

Walter de Gruyter · Berlin · New York 1994

Barry Wilkinson, Professor, Cardiff Business School,
University of Wales, College of Cardiff, U.K.

HF1416.6
.E18
W55

With 71 tables and 2 figures

1994

♾ Printed on acid-free paper which falls within the guidelines
of the ANSI to ensure permanence and durability.

Library of Congress Cataloging-in-Publication Data

Wilkinson, Barry, 1956—
    Labour and Industry in the Asia-Pacific : Lessons from the Newly-
Industrialized Countries / Barry Wilkinson.
    (De Gruyter series in organization ; international management,
organization and policy analysis ; 54)
    Includes bibliographical references.
    ISBN 3-11-012676-1 (alk. paper)
    1. Export marketing — East Asia — Case studies. 2. Export
marketing — Developing countries — Case studies. 3. Industrial
relations — East Asia — Case studies. 4. Industrial relations —
Developing countries — Case studies. 5. Industry and state —
East Asia — Case studies. 6. Industry and state — Developing
countries — Case studies. I. Title. II. Series: De Gruyter studies
in organization ; 54.
HF1416.6.E18W55   1994
382′.6′091724 — dc20
                                                  93-35002
                                                     CIP

Die Deutsche Bibliothek — Cataloging-in-Publication Data

Wilkinson, Barry:
Labour and Industry in the Asia-Pacific : Lessons from the Newly-
Industrialized Countries / Barry Wilkinson. — Berlin ; New York : de
Gruyter, 1994
    (De Gruyter studies in organization ; 54 : International management,
organization and policy analysis)
    ISBN 3-11-012676-1
NE: GT

Typesetting: Converted by Knipp Satz + Bild digital, Dortmund — Printing: Gerike
GmbH, Berlin. — Binding: D. Mikolai, Berlin. — Cover Design: Johannes Rother,
Berlin. — Printed in Germany.

For Julia and Lily

I owe you both one

Contents

Preface

At the time of writing the World Bank and the International Monetary Fund are reported to be in the process of reformulating their prescriptions for developing countries across the world on the basis of lessons from the East Asian Newly Industrialized Countries (*Financial Times*, 26 April 1993). Advanced Western nations are also looking to East Asia for lessons in how they might re-generate ailing industrial bases, and businesses the world over have been looking eastwards for some time to work out what advantages, now the 'cheap and docile labour' thesis has become less tenable, account for export competitiveness.

It has taken the West a long time to admit (and still many would not) that the Far Eastern economies are doing something which might be worthy of serious consideration, and that some aspects might actually be worthy of emulation. Now that East Asia *is* getting recognition as doing something unique, or at least different, it seems likely that the West will change. Western manufacturers are already desperately attempting to implement aspects of Japanese management systems (Oliver and Wilkinson 1992). Western governments have been slower to accept any lessons, but at the very least it now seems unlikely that the free market, non interventionist ideology which has dominated their thinking for over a decade can continue.

But while there is much for us as Westerners to learn, not everything in East Asia is rosy, and the East Asian nations are not without their own problems. The Asian NICs, on which the book focusses, have become even more highly dependent on Japan in an intra-regional division of labour and technology over the last ten years, and they now face the prospect of having to cope with the demands of independent trade unions and other interest groups in new international and domestic political climates. For each of the Asian NICs we explore these problems as they impinge on the inter-relations between the economic actors, broadly defined as the state, employers, and trade unions.

My interest in labour and industry in East and South East Asia derived from three years teaching and research at the National University of Singapore in the mid 1980s, where I experienced employment as one of the country's guest workers – albeit as a highly privileged professional. I was also able to observe first-hand the working lives of Singaporean employees, not just in the university, but in factories and on construction sites. Also during that time, and since then, I have been fortunate to have visited many other East Asian countries to conduct research and to share ideas with fellow academics and praticioners. These experiences have no doubt coloured my perspective, but nonetheless this book is written by a Westerner with a Western view of life – more specifically a Briton with a particular kind of outlook on how the world should be – and this is likely to be reflected in the sometimes sub-conscious choice of adjectives. I have, however, tried to present sufficient in the way of facts and alternative opinions for the reader to make his or her own interpretation of industry and labour in the East Asian NICs, informed by his or her own concerns.

One inevitably incurs many debts in writing a book, and in this case they are debts built up over a number of years. It is not possible to list all the people who have helped in one way or another, but I would like to give special thanks to the following: Park Duk Je of the Korea Air and Correspondence University, for sharing his ideas and for making it possible for me to undertake various works in Korea; the staff of the Korea Labour Institute for providing huge amounts of data and pointing me in the right directions; Tsai Ding Lin, and Kao Cheng Shu and his family of students at the University of Tunghai in Taichung; Chris Leggett, ex-National University of Singapore and now at the University of New South Wales, with whom I have collaborated on various projects; Choi Jong Pyo of Kon-Kuk University; Teresa Poon of Hong Kong Polytechnic and Gordon Redding of the University of Hong Kong; Nicole Woolsey Biggart of the University of California, Davis, who first convinced me that the East Asian economic cultures are as distinctly different from each other as are the Western economies, and her colleague Gary Hamilton; and closer to home Mair Price at the Cardiff Business School for being so professional and patient in turning my tables into legible form.

Barry Wilkinson
Cardiff, May 1993

List of Abbreviations

AFTA   ASEAN Free Trade Association
ANIC   Asian Newly Industrialized Country
APEC   Asia-Pacific Economic Cooperation
ASEAN   Association of South East Asian Nations

CFL   Chinese Federation of Labour (Taiwan)
CLA   Council of Labour Affairs (Taiwan)
CoWEC   Company Welfareism through Employers' Contributions
CPF   Central Provident Fund (Singapore)

DBS   Development Bank of Singapore
DLP   Democratic Liberal Party (Korea)
DP   Democratic Party (Korea)
DPP   Democratic Progressive Party (Taiwan)

EAEC   East Asian Economic Caucus
EC   European Community
EDB   Economic Development Board (Singapore)
EPB   Economic Planning Board (Korea)
EPZ   Export Processing Zone

FDI   Foreign Direct Investment
FKI   Federation of Korean Industries
FKTU   Federation of Korean Trade Unions
FTU   Federation of Trade Unions (Hong Kong)
FTU   Federation of Trade Unions (Taiwan)

GATT   General Agreement on Tariffs and Trade
GDP   Gross Domestic Product
GNP   Gross National Product
GSP   Generalized System of Preferences

HDB   Housing Development Board (Singapore)

IAC   Industrial Arbitration Court
IDB   Industrial Development Bureau (Taiwan)
IDB   Industry Development Board (Hong Kong)
IMF   International Monetary Fund
ISA   Internal Security Act (Singapore)
ITRI   Industrial Technology Research Institute (Taiwan)

JCC   Joint Consultative Committee

JETRO	Japan External Trade Organization
JIT	Just-in-time System
KDI	Korea Development Institute
KEF	Korea Employers' Federation
KMT	Kuomintang
Legco	Legislative Council (Hong Kong)
LMC	Labour-Management Council
LRC	Labour Relations Commission (Taiwan)
LSL	Labour Standards Law (Taiwan)
MFA	Multi-fibre Arrangement
MITI	Ministry of International Trade and Industry (Japan)
NAFTA	North American Free Trade Association
NCB	National Computer Board (Singapore)
NFTU	National Federation of Trade Unions (Korea)
NPB	National Productivity Board (Singapore)
NPC	National Productivity Centre (Singapore)
NTUC	National Trades Union Congress (Singapore)
NWC	National Wages Council (Singapore)
ONTA	Office of National Tax Administration (Korea)
PAP	Peoples' Action Party (Singapore)
QCC	Quality Control Circle
R&D	Research and Development
SATU	Singapore Association of Trade Unions
SDF	Skills Development Fund (Singapore)
SDU	Social Development Unit (Singapore)
SIAPA	Singapore Airline Pilots Association
SNEF	Singapore National Employers Federation
TPFL	Taiwan Provincial Federation of Labour
TQC	Total Quality Control
UPP	United Peoples' Party (Korea)
Urbco	Urban Council (Hong Kong)
VITB	Vocational and Industrial Training Board (Singapore)
WEC	Work Excellence Committee
WIT	Work Improvement Team

List of Tables and Figures

Introduction

It is with good reason that Western eyes are fixed on East Asia. The economic success of Japan has been followed by the rapid emergence of the highly export oriented Newly Industrialized Countries (ANICs) of Singapore, Korea, Taiwan and Hong Kong, then recently the Association of South East Asian Nations (ASEAN) of Malaysia, Thailand, Indonesia and the Philippines. And in the 1990s, the biggest tiger of them all, China, together with the Indo-Chinese economies of Vietnam, Cambodia, Laos and Myanmar, are tentatively but rapidly opening to contribute to and benefit from what is now the undisputed growth centre of the world. It is not just the developing world which looks on with interest. The advanced Western nations are also looking for lessons from the Asia-Pacific, and those 'Pacific-Western' developed nations of Australia and New Zealand would appear increasingly to identify themselves with the East Asian region and show a preference for pinning their economic future on the rising East rather than the declining West.

But it is less East Asia's rapid economic growth and business success *per se* which has been the cause of Western attention, and more the fact that the West's chronic economic problems are related to a crisis of world competitiveness which has been highlighted, and arguably to some extent caused, by the Asia-Pacific. It was with a confidence in their economic and technological superiority that the West, especially the United States, led the opening of world markets and encouraged the massive growth in international trade and capital mobility following World War II. Ironically it was also the West, and again especially the US, which provided the military and economic aid necessary to make East and South East Asia a bulwark against the international socialism which was spreading through Indo-China in the immediate post-war period. That East Asia might challenge American economic superiority within the space of three decades was contemplated by few. By the early 1970s East Asia was showing signs of winning in the international trade game: Japan was already coming to dominate various market sectors, but the West was complacent in a context of continued world growth. In the 1980s complacency disappeared. Faced with huge trade deficits with Japan and, even more alarmingly, increasingly with the ANICs, explanations for what went wrong were sought.

While some looked to the East, and especially Japan, for lessons in economics and business management, others sought to place blame for the West's problems of chronically high unemployment, industrial decline and trade deficits on the 'unfair' competition the East was unleashing on the West through gross labour exploitation, barriers to imports, and the conspiracies of government-business elites to carve up international markets and dominate the world economically.

The strong states the West had supported to prevent the world being over-run by the red menace were now guilty, it was implied, of betrayal. East Asia was exporting not just high quality and competitively priced consumer goods, but unemployment and economic malaise.

The response of advanced Western nations since the mid 1980s has been to attempt to shift the balance of competitive advantage back towards the West through forcing the appreciation of East Asian currencies, insisting on a liberalization of Asian markets, and making Western market penetration more difficult – especially through non-tariff barriers. In the meantime, when not baying for more protection against the East Asian onslaught, Western companies have been attempting to revive their own flagging fortunes by learning from the East, and especially the Japanese, about how to source raw materials, produce goods efficiently, and market them across the world.

The new protectionist sentiment in the West has not yet halted the growth of East Asian exports to the West, but for some East Asian economies at least it has slowed that growth, causing exporting problems, and in the process contributed to the urgency with which East Asian countries are attempting to restructure by moving into higher value knowledge intensive areas. Actions can be taken against the 'dumping' of mass produced standardized computer chips or electronic consumer goods, but not (yet) against exports of unique or custom designed products with an indigenous research and development content. But while Japan has an R&D capability to match or even surpass that of Western countries in increasing numbers of areas, the ANICs, on which this book focusses, still have a long way to go.

It is within this world economic context that the Asia-Pacific continues to develop, and the first chapter of this book considers this context in detail. The first chapter also explains in detail the inter-dependencies within the Asia-Pacific region: while being dependent on the West for export markets, intra-regional dependencies are less to do with markets for finished goods, and more with a hierarchical division of capital, labour and technology in which Japan, the ANICs, and the ASEAN countries (except Singapore) represent three tiers. In spite of significant and continuing political differences within the region, such are the economic inter-dependencies that it is increasingly appropriate to talk of competition from the Asia-Pacific *region* than from individual countries. The complex intra-regional division of labour and technology takes advantage of the varying assetts of the different countries, such that any finished exported consumer good is likely to have efficient labour and materials inputs from at least several different East Asian countries.

But understanding East Asian economic success and the nature of East Asian development demands more than an understanding of conventional economics, whose theories have failed dismally to account for the spectacular growth of the ANICs in particular. While a detailed explanation of the ANICs' economic structures and trade relations is provided, the country chapters attempt to describe the characteristics, roles, and inter-relationships between, the actors within each economy – state, employers and labour – who have been responsible for that success. As soon as we do this, the surface similarities between the East Asian economies begin to fall apart, to reveal diverse state roles, patterns of capital accumulation, organizational forms, and industrial relations. Further, these are changing – not least because of recent political transformations – and will continue to change through the 1990s. The intention is to provide an account which draws attention to the internal dynamics of the ANICs, rather than provide a static explanation, and to the conflicts of interest and ideology which underlie the common interest in economic growth, the outcome of which will influence the future of the economies.

While the book draws eclectically on various theories to help explain the roles of, and inter-relationships between, the economic actors in the ANICs, the concluding chapter focusses on the limits of univariate explanations of East Asian economic development before providing a comparative commentary on contemporary developments.

Chapter One: The Asia-Pacific Economy

This chapter locates the East Asian newly industrialized countries in the broader Asia-Pacific region and the world economy in order to provide the recent historical and contemporary context for detailed consideration of their specific national economies and capital-state-labour relations in later chapters. It begins by documenting the spectacular economic performance of the Asia-Pacific region since World War II, and focusses on the basis of growth – the penetration of export markets for manufactured goods. A discussion of intra-regional economic inter-dependencies suggests a 'semi-peripheral' status for the newly-industrialized countries between the 'core' Japan and the 'peripheral' South East Asian nations, though there are significant qualifications to this crude characterization. Special attention is given to Japan's activities in the Asia-Pacific and the potential problems as well as benefits these create. As a caveat, the key features of industry and labour in Japan are described. While a detailed explanation of the internal workings of the Japanese economy are beyond the scope of this book, it is important to provide a characterization for two reasons: first, the East Asian NICs are *not*, as is still too frequently assumed, 'new Japans', and readers may wish to compare and contrast Japan with the ANICs. Secondly, the Asia-Pacific economies have nonetheless selectively borrowed ideas from Japan – as in Malaysia's *Look East* policy and Singapore's adoption of enterprise unionism. Hence a brief discussion of industry and labour in Japan is useful to this contextual chapter. Finally in chapter one, the question of the prospects for the creation of a powerful Asia-Pacific economic alliance is explored.

This book is concerned primarily with industry in the four East Asian newly industrialized countries (ANICs) of Singapore, Hong Kong, South Korea and Taiwan, and discussion in this chapter is limited to those nearby countries whose national economies are closely inter-related in an intra-regional division of labour and technology. As well as Japan, these are four member states of the Association of South East Asian Nations (ASEAN). Singapore is a member state of ASEAN, but for the purposes of this book is characterized as an ANIC. For brevity, we will use the terms ANICs to refer to the newly-industrialized countries, and ASEAN4 to refer to Malaysia, Thailand, Indonesia and the Philippines. The nine Asia-Pacific countries of Japan, the ANICs and the ASEAN4 will be referred to collectively as the AP9.

This is not to deny the future potential importance of presently undeveloped countries such as Vietnam, North Korea and Papua New Guinea, nor the current relevance of the concept of a 'Pacific Basin' which takes in West coast America, Canada, Australia and New Zealand as well as the Asia-Pacific. But a line has to be drawn somewhere and it seems sensible to restrict analysis primarily to those East

Asian nations which in recent decades have grown most rapidly and economically have been the most inter-dependent. The most important ommission is of course China, whose economy (political developments willing) is poised to take off with potentially enormous regional and world economic consequences during the next two or three decades. China will be discussed later in the book, especially in relation to Hong Kong and Taiwan whose futures are so closely connected to mainland developments, but is given only brief attention in this chapter on the grounds that the discussion must be sensibly limited.

Economic Growth

As a major industrial power Japan was alone among the Asia-Pacific countries prior to World War II. Most of the rest were colonies subject to government from various nation-states, including of course Japan itself, and although the colonialists left behind, in some cases, significant infrastructures, the Asia-Pacific nations remained largely dependent economically on agriculture and the primary production of raw materials, or (in the cases of Hong Kong and Singapore) entrepot trade. Yet probably by the 1960s, and by all accounts by the late 1970s, the Asia-Pacific region had become *the* growth centre of the world. The rapid growth was treated with scepticism by many, but the optimists declared the twenty first century would be an 'Asia-Pacific century' – by the year 2000 the region would be as great as the US and Europe as an economic power (de Bettignies 1982; Lee Kam Hon 1989; Linder 1986). In the 1990s, even the sceptics might grudgingly agree that the Asia-Pacific century has arrived already.

Initially fixed on Japan, eyes were gradually turned to the ANICs and then to the whole region as economists and sociologists sought explanations of relative economic success, governments sought models which might guide their own national economies, and business leaders sought lessons in the management of organizations.

Industrial Growth

Trends in economic growth speak for themselves and are shown in table 1.1.

Apart from the Philippines, whose debt-ridden economy has faced severe problems due to endemic corruption and political turmoil which curtailed growth over the last decade or so, the growth performance of the AP9 has been spectacular and continues into the 1990s. The newly found wealth of the region is reflected in GNP per capita figures which indicate that the ANICs are rapidly catching up with the advanced West (table 1.2).

The rapidity of the industrialization which largely accounts for growth is indicated in table 1.3.

Table 1.1:   Annual Average GDP Growth in Selected Countries, 1965-1990 (%)

	1965-80	1980-89	1990
US	2.7	3.3	0.9
UK	2.9	2.6	1.2
Japan	6.6	4.0	5.6
Singapore	10.0	6.1	8.3
Korea	9.9	9.7	9.0
Taiwan	9.9	8.0	5.2
Hong Kong	8.6	7.1	2.5
Malaysia	7.4	4.9	9.4
Thailand	7.3	7.0	9.8
Indonesia	7.0	5.3	6.5
Philippines	5.9	0.7	NA

Sources: Council for Economic Planning and Development, Republic of China, *Taiwan Statistical Data Book 1992;* Ministry of Trade and Industry, Republic of Singapore (1991).

Table 1.2:   Per Capita GNP in Selected Countries, 1990 (US$)

US	22,101
UK	17,213
Japan	23,965
Singapore	11,753
Korea	5,562
Taiwan	7,954
Hong Kong	12,254
Malaysia	2,270
Thailand	1,387
Indonesia	572
Philippines	715

Source: Council for Economic Planning and Development, Republic of China, *Taiwan Statistical Data Book 1992.*

Readily apparent from table 1.3 is the time lag in industrial development between Japan, the ANICs, and the ASEAN4. Also apparent is the growth in services among the ANICs, some of whose economists and government leaders, perhaps ambitiously but not without grounds, have for several years been characterizing the shifts in economic structure as indicative of the emergence of *post-industrial* societies. Also noteworthy is the fact that Japan, like Germany but unlike the US

Table 1.3: Structure of GDP in Selected Countries by Sector, 1965 and 1989 (%)

	Agriculture		Manufacturing Industry		Other Industry		Services	
	1965	1989	1965	1989	1965	1989	1965	1989
US	3	2	28	17	10	12	59	69
UK	3	2	34	20	12	16	51	62
Germany	4	2	40	32	13	4	43	62
Japan	10	3	34	30	10	11	46	56
Singapore	3	0	15	26	8	11	74	63
Korea	38	10	18	26	7	18	37	46
Taiwan	24	5	22	36	8	7	46	52
Hong Kong	2	0	24	21	16	7	58	72
Malaysia*	28	21	16	20	11	17	45	42
Thailand	32	15	14	21	9	17	45	47
Indonesia	56	23	8	17	5	21	31	39
Philippines	26	24	20	22	8	11	46	43

* Figures for Malaysia are for 1975 and 1985.

Sources: Council for Economic Planning and Development, Republic of China, *Taiwan Statistical Data Book 1992;* Limqueco et al. (1989).

and UK, has maintained manufacturing industry at a relatively high level in the home country in spite of the recent rapid expansion of Japanese manufacturing capacity overseas, and is one indication of Japan's success in up-grading its home industrial base towards the highest value products and activities.

In the ANICs, the post-colonial administrations (Hong Kong is the exception) established during the two decades following World War II were quick to add an emphasis on the export of manufactured goods to their initial import substitution strategies of development. Foreign capital, often in the form of direct investment, was attracted by the availability of cheap factors of production, accomodating governments, and compliant labour, and the goods produced had ready markets in the capital-source countries and elsewhere in the world. The ANICs may be considered fortunate in the timing of their industrialization and export efforts because of the generally favourable world economic situation for large parts of the 1960s and 1970s (Nolan 1990), but strong export-led growth continued through the 1980s even as most advanced Western nations faced crises of industrial competitiveness of massive proportions.

The ASEAN4, on the other hand, were about a decade behind the ANICs in their own industrial take-off, and hence entered export markets at a less favourable time

(Robison 1989). Despite this, manufactured goods exports have grown rapidly for these countries too. Table 1.4 shows the massive growth of the importance of manufactured over other exports for the ASEAN4 and the ANICs since the 1960s.

Table 1.4:   Manufactured Goods as a Proportion of Total Exports in the ANICs and the ASEAN4, 1965-1989 (%)

	1965	1970	1975	1980	1985	1986	1987	1988	1989
South Korea	59.4	76.7	81.6	89.9	91.4	92.0	92.4	93.1	93
Hong Kong	87.1	92.9	93.2	92.4	91.6	92.1	92.4	91.6	96
Taiwan	41.5	76.1	81.1	87.9	90.5	91.0	91.8	NA	92
Singapore	34.4	30.5	43.3	53.9	58.4	65.5	71.7	74.4	73
Malaysia	6.0	7.4	17.9	19.0	27.3	37.3	39.5	43.9	44
Philippines	5.7	7.6	17.2	37.0	57.1	58.0	NA	62.2	62
Thailand	4.8	10.7	18.1	29.0	39.3	44.6	52.5	NA	54
Indonesia	NA	1.4	1.2	2.4	13.2	19.5	26.2	30.9	32

Source: Hirata (1992).

By the end of the 1980s, the combined exports of the ANICs were reaching levels comparable with those of Japan. The significance of this fact lies in a combined population for the ANICs of little more than a half of Japan's, and far lower levels of per capita GNP: the ANICs are hence far more export-dependent than Japan. The ASEAN4 as yet lag behind the ANICs in terms of exports, and especially manufactured exports, but their export performance is nonetheless remarkable. This is confirmed in table 1.5 which shows the ratio of exports to GNP for the AP9 in 1989.

The differences between individual countries apparent in table 1.5 need to be treated with care, since exports, unlike GNP, do not take account of value added. Nonetheless, and especially when the figures for the ANICs, the ASEAN4, and the AP9 are looked at as sub-totals, and in the light of the inter-dependence of the region as a manufacturing force, the export orientation is clear: the value of exports from the AP9 is one and a half times greater than US exports despite a GNP only two thirds the size. We will now examine the export orientation in more detail.

Export Orientation

The growth of exports, and particulary manufactured exports, has been greater for the Asia-Pacific than any other region for the past three decades. Of course at the same time imports have also grown remarkably quickly. Over the two decades of the 1970s and 1980s world trade expanded enormously, but of key importance

Table 1.5:   Ratio of Exports to GNP in Selected Countries, 1989

	GNP (US$ million)	Population ('000 persons)	Exports (US$ million)	Exports: GNP ratio (%)
US	5,248,200	247,347	346,948	6.6
UK	843,937	57,239	152,403	18.1
Japan	2,892,476	123,121	275,040	9.5
Singapore	28,888	2,680	44,600	154.4*
Korea	211,173	42,379	62,283	29.5
Taiwan	150,238	20,006	66,304	44.1
Hong Kong	64,036	5,674	73,076	114.1*
ANICs Total	454,335	70,739	246,263	54.2
Malaysia	35,278	17,353	25,053	71.0
Thailand	68,189	55,438	20,059	29.4
Indonesia	90,015	179,313	21,773	24.2
Philippines	41,919	60,142	7,774	18.5
ASEAN4 Total	235,401	312,246	74,659	31.7
AP9 Total	3,582,212	506,106	551,617	15.4

* Export figures for Singapore and Hong Kong are swelled considerably by re-exports. Domestic exports are US$ 28,731 million for Hong Kong, and US$ 28,330 million for Singapore, giving domestic export: GNP ratios of 44.9 and 98.1, respectively.

Sources: Calculated from data in Council for Economic Planning and Development, Republic of China, *Taiwan Statistical Data Book 1992*; Census and Statistics Department, Hong Kong (1990); Ministry of Trade and Industry, Republic of Singapore (1990).

here is the fact that trade between the AP9 and the rest of the world grew around twice as fast as world average trade growth. Table 1.6 demonstrates the emergence of the AP9 as major players on the world economic stage.

Examining table 1.6 we see that in 1989 Japan had a trade surplus (which has since grown) of US$ 65 billion with the rest of the world, US$ 49 billion of which was accounted for by the surplus with the US alone. The ANICs between them had a surplus of US$ 10 billion with the rest of the world, but this depended heavily on positive balances with the EC12 (US$ 10 billion surplus) and most especially the US (US$ 35 billion surplus). The ASEAN4 on the other hand were almost in trade balance, but still depended on surpluses with the EC12 (US$ 2.5 billion)

Table 1.6:　Trade Matrix for All Commodities, 1970 and 1989 (US$ million)*

From	To	AP9	Japan	ANICs	ASEAN4	US	EC12	World
AP9	1970	8,290	2,006	4,000	2,284	8,948	4,095	30,206
	1989	183,229	49,039	95,754	38,436	183,105	93,353	646,928
		(22.1)	(24.4)	(23.9)	(16.8)	(20.5)	(22.8)	(21.4)
Japan	1970	4,042		2,647	1,395	6,015	2,332	19,318
	1989	69,087		52,511	16,576	93,954	47,986	274,597
		(17.1)		(19.8)	(11.9)	(15.6)	(20.6)	(14.2)
ANICs	1970	1,903	746	502	655	2,029	1,021	6,376
	1989	77,804	30,876	28,162	18,766	73,804	34,058	247,493
		(40.9)	(41.4)	(56.1)	(28.7)	(36.4)	(33.4)	(38.8)
ASEAN4	1970	2,346	1,260	851	234	904	742	4,512
	1989	36,338	18,163	15,081	3,094	15,347	11,309	74,767
		(15.5)	(14.4)	(17.7)	(13.2)	(17.0)	(15.2)	(16.6)
US	1970	6,901	4,569	1,486	846		11,952	42,590
	1989	91,671	44,584	38,458	8,629		86,570	363,807
		(13.3)	(9.8)	(25.9)	(10.2)		(7.2)	(8.5)
EC12	1970	3,457	1,410	1,116	931	9,612	61,893	116,037
	1989	54,289	23,215	24,232	8,811	84,477	677,825	1,133,700
		(15.7)	(16.5)	(21.7)	(9.5)	(8.8)	(11.0)	(9.8)
World	1970	29,467	16,993	8,157	4,317	35,956	111,893	282,638
	1989	522,608	209,635	237,457	75,516	493,652	1,165,800	2,912,200
		(17.7)	(12.3)	(29.1)	(17.5)	(13.7)	(10.4)	(10.3)

* Figures in parentheses show the rate of expansion between 1970 and 1989.

Source:　Adapted from Hirata (1992).

and the US (US$ 6.7 billion) for their healthy situation. Hence the (manufactured) export dependence of the AP9 on the advanced Western countries, and especially the US, is quite remarkable.

Within the AP9 trade relationships are equally interesting and the figures equally telling. In 1989 the ASEAN4 had a US$ 1.6 billion surplus with Japan and a US$ 3.7 billion deficit with the ANICs. The ANICs on the other hand had a combined US$ 22 billion deficit with Japan. The ASEAN4's small surplus with Japan clearly relates to its provision of primary goods to a country short on natural resources. The ANICs' deficit with Japan is accounted for by a failure to penetrate the Japanese market with their own manufactured goods sufficiently to balance their dependency on imports of Japanese capital goods and technology.

The clear picture which emerges is an Asia-Pacific region which internally is highly inter-dependent in terms of a division of labour and technology, but which in turn is externally dependent on trade with the advanced Western nations. Asian economic inter-dependencies are explored in detail below.

Success of the region in the international trade game is unequivocal, and unsurprisingly has brought with it trade friction and accusations of unfair trade practices from Europe, and particularly from the US which ironically played such a key role in giving the Asia-Pacific its post-war political and economic shape.

Japan has been at the forefront of attacks, facing around 200 dumping cases brought by the US and EC in the decade to 1992 (*The Independent*, 6 February 1993). The ANICs have also been subject to severe criticism. In 1987 for instance the Finance Ministers and Central Bank Governors of the G7 industrial nations (US, Canada, UK, Germany, France, Italy and Japan) said the ANICs had 'greatly benefited from the openness of the international trading system and should now be prepared to assume greater responsibility'. This meant they should 'reduce trade barriers and allow their currencies to reflect fully the underlying strength of their economies' (*New Straits Times*, 18 April 1987). The realignment of currencies among the ANICs was not as dramatic as the G7 would have wished (Taiwan's currency strengthened the most – 32 per cent against the dollar between 1984 and 1990), but Japan's currency was forced up almost two-fold in the mid to late 1980s [table 1.7].

Japan's response to *endaka* (the high Yen crisis) is already legendary. There was a massive outflow of capital in the form of foreign direct investment in the late 1980s, but at home manufacturers managed to cut costs and improve efficiencies sufficiently to maintain export growth: one report by the Fuji Bank suggested that Japanese factories reduced the break-even point for the profitability of their exports from ¥ 210 to the dollar in 1985 to ¥ 114 in 1988 (*Financial Times*, 20 May 1989). The country's surplus for the 1992 calendar year, after falling at the turn of the decade, had balooned to US$ 107 billion and showed signs of growing further. Further action from the EC, and from the US under a new Clinton administration, seems inevitable.

Table 1.7:   Exchange Rates for Japan and the ANICs, 1984-1990 (National Currency
             Units per US$)

	1984	1985	1986	1987	1988	1989	1990
US	1.000	1.000	1.000	1.000	1.000	1.000	1.000
Japan	237.4	238.5	168.4	144.6	128.2	138.1	145.0
Singapore	2.133	2.200	2.177	2.106	2.012	1.950	1.813
Korea	806.0	870.0	881.4	822.6	731.5	671.5	707.8
Taiwan	39.60	39.85	37.84	31.84	28.59	26.41	26.89
Hong Kong	7.819	7.791	7.804	7.798	7.807	7.801	7.790

Source: Bureau of Labour Statistics, US Department of Labour (1991).

In response to political demands and upward pressure on their currencies, and equally importantly due to labour shortages and rising wages, the ANICs also accelerated investment outflows and the move towards higher value added (explored below), but again their trade surpluses with the advanced Western nations have remained stubbornly large.

Before discussing the implications of any further political pressure or action which might be taken by the West against Japan and the ANICs, we will turn attention to economic relations *within* the Asia-Pacific region.

Economic Inter-dependence

The massive growth in exports from the AP9 to the advanced West since the 1960s was based on the export of manufactured consumer goods, though lately the export of high value capital goods such as machine tools, robotics and sophisticated computers and automated equipment has increased markedly, primarily from Japan and very recently also from the ANICs. Economic relations *within* the AP9 region, on the other hand, has been less to do with trade in manufactured goods for mass consumer markets (though this is not unimportant) and more with the emergence of a division of labour and technology which allows the whole region to export to the rest of the world. Indeed, such is the inter-dependence within the region that it becomes increasingly difficult to separate out any single East Asian country for sensible discussion of its economy.

Economic Tiering

GNP per capita and economic structure data (tables 1.2 and 1.3) suggest a clear tiering of the AP9 between Japan, the ANICs and the ASEAN4. The structure of exports further confirms different situations and roles for the countries in the three tiers (table 1.8).

While all of the AP9 have greatly increased manufactured exports and, therefore, reduced the percentage share of primary goods in their export structures, the ANICs have been quicker to make the transformation than the ASEAN4, and the importance of their role in providing raw materials is now negligible. In 1989, Singapore still registered 27 per cent in the two primary categories, though these figures refer mostly to the export of petroleum and chemical products which have been processed by capital intensive methods for export. The most remarkable ANIC in terms of the rapidity of industrialization and growth of exports is Korea. Industrialization proper in this country got under way only in the early 1960s following the ravages of war and political turmoil (Park Duk Je 1992), but by 1989 we see an export stucture similar to the other ANICs. The ASEAN4 on the other hand still rely primarily on the export of primary goods, especially Malaysia and Indonesia, reflecting their more recent export orientations.

Also apparent from table 1.8 is a shift in *manufactured* export structure. Although a crude indicator, textiles and clothing are often contrasted with machinery and transport equipment categories to indicate levels of technological sophistication, capital intensity, value added and workforce skills. The 'sweated industries' of clothing and textiles has greatly reduced in significance in Japan since 1965, and the exceptionally high figure for machinery and transport equipment in 1989 reflects Japan's well known dominance of key international markets for products such as automobiles and electrical consumer goods.

In the ANICs the traditional textiles and clothing sector has reduced somewhat as a proportion of exports, but remains highly significant in absolute terms. The ANICs in fact have continued to dominate export markets not only for textiles but also other low technology products such as footwear, toys, and household appliances (Kim Won Bae 1991). However, there has been a tendency recently to sub-contract the most labour intensive aspects of production or to relocate manufacturing facilities to the ASEAN4. In the case of Hong Kong, whose textiles and clothing sector remains the most important manufacturing sector, extensive sub-contracting linkages have been developed in mainland China, and particularly the nearby Guangdong province, which take advantage of the vast reserves of cheap labour. Figures are not easily available, but it has been suggested that in the late 1980s around half the workers employed by Hong Kong firms were in China (Kim Won Bae 1991). Most of these are employed in manufacturing: one estimation was that by the late 1980s Hong Kong manufacturers employed twice as many workers in China as they did in Hong Kong (*The Independent*, 23 May 1988). By focussing the higher value activities of the sector within Hong

Table 1.8: Structure of Merchandise Exports in the Asia-Pacific, 1965 and 1989 (share of merchandise exports in %)

| | Percentage share of merchandise exports | | | | | | | | | |
| | Fuels, minerals and metals | | Other primary commodities | | Machinery and transport equipment | | Textiles and clothing | | Other manufacturing | |
	1965	1989	1965	1989	1965	1989	1965	1989	1965	1989
US	8	6	27	16	37	43	3	2	25	32
UK	7	10	9	8	42	40	7	3	35	37
Germany	7	4	5	6	46	49	5	5	37	36
Japan	2	1	7	1	31	65	17	2	43	30
Singapore	21	18	44	9	10	47	6	5	18	21
Korea	15	2	25	5	3	38	27	23	29	32
Taiwan	2	2	28	6	15	36	25	15	29	42
Hong Kong	1	1	5	2	7	23	52	39	25	34
Malaysia	34	19	60	37	2	27	0	5	4	12
Thailand	11	3	86	43	0	15	0	17	3	22
Indonesia	43	47	53	21	3	1	0	9	1	22
Philippines	11	12	84	26	0	10	1	7	5	45

Source: Council for Economic Planning and Development, Republic of China, *Taiwan Statistical Data Book 1992.*

Kong and automating production, a significant labour productivity advantage has been maintained (Hooley 1988) and the country has been able to continue its dominance. (Nonetheless, as we will discuss in chapter five, Hong Kong is probably the most backward of the ANICs in terms of technological sophistication in manufacturing industry.)

The growth in importance of the machinery and transport sectors in the ANICs reflects a diversification of industry and a shift to higher technology and higher value added products since the 1970s. White goods, automobiles and electronic consumer goods are all highly visible examples of the ANICs' shifting economic and export structures. Less visible but also important is the incursion of the ANICs into the markets for product components such as semiconductors and TV picture tubes which previously would have been imported, and for producer goods such as machine tools (Wade 1990).

The ASEAN4 have been slower to reduce their export dependence on primary goods, though they started from much higher bases of dependency. In these countries the growth of the textiles and clothing sector has been a result of the inevitable shift of capital and production capacity away from Japan and the ANICs as labour costs have become prohibitive. This was a trend recognized during the 1970s (Kim and Terpstra 1984). Interestingly, with the exception of Indonesia until the end of the 1980s, the ASEAN4 have at the same time developed a capacity for the production and export of machinery and transport equipment. However, in the latter sector, the labour intensive aspects of production, and particularly the final assembly of standardized mature products whose high value components are sourced from the ANICs or Japan, account for the bulk of activity (Abdullah 1991).

Very clearly then, there has been an advance of the whole AP9 from primary to manufacturing production. But within the AP9 there is a strong tiering of activities reflecting different stages of economic development and hierarchical economic relations: Japan has been the clear leader in shifting to technology and skill intensive manufactures; the ANICs have now virtually shed their dependence on exports of primary goods but are still in the process of shifting from low to high value added manufactures; and the ASEAN4 have only recently embarked on their export oriented industrialization programmes.

Divisions of Labour and Technology

While AP9 intra-regional trade in consumer goods is far less important than trade between the AP9 and the advanced Western nations, economic inter-relations are close, growing, and of crucial importance. This becomes clear when we examine patterns of foreign direct investment (FDI) and production inter-linkages.

While the US was the most important investor in the immediate post-colonial period, Japan gradually extended its own overseas investments in East and South

East Asia during the 1960s and 1970s as its economy recovered after World War II, then rapidly overtook the US as the most important source investment capital during the 1980s. In 1987 for instance Japanese direct investment in Malaysia accounted for 30.8 per cent of total FDI inflow (US 8.2 per cent), in Singapore 41.4 per cent (US 37.5 per cent) and in Thailand 69.4 per cent (US 16.8 per cent) (Chew Soon Beng et al. 1992). Table 1.9 shows the rapid growth in Japanese FDI in the Asia-Pacific from the 1950s.

Indonesia was the favoured location up to the early 1980s, though investments here were focussed mostly on mining and the primary processing of raw materials (Higashi and Lauter 1990; Saravanamuttu 1988). Hong Kong also has a high proportion of non-manufacturing investment (the bulk of the investment is in services and real estate). If we ignore these two countries, the manufacturing share of accumulated FDI from 1951 to 1988 becomes 57.1 per cent for the ANICs and 79.4 per cent for the ASEAN nations – both very high percentages compared with Japanese FDI in the advanced Western nations.

The manufacturing investments in which we are primarily interested have been well spread throughout the region, but a discernible trend for 1987 and 1988 over 1985 and 1986 was the shift in preferred location for manufacturing investments from the ANICs to the ASEAN4. This was clearly related to rising labour costs and labour shortages in the ANICs during the 1980s – a number of Japanese companies simply transferrred assembly plants from one country to another – and also relates to the ASEAN4 nations' attempts during the 1980s to improve their investment climates for international export oriented capital (Higashi and Lauter 1990).

The new trend of Japanese FDI in the Asia-Pacific has in fact accelerated sharply since 1988. In 1990, the ASEAN4 received around two and a half times more FDI from Japan than the ANICs, as shown in table 1.10.

The figures in table 1.10 are not directly comparable to those in table 1.9: table 1.9 indicates implemented investments and table 1.10 approvals which are not necessarily implemented during the year. Nonetheless the trend is striking and clear: since the late 1980s Japan has been by-passing the ANICs to invest directly in the ASEAN4, which are becoming the new export platforms for Japanese manufacturers. This means the ANICs are facing increased competition from 'Japan-Asia' (a term popularly used by economists in Korea to describe Japanese productive capacity in the ASEAN4) for export markets.

Alongside the emergence of *Japan-Asia* another phenomenon has emerged – one which is only recently becoming possible to discern in official statistics but is nonetheless real. This is the recent and very rapid development of direct investment from the ANICs to the ASEAN4 and China. Kim and Terpstra (1984) documented the beginning of outward flows of FDI from the ANICs in 1967: these had reached an annual flow of US$ 273 million by 1980, and over half of the accumulated total went to the ASEAN4 (15 per cent went between the ANICs). Although these figures were significant, they were relatively small compared with

Table 1.9: Trends in Japanese Foreign Direct Investment in the Asia-Pacific, 1951-1988 (US$ million)

	1951-1980	1981-1984	1985-1986	1987-1988	Cumulative total (1951-1988)
Singapore total	936	994	641	1,242	3,813
(manufacturing)	(688)	(664)	(197)	(441)	(1,990)
Korea total	1,137	412	569	1,130	3,248
(manufacturing)	(780)	(128)	(180)	(501)	(1,589)
Taiwan total	370	277	405	740	1,791
(manufacturing)	(348)	(229)	(383)	(518)	(1,477)
Hong Kong total	1,096	1,704	633	2,734	6,168
(manufacturing)	(184)	(49)	(66)	(193)	(492)
ANICs total	3,539	3,387	2,248	5,846	15,020
(manufacturing)	(2,000)	(1,070)	(826)	(1,653)	(5,548)
Malaysia total	451	595	237	550	1,834
(manufacturing)	(293)	(466)	(97)	(494)	(1,350)
Thailand total	396	315	172	1,109	1,992
(manufacturing)	(292)	(215)	(113)	(836)	(1,456)
Indonesia total	4,014	4,001	658	1,131	9,804
(manufacturing)	(1,527)	(743)	(93)	(593)	(2,955)
Philippines total	615	217	81	207	1,120
(manufacturing)	(236)	(76)	(57)	(141)	(510)
ASEAN4 total	5,476	5,128	1,148	2,997	14,750
(manufacturing)	(2,348)	(1,500)	(360)	(2,064)	(6,271)
China total	25	162	326	1,523	2,036
(manufacturing)	(2)	(30)	(45)	(273)	(350)

Source: Calculated from Japanese MITI and Japanese Ministry of Finance data.

Table 1.10:   Asia-Pacific Trade with Japan and Japanese Direct Investment in the Asia-Pacific, 1990 (US$ million)

	World trade		Trade with Japan		Direct investment inflow*	
	Exports	Imports	Exports	Imports	Total	From Japan
Singapore	52,752	60,899	3,581	10,739	1,223	391
Korea	60,457	68,453	11,743	17,499	803	236
Taiwan	67,214	54,716	8,506	15,461	2,302	839
Hong Kong	82,144	82,428	2,182	13,106	3,971	1,282
ANICs	262,567	266,496	26,012	56,805	8,299	2,748
Malaysia	29,409	29,251	5,411	5,529	6,517	1,557
Thailand	22,805	33,741	4,161	9,150	14,128	2,706
Indonesia	25,675	21,931	12,744	5,052	8,750	2,241
ASEAN3**	77,889	84,923	22,319	19,731	29,395	6,504

*   Approvals registered by recipient countries.
** Data for the Philippines not available.

Source: Adapted from JETRO (1992).

the Japanese FDI which, for good reason, attracted all the attention. However, in the late 1980s outflows of FDI from the ANICs suddenly grew rapidly. Official figures put Taiwanese and Korean overseas capital outflows at only just over US$ 200 million for 1988, but Clifford and Moore (1989) estimated the real figure for Taiwan was somewhere between US$ 2.2 and US$ 3.5 billion (most investments go through unofficial channels to avoid tax) and that for Korea stood at US$ 1.2 billion in paid-up capital (this understates the actual size of investment projects). According to government figures Korean FDI for 1990 was US$ 2.3 billion (*Korea Times*, 15 October 1991). Outbound FDI from Taiwan on the other hand was US$ 7 billion in 1989 and US$ 5.2 billion in 1990. Of the cumulative total of Taiwanese FDI in mid 1992, US$ 5 billion went to Malaysia, US$ 3.4 billion to Thailand, and US$ 2.8 billion to Indonesia (*Far Eastern Economic Review*, 9 April 1992). Hence most outbound FDI from the ANICs has gone to the ASEAN4 and China (Taiwan was Malaysia's biggest source of inward investment in 1989 [Lubeck 1992]), though substantial amounts have also been aimed at Europe and the US in anticipation of the need to circumvent trade barriers (*Korea Times*, 19 October 1991; McDermott 1992).

    The size the ANICs' outward investments at the turn of the decade are confirmed by figures from investment host countries compiled by JETRO: of the US$ 30.4

billion approved FDI directed to the ASEAN4 during 1990, the ANICs accounted for US$ 14.9 billion – double that from Japan and the US combined. In the same year the ANICs invested US$ 2.9 billion in China, and investments in Vietnam began to become popular, especially from Hong Kong and Taiwan, from 1991. By May 1992 Taiwan and Hong Kong between them had invested US$ 1.3 billion in Vietnam. Hence within the Asia-Pacific region the ANICs have become major net exporters of capital, a phenomenon which would have been predicted by only the bold few even just ten years ago. Intra-regional direct investment flows in the Asia-Pacific for 1990 are summarized in figure 1.1. (Reverse flows of FDI are not shown since they are neglible.)

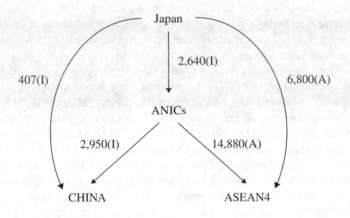

Figure 1.1: Direct Investment Flows in The Asia-Pacific in 1990 (US$ million)
            I = Implementation basis of calculation.
            A = Approvals.

Source: JETRO (1992).

Intra-regional trade figures also reflect inter-dependencies within the Asia-Pacific region. Table 1.10, which gives figures for 1990, suggests that 1989 (table 1.6) was no abberation: the combined trade deficit of the ANICs with Japan was getting even more marked – over US$ 30 billion compared with around US$ 20 billion in 1989 – and in the first half of 1991 each of the ANICs had deficits with Japan of over US$ 4 billion. Japan's surplus is explained largely by the ANICs' reliance, despite increases in their own capacity, on Japanese machinery and high value components which are necessary to their own production processes (Hanazaki 1992). And as the ANICs rapidly try to reduce labour intensity because of labour shortages, the investment in capital equipment is faster than can be supplied internally. For instance of Korea's US$ 18.6 billion imports from Japan in 1990, a huge US$ 10.8 billion-worth were of capital goods (Bank of Korea, *Monthly Balance of Payments*, October 1991).

Of course, the ASEAN4 nations are even more dependent on Japan (and the AN-ICs) for capital equipment and components, though obviously capital goods do not show up on trade figures when they are a part of direct investments. The ASEAN4's receipt of direct investments, together with exports of non-manufactured goods, helps explain their small surplus with Japan. Also significant is Japan's recent tendency to import goods manufactured or assembled by Japanese companies in the ASEAN4, which added up to around US$ 1.5 billion in 1990.

Inter-dependence between the AP9 is clear from the above discussion, but perhaps is most vividly illustrated in the concept of the 'growth triangle' which has emerged through the collaboration of Singaporean, Indonesian and Malaysian governments. Just as Hong Kong has served as a base for local and foreign capital to take advantage of cheap labour and potential markets in mainland China, Singapore is now attracting and retaining multinationals by promoting itself as a base for investments which can take advantage of the nearby Johore and Riau regions of Malaysia and Indonesia (Ministry of Trade and Industry, Republic of Singapore 1990). The idea is that Singapore provides the advanced infrastructure, communications facilities and professional expertise – Singapore recently introduced special tax incentives for companies setting up operational headquarters in Singapore (Tokunaga 1992) – while Malaysia and Indonesia supply land, energy and (relatively cheap) labour. In 1990 a joint venture of Singaporean and Indonesian companies actually established an industrial park on Batam Island which is owned by Indonesia but lies only 20 kilometres from Singapore: many multinational companies have been attracted already by the ready availability of the advanced services Singapore can offer and the cheap Indonesian labour (paid around US$ 60 per month in 1991) which is shipped in to spend spells working and living on the island in purpose-built dormitories. One hundred per cent foreign ownership is guaranteed for the first five years, and 95 per cent thereafter. By 1996, the park is expected to have around 100 factories employing around 50,000 Indonesian workers, mostly in electronics. The advantages for the multinationals are obvious – labour rates are around 20 times cheaper than Japan, but, according to a Sumitomo Electric Industries spokesperson: 'If you consider productivity of Japanese workers as one hundred, workers here are measured at eighty five. In the future the productivity levels of the two places would be similar' (cited in *Korea Times*, 14 September 1991). More recently plans have been laid to develop other nearby islands along the same lines. Karimun is expected to become a centre for heavy industry, and Bintan is to be developed for light industry and tourism (*Far Eastern Economic Review*, 27 February 1992).

Changing Patterns of Dependency

On the basis of a study of FDI from Japan to the ANICs and the ASEAN4, and from the ANICs to the ASEAN4 between 1967 and 1980, Kim and Terpstra (1984, p.1) suggested that:

the extent of intra-regional foreign direct investment is greater in the Asian Pacific region than in any other region (and) the Asian Pacific region has evolved into an interactive international production system comprising three tiers of countries: Japan, the ANICs, and the four developing countries (the ASEAN4).

They documented a shift in production capacity in electronics from Japan to the ANICs, and in textiles from the ANICs to the ASEAN4. By the 1990s inter-dependence was even greater, and the division of technology and labour more complex. Traditional industries such as footwear, textiles and clothing, have not been shifted wholesale, but the more labour intensive aspects have increasingly been transferred – a process still on-going today. And in electronics and other higher value sectors (especially automobiles) both Japan and the ANICs have been shifting final assembly of standardized mature mass produced goods and the manufacture of various components to the ASEAN4 in response to labour shortages at home and to take advantage of cheaper labour and factory space overseas. In Thailand, electronics at 16.5 per cent was the top export category in 1991, up from 10 per cent in 1988, due to massive Taiwanese, Korean and Japanese investments in 'screwdriver' factories (*Far Eastern Economic Review*, 30 January 1992). Some heavy industries such as chemicals have also been relocated, in part to avoid the protests of environmental pressure groups in the home country (Clifford and Moore 1989). But while the pattern of inter-dependencies has changed over the past decade in complex ways, the tiering between Japan, the ANICs and the ASEAN4 is as stark as ever. We will now attempt a brief characterization of the recently emergent inter-dependencies.

Japan has established itself as undoubted economic hegemon. Saravanamuttu (1988, p.139-40) quotes Constantino as follows:

Japan's war time version of a Greater East Asia Co-Prosperity Sphere is now a peace time reality, thanks to war reparations ... (and) modern instruments for economically dominating formally independent countries, namely: foreign trade, foreign investment and foreign aid.

Such statements are sweeping generalizations, but Japan's central role in the new East Asian (and world) order can no longer be disputed. The way in which the 'modern instruments' referred to by Constantino work in subjugating independent nation states is best explained by reference to divisions of labour and economic dependencies.

Frobel et al.'s (1980) classic work documented a 'new international division of labour' associated with the internationalization of capital following World War II. Capital mobility undermined colonial economic relations whereby the industrialized countries more or less ruthlessly exploited local populations and appropriated raw materials from subject undeveloped nations, and led to a sub-division of manufacturing processes at different industrial sites throughout the world. However, for the dependency theorists (or as Saravanamuttu calls them *dependentistas*) the former colonies continued to be subordinated to the advanced countries because they remained dependent on foreign capital, technology and expertise. To the extent that the *dependentistas'* analysis holds true, so does the characterization of Japan as the new hegemon and core country and the rest in East Asia as peripheral (or 'semi-peripheral' in the case of the ANICs) and dependent on Nippon. As we have documented, in the 1980s Japan became the most important source of capital for the ANICs and the ASEAN4, usurping Europe and even the United States.

Of course, Japan has also become a key provider of international capital for the 'advanced' Western nations, and because Japan's capital outflows are not matched by inflows (Japan's capital outflow to inflow ratio was a massive 20:1 compared with 1.04:1 for the US and 1.59:1 for Germany in 1990 [JETRO 1992]) Japan has been attacked by the West for not playing the international trade game fairly, and accused of attempting to dominate Western economies in a similar manner to its domination of Asian economies. (For recent commentaries on the arising debate see Williams et al. 1992 and Munday et al. 1992.) However, if Japan's new relations with the advanced West have caused a jumble in the *dependentistas'* cupboard, so has the apparent escape of the ANICs from purely dependent roles in the international division of labour.

The ANICs emerged from colonialism (but note Hong Kong is still a colony) as undoubted dependent developers. After brief periods of import substitution, they rapidly turned attention to export oriented manufacturing as the engine of growth with more or less heavy reliance on American aid (in Korea and Taiwan) and on the increasingly mobile, and especially American, international capital for industrial development (Deyo 1981, 1989; Nolan 1990; Saravanamuttu 1986). Their dependency on foreign capital has not disappeared altogether – and in the case of Singapore is greater than ever – but the characterization of the ANICs as *mere export platforms* for multinational capital was never accurate, and lost all credibility in the late 1980s when they became net *exporters of capital*. Today, in addition to providing a platform for exports for multinational companies, the ANICs have at least three more roles (Gereffi 1992). First, there is the role of *component supplier*, where subsidiaries of foreign companies produce components specially for core company consumption, or local indigenous companies produce components such as semiconductors for sale on the open market. Second, there is what Gereffi calls the *commercial sub-contracting* role, whereby the ANICs are effectively franchized to produce goods to be labelled and marketed by (especially) European and American companies. (British readers wearing Reebok sports shoes displaying the Union Jack might not be aware that they were made in Korea, and that the manufacturer H.S. Corp. sells its own brand – 'Le Caf' – at much cheaper prices.) Third, increasing numbers of indigenous ANIC companies have managed to evolve into fully fledged *independent exporters*. Korean companies such as Goldstar, Hyundai and Samsung have been the most visibly successful in this regard, and while their products might as yet be scorned by some elements of the Western middle classes as 'poor man's copies' of Japanese or Western equivalents, their emergence surely signals the beginning of the end of Western perceptions of the ANICs as Third World countries. Indeed, many Korean and Taiwanese companies, like their Japanese counterparts, are now establishing manufacturing operations in Europe and the US in order to circumvent the trade barriers increasingly threatened to guard the West from competitively superior products.

While the *export platform* role for the ANICs is declining in importance (and hence their characterization as 'semi-peripheral' becomes increasingly qualified) the ASEAN4 are taking on 'traditional industries' such as textiles and 'dirty industries' such as chemicals, and are welcoming the responsibility of assembling standardized mature products for sale and consumption in the advanced West and the wealthier Asia-Pacific countries. As we have documented, Japanese and other multinational capital is pouring into the ASEAN4 nations where land and labour is plentiful and cheap, by-passing the ANICs (except Singapore) which are concentrating on higher value activities: the ANICs themselves have also become key sources of capital for the ASEAN4 nations, which are becoming their (as well as Japan's and America's) export platforms and sources of (cheap) labour. For instance many of Goldstar's consumer electronics goods are assembled in Bangkok and Manilla, and H.S. Corp. now has some of its 'Reebok' sports shoes made in Thailand and Indonesia (Clifford and Moore 1989). Even more recently than the ASEAN4, other Asia-Pacific countries, particularly China and Vietnam, have developed *export platform* ambitions, and already made some progress in setting up their own export processing zones (JETRO 1992). Cambodia, Laos and Myanmar (Burma) have also showed signs of economic liberalization and baegan to open their doors to foreign investors in recent years (*The Economist*, 20 March 1993). It seems that the rest of South East Asia is following the ASEAN4 in pursuing the dependent development strategy which was so instrumental in the economic advance of the ANICs.

Economic Futures

The obvious practical questions which arise from the above characterization of changing inter-dependencies among the three tiers within the AP9 are: 'Can the ANICs beome Japan's?', and, 'Can the ASEAN4 become ANICs?'. Given that the Asia-Pacific nations have defied the logic of at least several economic theories in so short a space of time (Clegg et al. 1986), and given the complexity of the recent changes which we are only just beginning to acknowledge, let alone understand and explain, it might be foolish to offer answers. However, it is possible to point to some obvious potential obstacles which would have to be overcome if the grand ambitions of the Asia-Pacific nations are to be achieved. The most important are structural problems related to increasingly complex divisions of labour, problems of technology transfer, and the time and expense involved in developing a research and development capability. Another important potential obstacle according to some pundits, though their arguments are highly contentious, is the national culture of specific countries.

Divisions of Labour

As described above, the ANICs defied the logic of the original *dependentistas'* theories of underdevelopment, first by rapidly industrializing, and then by extending their roles well beyond mere *export platforms*. Their success has inevitably led to their present status of models of rapid growth and efficient industrialization for the rest of the developing world, which is now urged (for instance through the World Bank and the International Monetary Fund) to lay the conditions for growth through:

– locating manufacturing production for export markets as the engine of growth and the cornerstone of development policy;
– the state taking responsibility for laying down the social (especially education) and physical (roads, communications, etc.) infrastructure; and
– allowing the market mechanism to do its distributive and allocative work with minimum state intervention.

This model of growth was given further impetus with falling demand for primary exports and the collapse of commodity prices in the 1980s: the use of commodity export earnings to service the debts of developing countries became increasingly inadequate (Jansen 1991). Hence this model of growth would characterize the ASEAN4, in becoming *export platforms*, as taking the correct first step towards sustainable industrial and economic advance.

But the success of the ANICs does not necessarily confirm the wisdom of simple neo-classical or 'modernization' theories of economic development which ignore dependencies or treat them as benign. That the ANICs (and the ASEAN4) have escaped certain dependencies is undeniable, but these have been replaced by other dependencies, and it does not automatically follow that these, too, will be so easily escaped. Hence any assessment of the prospects for the Asia-Pacific economies must take account of present patterns of inter-dependency (Deyo 1987a; Limqueco et al. 1989). Present divisions of labour between Japan, the ANICs and the ASEAN4, as described above, suggest a 'core' Japan, a 'semi-peripheral' group of ANICs which are now taking on at least some 'core' characteristics, and a peripheral group of ASEAN nations which are now taking on some 'semi-peripheral' characteristics. So what is to stop the ANICs becoming Japan's and the 'ASEAN4' becoming 'ANICs'?

Among the ANICs, Singapore and Hong Kong must be singled out for separate consideration because in themselves their economies are simply too small to become 'like Japan'. Singapore deliberately, and Hong Kong more by accident of history (and less successfully than Singapore), have shifted to higher value production *and* developed roles as commercial and logistical bases for international capital to exploit cheap factors of production in South East Asia and on the Chinese mainland. Singapore in particular is also now promoting itself as a centre for the regional research and development activities of multinational corporations. As island city states with small populations and virtually no natural resources, both countries' futures will continue to depend heavily on the provision of niche services to multinational capital on the one hand, and the adjacent developing countries on the other. In these directions their success appears to be continuing. However, because of their specialized roles it would be nonsense to compare their advance directly with the advance of other larger nations, and indeed it is increasingly difficult to understand their economies separately from their 'hinterlands'. Their future development prospects, then, depend heavily on the further progress of the ASEAN4 and China as manufacturing centres and as markets.

Taiwan and Korea, on the other hand, are larger countries which have generated significant indigenous bourgeoisies capable of exporting a range of their own manufactured products to the rest of the world. The largest of the ANICs, Korea, was indeed given the status of 'Asia's next giant' (after Japan) in the popularly influential book by Amsden (1989). However, unlike Japan, both Korea and Taiwan remain highly export dependent (table 1.5), they still rely to a degree on foreign capital, and most impotantly here is their continued dependence on foreign technology. This was indicated above in the discussion of the ANICs' imports of capital equipment. Morris-Suzuki (1992a, 1992b) notes, in addition, the ANICs' continued dependence on key high technology componentry, particularly from Japan, for assembly into their products. The increasingly complex division of labour in the Asia-Pacific, she argues, will make it difficult for the ANICs to escape a role of 'peripheral intermediation' in the new international division of labour.

The ASEAN4 of course come well below the ANICs in the international division of labour, having embarked on export oriented industrialization later. Numerous scholars have commented that their late entry puts them at a significant disadvantage (Nolan 1990; Rigg 1991; Rodan 1989). And Douglass and DiGregorio (1991) claim that the end of the expansion of mass markets for standardized products characteristic of the 'Fordist' era leaves the ASEAN4 (and other developing countries) without clear foundation for their strategies.

The ASEAN4 have in fact already had some success in their intention of becoming export platforms, and Wu (1991) documents a growth of exports from the ASEAN4 to Japan and the ANICs faster than the growth in exports to the advanced West. Hence the success of ASEAN nations may depend as much on continued FDI and technology transfer from Japan and the ANICs, and on the further expansion of markets in *East Asia*, as it does on developments in the West. But while signs of rapid growth in Asia-Pacific consumption of mass produced standardized goods might give some grounds for optimism for the ASEAN4 (and incidentally raises serious questions about the 'post-Fordist' hypothesis), further development towards ANIC status could only come with a deepening of manufacturing capacity beyond the traditional industries, and beyond the mass assembly of components into finished or semi-finished goods for re-export. This in turn would appear to depend on a desire on the part of the ANICs and Japan (or other multinational capital) to shift higher value activities to the ASEAN4: for the most part indigenous bourgeoisies, unlike those of Korea and Taiwan, simply do not have the ability to shift in this direction independently (Lubeck 1992; Robison 1989).

Technology Transfer and R&D

Moving up a division in the international labour league tables depends heavily on technology acquisition, which is enabled primarily through FDI and licensing agreements. Japan acquired much of its own technological capability, and indeed became a significant innovator, prior to World War II (Morris-Suzuki 1992b). Then soon after the war, with the help of experts sent from the US on a mission to help re-build Japanese capitalism, the country emerged as a major exporter of manufactured goods which gradually acquired a reputation for their quality as well as their competitive prices (Oliver and Wilkinson 1992). Today Japan is world leader in increasing numbers of sectors, inexorably shifting its sights to the most advanced technologies and the highest value product areas.

Technology acquisition in the ANICs and the ASEAN4 has been much more recent, and is occuring in a context which poses far more obstacles than the Japanese faced. First, unlike the case in pre-war Japan, 'technology transfer' has been much more likely to take place within the confines of multinational corporations. Korea and Taiwan did manage to make significant technological acquisitions in the 1960s and 1970s through licensing to independent firms in some sectors (Wade 1990; Westphal et al. 1984) but this is becoming increasingly difficult and expensive as multinationals have become more wary of 'giving away' the technological basis of competitive advantage. Secondly, multinationals and their home governments have increasingly taken an interest in 'intellectual property rights' (Ting Wen Lee 1988; Kaplinsky 1991) in an attempt to prevent other countries simply copying innovations. Thirdly, it appears to be less likely today (though substantial further research is needed here) that international investors (especially Japanese) will actively extend vertical linkages for component production and business services to indigenous firms, preferring to import components or persuade their existing home country suppliers to set up manufacturing capacity nearby (Morris-Suzuki 1992a).

The net result for the ANICs' and the ASEAN4's indigenous manufacturers, to use Morris-Suzuki's terminology, is an increasing difficulty in 'de-packing' and 'modifying' technology, and for the ASEAN4 in particular is the problem of being recipient of only standardized technologies considered 'obsolescent' by the more advanced nations. (That the US and some European nations, notably the UK, could in this regard be in the same position as the ASEAN4 for increasing numbers of manufacturing sectors which have come to be dominated by the Japanese, is a phenomenon of great import which is beyond the scope of this book.)

If the ASEAN4 are to face more problems in 'de-packing' and 'modifying' technology than did the ANICs a decade or more earlier, then R&D capabilities become crucial to any advancement beyond the status of dependent developer and export platform. R&D capabilities are important to the ANICs as well. Singapore's stated ambition, and perhaps *laissez faire* Hong Kong's implicit ambition, is to attract the regional R&D of multinational corporations to become the *brain centre* of South East Asia. Taiwan and Korea on the other hand have significant local bourgeoisies who are being encouraged by their governments to develop company-based R&D capabilities so they can compete head-on with Japan in at least some product areas. The Korean government, for instance, has a stated ambition of making Korean electronics companies leaders in product development, and becoming world number one in consumer electronics in the 1990s (*Korea Times*, 19 October 1991). But while Singapore and Hong Kong may achieve some success in their limited ambitions, and while Korea and Taiwan may (be allowed by Japan to) advance in some relatively low value areas – e.g. consumer electronics (but not super-computers and artifical intelligence) and civilian aircraft manufacture (but not jet fighter aircraft manufacture), the R&D capability which would be necessary for the ASEAN4 to 'become ANICs', or the ANICs to 'become Japan's' is still quite a way off.

Japan's shift from the status of 'pursuer' to 'pioneer' is reflected in levels of R&D spending now comparable with or exceeding all of the advanced nations (Gow 1989), and an advantage for Japan, like Germany, is that the defence sector does not take a large slice of that expenditure. The ANICs have achieved substantial growth in R&D expenditures during the 1980s – Korea and Taiwan's expenditures as a proportion of GNP are now approaching two per cent – and most of this is in experimental engineering and applied technology targetted at specific industries (Council for Economic Planning and Development, Republic of China 1992). The ASEAN4, however, have made little progress in the 1980s, being 'stuck' at around half a per cent of GNP, and with many times less the number of researchers (Morris-Suzuki 1992b).

The ASEAN4's problem of acquisition of technology and R&D capability will not disappear easily: while the ANICs were relatively strong on the manpower supply side in terms of workforce skills and educational levels back in the 1950s (and today have some of the most highly educated workforces in the world) the ASEAN4 began their industrialization with less educated populations, and are now trying to advance technologically in more difficult circumstances (Nolan 1990). The 'technological gap' is massive, and circumstances suggest a 'technological leap' will be considerably more difficult now than in past decades.

National Cultures

Differences of *national culture* which might provide impediments to growth and development for some countries are extremely difficult to specify just as they are so obviously of some importance. The hypothesis which claims a cultural basis for economic activity and competitive ability is derived theoretically from Max Weber (Weber 1930, 1951). Weber's sociology of capitalism is complex, but put simply he argued that while Protestantism underpinnned Western capitalist development, the Eastern religions and ideologies, particularly Confucianism, failed to provide ideological justification for the dynamic of capital accumulation, and the behaviour and social relations which they informed stood in the way of rational capitalistic relations. However, while the *culturists* of the 1950s, after Weber, explained economic backwardness in East Asia by reference to Confucianism and the feudal traditions the ideology informed, today's *culturists* are more likely to find an explanation of East Asian economic success precisely in the same Confucianism. The irony of such a shift is explored by Berger (1987).

Weber, say the *new culturists*, was right in arguing for a cultural basis for capitalism, but wrong in his pessimism about Confucianism. Confucian, or more accurately *neo-Confucian*, ideology provides an underpinning for capitalism in its concept of a 'ceaseless pursuit of renovation' which provides a motivational mechanism paralleling Western Calvinism (Shepard et al. 1989). Further, the 'humanistic bureaucracies' of East Asian capitalist organizations which create the enthusiasm, commitment and loyalty among staff so important in their success (Pascale and Athos 1982) derive from the neo-Confucian promotion of 'righteousness' (*yi*) over profit (*li*). For Shepard et al. (1989, p.319) 'seeking employee welfare can be as strong a motivating mechanism for capitalistic activities as the profit motive'.

If the *new culturists* are correct, then the future prospects for the ASEAN4 are poor. How could Filipino Catholics, Thai Buddhists, and Indonesian and Malay Muslims ever hope to compete with the neo-Confucian Japanese, Koreans and Chinese? But the claim for a simple causal link between culture, management style and economic success is less the result of detailed historical analysis and more that of post-hoc rationalization. Indeed, Kolm (1985) has found a *Buddhist* explanation for growth, and as Lubeck (1992) points out, *Islamic* texts have been re-interpreted to rationalize disciplined capital accumulation. Readers who are *Catholic* or inclined religiously in any other way need not be down-hearted because:

Since all cultural traditions contain valuable lessons about honesty, discipline, and authority ... anyone committed to a cultural explanation can, with some diligence, discover a tradition or verse from a sacred text to make the causal connection – from cultural value to observed behaviours – once a state achieves industrialization (Lubeck 1992, p.190).

This is not to deny the importance of an understanding of religion, ideology and feudal tradition in explanations of the rise of particular economic forms and the relations between capital, state and labour, but it is to criticize the simplistic causal argument which, as well as being potentially racist, is wrong.

More careful explanations of the links between culture and economic development in Japan and the ANICs have attempted to trace the historical links between feudal traditions and the ideologies which informed them on the one hand, and specific forms of capitalist organization on the other, but also taking into account the political and social institutions which influence hierarchical and market relationships within a country. Hamilton and Kao (1987) have argued that such an *institutional* approach was the original intent of Weber, who has been grossly misinterpreted by naive culturists. From the *institutional* perspective, what is important for economic success is not so much having a particular culture, but being able to organize business, state-capital, management-union, etc. relations in a manner which can take advantage of, or resonate with, culturally-derived beliefs and patterns of behaviour (Biggart and Hamilton 1990). Hence a culture *in itself* is never necessarily an impediment to growth, and potentially is a powerful resource upon which to draw.

Put this way, explanations of developments in national economies, and understandings of the abilities of nations to overcome the structural obstacles to futher economic advance, demands a detailed historically-specific understanding of the roles of, and relationships between, the different actors in the economy. In the chapters which follow we will explore these through analyses of the three principal actors – the state, capital and labour – for each of the ANICs.

In the light of this brief discussion, and for the purposes of this chapter, we will *not* characterize national cultures as impediments to the further advancement of the ASEAN4 or any other countries. But culture, and the ideologies used by capital and states as rationalizations or justifications for particular relationships and courses of action (including the repression of labour and opposition movements) will be subjects to which we return throughout the book and give special consideration in the final chapter.

Japan: Inside the Hegemon

The discussion so far has demonstrated the importance of economic inter-dependencies between Japan and the rest of the Asia-Pacific. In the light of this discussion it should hardly be surprising that many Asia-Pacific nations have looked to Japan for lessons in the management of their own economies – hence the importance of this section. Equally important is being able to distinguish patterns of development and the roles of state, capital and labour in Japan from those in the ANICs. There has been an important element of selective borrowing from Japan, especially by Singapore, but there are fundamental differences of key features. The following brief discussion of the roles of state, capital and labour in Japan may hence be usefully compared and contrasted with the more detailed discussions of the economic actors in the ANICs in chapters two to five.

The State

Although it is the private sector in Japan which dominates economic activities, the state has played a central role in economic coordination and in the development and implementation of long term industrial policy. Wolf's (1985) identification of a 'Japanese conspiracy' and a 'plot to dominate industry world wide' may or may not be a fully accurate characterization, but the closeness of collaboration between state and business elites should not be underestimated. A key institution is the Ministry of International Trade and Industry (MITI) which selects target industries, products and technologies, then channels government funds for R&D, export subsidies and the like into the areas identified as strategically important (Sethi et al. 1984). Gow (1989) explains how the government shifted from the promotion of heavy and traditional industries such as ship building and syn-thetic fibre production in the 1950s and 1960s to ever more advanced sectors, most recently biotechnology, artificial intelligence, jet fighter aircraft, and other exceptionally high value and R&D intense areas. State support of industry has been forthcoming in the form of long term, low interest loans from the Bank of Japan and the Industrial Bank of Japan. But perhaps of greater importance than financial incentives, government loans and bureaucratic guidance, is the extent of institutional cooperation between state organizations, manufacturing and finance capital. Japan's large and influential business associations, which are made up of leaders of the country's giant corporations, interact frequently and closely with MITI and the Ministry of Finance in the development of industrial policies (Orru 1991).

In very recent years the state has been involved in a radical restructuring of the Japanese economy. This was necessary because of increasing political pressures from the US and the EC which forced up the value of the Yen (see table 1.7) and led to the introduction of 'voluntary' restraints on exports in a variety of sectors.

The response of the state was encapsulated in the *Maekawa* report, the contents of which were implemented in the late 1980s and early 1990s. FDI, especially in Europe and North America, was systematically accelerated: the role of the government's Import-Export Bank of Japan was key here, changing from export promoter in the early 1980s to FDI promoter in the late 1980s. MITI was enabled to provide insurance protection against risks or losses from overseas investments under the 1987 Trade Insurance Act (Tokunaga 1992). The massive outflow of capital from Japan in the late 1980s is well documented (Munday et al. 1992). On the home front, domestic demand-led growth was encouraged, and companies were set a target of an average 1,800 hour working year for their employees. At the time of writing little progress towards this target had been documented, and the National Defense Counsel for Victims of *Karoshi* (death from overwork) was still campaigning vigorously. But there were signs that at least companies were successfully persuading their employees that taking occasional holidays was no longer taboo. At the same time, and again in line with the recommendations of the *Maekawa* report, while Japan's mature industries were being transferred overseas, manufacturers at home were encouraged to develop even more sophisticated higher value products via a range of incentives. This is a process which is ongoing in the 1990s.

The Japanese state has also had a crucial involvement in creating the 'industrial harmony' for which Japan is renowned. The historical emergence of the ubiquitous enterprise union had little to do with company loyalty, and much to do with the repression of the independent labour movement. Littler (1982) has documented a key role for the state in suppressing 'dangerous groups' and 'dangerous thoughts' in the late 1910s and early 1920s when industrial conflict was commonplace. Following World War II, the US occupation forces liberalized trade union activity, but gave blessing to purges of the Communists who had surfaced to lead the union movement in the 1950s (Gordon 1985; Morishima 1982). Anti-labour legislation was introduced, and in 1950 alone 12,000 workers were sacked from Japanese companies on the grounds that they were Communists (Clegg et al. 1990). Enterprise unions had in fact been sought by the Japanese left, who saw them as precursors to factory soviets, and in the late 1940s some enterprise unions secured agreements which gave them serious roles in enterprise decision making over issues such as investment and staffing (Kenney and Florida 1988). But in the 1950s moderate, company oriented unions were installed, with roles in the discipline and socialization of labour rather than the protection of workers' rights.

More generally, the state had a role in the propagation of an ideology of industrial harmony which was vigorously pursued through the *Kyochokai* (the Cooperation and Harmony Society) during the inter-war years (Kinzley 1991). And the state orchestrated and encouraged the adoption of life-time employment, seniority wages systems, and company welfareism at different points in Japanese history in the attempt to foster company loyalty and pre-empt 'Western-type' class struggle (Kinzley 1991; Littler 1982; Morishima 1982).

Hence while the Japanese state has had relatively little direct involvement in industry by way of direct ownership, its ability to guide industrial development through a mix of incentives and collaboration with the business elite has been crucial, as has the state's role in controlling the labour movement and ensuring employer prerogatives through a mix of ideological dissemination, surveillance of radical groups and, where necessary, simple and brutal repression.

Employers

After World War II the Japanese *zaibatsu* were dismantled by the American occupation forces, but gradually the networks of reciprocal shareholdings and banking links were re-generated so that a high concentration of economic power is again characteristic (Okumura 1991). However, this economic power is vested less in individual shareholders than in a managerial elite which enjoys a high degree of autonomy from owners and the stock market. The structure of ownership, and particularly the mutual shareholding typical between financial and manufacturing companies, gives Japan's giant corporations long term planning horizons and allows a concern with market share rather than short term profitability.

Dore (1973) has celebrated the emergence of long term 'high trust' relations between the major corporations and their tiers of suppliers, who are often dedicated to the parent company and are organized into *keiretsu* groups. Monopsony, and sometimes a direct stakeholding in *keiretsu* companies, means large companies can gain the benefits of vertical integration, but without the costs (Sako 1987). Parent companies typically have exceptionally close relations with their suppliers, and are willing to share technology and help develop their competences, giving the benefits which might accrue from vertical integration via 'obligational contracting'. At the same time, wages and working conditions in the smaller companies are relatively poor; hence a major potential cost of vertical integration is avoided (Oliver and Wilkinson 1992).

Another way in which Japanese companies differ from most of their Western counterparts is in their manufacturing organization. The 'just-in-time' (JIT) system, as it became known, was established at Toyota in the 1950s then diffused through Japanese industry in the 1960s and 1970s. JIT is a form of manufacturing organization which is market-led and which operates on the basis of minimal stocks, work-in-progress and inventories. Close and collaborative relations with suppliers are clearly a prerequisite for JIT, as are stable industrial relations and clear managerial prerogatives because of the vulnerability of the system. These are provided via obligational contracting and enterprise unions (Oliver and Wilkinson 1992). Total quality management, the Western inventors of which have expressed exasperation at the failure of US and European companies to adopt the methods, is also widely practiced. Employee involvement in quality and productivity improvements is facilitated by life-time employment and welfareist practices for core workers which contribute to a low level of employee turnover and the knowledge that improving productivity does not necessarily mean a shedding of labour. On-the-job training, job rotation and team work are widely practiced, and a range of small group activities take place inside and outside the workplace.

Life-time employment, seniority wages and promotion systems and company welfareism in the larger corporations have been widely debated by advocates and critics: less well known, but increasingly well documented, are rigorous systems of selection and induction, the increasing use of personal appraisal, and other pressures on employees which lead to over-working. Selection into the core work force of a large corporation is highly competitive, and educational attainments are key. Such are the benefits of permanent employment in such a firm over scraping a living on the periphery that there is strong competition to gain entry even into the best kindergartens, and cramming classes for four to five year olds are commonplace (Ouchi 1981). But educational attainments alone are not sufficient. Companies are reported to make routine use of private investigators to ensure the candidate is of an acceptable background by checking on family, friends and neighbours, and 'moderate views' and a 'balanced personality' are sought (Pucik 1985; Robbins 1983). Those fortunate enough to be selected are then put through an induction programme which involves familiarization with the company philosophy, and which in some companies might more accurately be described as indoctrination. Azumi (1969) compares company indoctrination with that given in religious orders and military schools.

Inside the organization, the rate of promotion and the level of pay is determined partly by seniority, but also, and increasingly, by personal assessments – the *satei* system. Under *satei*, the immediate superior (the team leader for shop floor workers) assesses employees' performance together with factors such as their work attitudes, eagerness, self sacrifice and team involvement. Endo (1991) and Ogasawara (1992) have argued that *satei* leads to intense individual competition, subservience to management, and even a tendency to work overtime or during holidays without officially recording the fact because it would be seen as a sign of weakness. Tight manning practices, and public displays of targets, performance, absence and lateness add to the pressures on employees, and the work experience can be stressful. Domingo (1985) argues that the culture and values of the Japanese predisposes them to enjoying a stressful work environment. The National Defense Counsel for Victims of *Karoshi*, on the other hand, would disagree.

Hiroshi Kawahito and his colleagues at the National Defense Counsel, which is made up mostly of liberal minded doctors and lawyers, have pointed out that the officially recorded average annual working hours in Japan – which at 2,168 in 1987 were in any case high by Western standards – contrasted with the average 2,400 hours per year indicated from the results of a government survey study based on questionnaire data from households rather than workplaces. They explain the massive discrepancy simply in relation to the reluctance of employees to officially record overtime or weekend and holiday work. Unrecorded and unpaid working

hours are known as 'service overtime'. They estimate that Japanese males work
an average of 2,600 hours per year, and white collar males in some sectors (the
'salarymen') 3,000 hours per year. On top of these hours they often engage in
work-related study and small group activities outside work. The conclusion is that
'almost all of the active waking hours of working age males are spent working for
their companies' (National Defense Counsel for Victims of Karoshi 1990, p.66).
Failure to persuade the Japanese trade union movement to join the campaign to
get *karoshi* legally recognized as a work-related medical condition has led to
the Defense Counsel switching its campaign to publicizing the plight of *karoshi*
victims internationally. They have had some success in raising the awareness of
international business, political and trade union communities, and it is possible
that complaints from these communities has been a factor in the government's
recently announced target of a 1,800 hour working year.

   The maintenance of efficient business organizations with high degrees of labour
flexibility, discipline, worker participation in group activities, and long working
hours, are of course dependent on strong managerial prerogatives. These were
established in part by the repression of independent trade unions, though alone
this is insufficient to explain the apparent dedication of Japanese employees.
Japanese values – for instance the spirit of *gambare* (endurance) and the equation
of company loyalty with national loyalty – may have an influence. This was
explored in a fascinating piece of research (reported in Turpin 1991) whose
findings contrasted the values of 3,600 Japanese and 400 European executives.
Among the survey's questions was, 'What is your favourite word in life?'. For the
Europeans, 'love', 'family', and 'fun' topped the list; for the Japanese 'effort',
'persistence', and 'thank you'. However, as mentioned earlier in this chapter,
the simple *culturist* argument is fraught with difficulties. Further clues as to
the sources of managerial prerogatives and employee obedience come from a
consideration of the Japanese form of trade union organization.

Labour

Japan had 12.2 million trade union members in 1990 – 25.9 per cent of the work
force. Over 90 per cent of the total membership belonged to enterprise unions,
and these are concentrated in large organizations. Enterprises employing less than
100 workers where wages and working conditions are relatively poor, are 95
per cent non-union. National level union federations – of which there have been
only two since 1987 – are relatively weak (Oliver and Wilkinson 1992). Today
Rengo oversees the mainstream union movement, while *Toitsu Rosokon*, with a
small membership, is a peak organization linked to the Japanese Communist Party
(Clegg et al. 1990). Some enterprise unions have been successful in gaining an
influence over labour deployment, overtime working, and even work scheduling.
This was reported to be the case for instance at Nissan until the mid 1980s when,

in the context of a crisis of company competitiveness, the union leadership was toppled and managerial prerogatives re-established (Ishizuna 1990; Tabata 1989). Tabata (1989, p.28) concluded that 'all enterprise-based unions in Japan ... seem to be showing the same tendency, with their functions on the wane'.

More typically, enterprise unions are closely controlled by the company, and supervisors and middle managers are often also trade union representatives (Moore 1987). Supervisors and team leaders are given a key role in maintaining order on the shop floor, and may be given training in how to identify 'trouble makers'. Yamamoto (1989) documents the practice of 'tailing' suspect workers outside the work place to check whether they are involved in 'subversive' activities, and the training of supervisors in the arts of informally pressurising 'problematic persons' to either become 'well cultured, mature human beings', or to leave the company.

Worker discipline and obedience, then, might best be explained by the strong labour market segmentation in the Japanese economy which makes widespread unionization difficult and might give unionized workers a feeling of being privileged; by the rigorous procedures of selection and indoctrination; by the extensive and direct communications between management and work force; by the use of peer pressures via 'team work'; and by a detailed surveillance of individual activites by key employees. The main point here is that 'industrial harmony' is not a 'natural' state of affairs in Japan. 'Harmony' has been actively created by employers, sometimes with the crucial support of the state, and is re-created on a daily basis through propaganda, peer controls and work place surveillance.

If Japan *has* been successful in creating close cooperation among the actors within its own industrial system, since World War II it has not taken a great interest in contributing to the creation of cooperative bonds among the countries of the Asia-Pacific, in spite of the high and growing levels of economic inter-dependence. The final section of this chapter will describe the tentative steps taken towards the creation of Asia-Pacific-wide collaborative institutions, and explain the obstacles to the emergence of a cooperative body on a par with NAFTA or the EC.

Economic Alliances

Export oriented growth obviously depends on a degree of freedom of world trade, and the reduction in tariffs under the influence of GATT in recent decades has greatly favoured the advance of the AP9. However, non-tariff barriers (especially 'voluntary' export restraints) have proliferated in the 1980s and early 1990s, and as documented above some Asia-Pacific countries have seen their currencies revalued upwards as a result of political decisions made by the advanced Western nations. It is in the light of the possibility of the erection of further significant barriers to trade, or more political measures to skew the balance of advantages in international trade back towards the West, that the East Asian nations have increasingly considered cooperating as a force in world trade negotiations.

Western Alliances

Political pressures from the West (mentioned earlier) on Japan and the ANICs
to introduce measures to reduce their trade surpluses have been one factor in the
acceleration of capital outflows – to the ASEAN4 and China, and also to the US
and Europe – since the late 1980s. Upward pressures on East Asian currencies, and
the US's decision to remove the ANICs from the generalized system of preferences
(GSP) in 1989 were probably the most publicized moves. (The EC intends to take
away the ANICs' GSP statuses in 1994.) 'Voluntary export restraints', such as the
limit on Japanese car exports to the EC of 1.23 million units per year until the end
of 1999 (*Japan Times*, 2 August 1991) have also had their impact. So too have
have other moves such as the US's ideological attacks on a 'Japan Inc.' conspiracy,
and on the Korean frugality campaign which persuades the Korean population not
to squander money on luxury Western imports. Europe has also made ideological
attacks. The then Prime Minister of France, Edith Cresson (cited in *Business
Week*, 3 June 1991) summed up the feeling of significant political elements within
Europe towards the Far East when she commented:

The Japanese have a strategy of world conquest. ... They have finished their job in the US.
Now they're about to devour Europe.

Another major factor accounting for capital outflows, however – and certainly
those targetted at the ASEAN4 and China – has been rising labour costs and
severe labour shortages at home. For Japan and the ANICs the two factors of
Western political pressure and local economic circumstance could be said to have
happily coincided, so that outward investment has not (so far) led to high home
unemployment. But the trade deficits of the US and Europe with Japan and the
ANICs have not gone away, and political pressures for further action have been
growing. It may be premature yet to talk of the emergence of trade blocs, but the
North American Free Trade Association (NAFTA) which takes in the US, Canada
and Mexico, and the European Community (EC) have become stronger in their
ability to put on a united ideological and political front with the rest of the world.
    The response of the Asia-Pacific has so far been at the national level: in spite
of deepening economic inter-dependencies between nations within the region,
the political will for multilateral economic action has been overshadowed by
differences between the countries. There have nonetheless been some attempts to
establish economic alliances, and given their future potential importance they are
worthy of brief discussion.

ASEAN

The Association of South East Asian Nations (ASEAN) was established as early
as 1967, but remains today a relatively weak actor in the international economic

community. For the first ten years it was concerned almost entirely with regional political conciliation as the fledgling independent states of Singapore, Thailand, Malaysia, Indonesia, the Philippines and Brunei tried to find their way in the world (Thailand was the exception in never having been colonized). Limits on cooperation on the economic front since then are related to three factors: a continued emphasis on political matters; a lack of homogeneity of economic goals; and most importantly the dependence of individual ASEAN nations on external finance, technology and trade (Muraoka 1986). As Saravanamuttu (1988, p.218) puts it:

State and local interests could in the long run benefit from a self-reliant and self-sustaining regional ASEAN economy but their present links and dependence on the international bourgeoisie and on the Western alliance for military protection are too important to jettison just yet.

Indeed, while the fortunes of individual ASEAN nations are tied closely to those of the Asia-Pacific as a whole, ASEAN's own intra-regional trade has remained remarkable low – always below 20 per cent of its total world trade from its inception. In 1991 intra-ASEAN trade was still less than 20 per cent of total ASEAN trade. This, together with the reliance of individual ASEAN states on external countries for investment, technology, and markets for exports, will mean a continuing problem of finding a basis for political collaboration on the economic front: the ASEAN economies are competitive rather than complimentary (Rigg 1991).

The most important recent attempts at ASEAN politico-economic collaboration are represented in the 'growth triangle', and in the concept of an ASEAN Free Trade Association (AFTA). The growth triangle, described earlier, with Singapore at the centre and Indonesia and Malaysia providing cheap factors of production, may mean more economic *inter-dependence*, but not of the sort which necessarily leads to common economic *interests*. Malaysian and Indonesian commentators have already voiced unease at the hierarchical nature of the relationship implied by the triangle, and Malaysia's Prime Minister Mahathir has commented that 'cross-border investment must not become an excuse to relocate sweatshops and environmentally harmful industries to lesser developed nations' (*Far Eastern Economic Review*, 7 January 1993). The first step towards AFTA came in January 1993 with a series of modest tariff cuts which were to lead gradually to free intra-ASEAN trade by the year 2000. But even these did not stick: straightaway the ASEAN countries were arguing about the details and the timing of the cuts.

East Asian Economic Caucus

In recent years, and pushed most vociferously by Malaysia, the concept of an East Asian Economic Caucus (previously the East Asian Economic Grouping) has emerged as a response to the single European market and NAFTA. The EAEC takes in Japan and the ANICs as well as the ASEAN4, and Malaysia's Prime Minister, Mahathir Mohamad, has suggested the new grouping could become an 'economic bloc'. This comment caused upset among world trade negotiators who prefer less provocative nouns to describe alliances (Hirata 1992), and Japan has displayed extreme reluctance to endorse the EAEC concept.

Just as ASEAN is limited in its ambitions by political differences, inter-nation competition, and the lack of a significant common market, so is the EAEC. For a start, Taiwan does not have official diplomatic relations with any of the EAEC nations. More importantly, intra-ANICs trade was less than 10 per cent throughout the 1980s (Hanazaki 1992); intra-AP9 trade is similarly low (see table 1.6). Further, the political antagonisms between Japan and much of the rest of South East Asia which derived from the colonial period and World War II have been slow in healing. For instance Japanese war atrocities are still popular reading in Korea, whose government is still demanding apologies from Japan.

Of course, memories of colonialism, war and other international conflicts have a habit of being forgotten when the economic need arises, but as long as East Asian trade is with the rest of the world rather than within the EAEC, liberalization of inter-EAEC trade would have a limited effect, and any attempt to exert power as a group in world trade negotiations could back-fire. The key point is that the inter-dependencies among the Asia-Pacific countries are hierarchical ones to do with technology and direct investment flows, rather than lateral ones to do with trade in finished goods. Hence while EAEC nations may have some interest in negotiating with NAFTA and the EC as a group, the types of inter-dependency which enjoin the EAEC nations are not wholly conducive to political collaboration. The future for the EAEC is then, uncertain. So much depends on the extent to which NAFTA and the EC take on more the character of economic blocs and thereby force the Asia-Pacific countries to ignore their differences and look inwards for solutions to economic problems.

Asia-Pacific Economic Cooperation

The most recent attempt at forming an economic alliance which spans the East Asian nations is 'Asia-Pacific Economic Cooperation' (APEC) which was formed in 1988. As well as the AP9, APEC includes Brunei and China, and also the non-Asian Pacific Rim countries of the US, Canada, Australia and New Zealand. Unsurprisingly, wildly conflicting opinions have been expressed by the different countries (*Korea Times*, 13 November 1991), and the accomodation of China has been particularly difficult. At APEC's first full ministerial level meeting in Seoul in November 1991, representatives from China, Taiwan and Hong Kong met for the first time as APEC members. To appease China, Taiwan had to call itself 'China-Taipei', and both Taiwan and Hong Kong referred to themselves as 'economies' rather than sovereign states. To avoid awkwardness for the 'three Chinas', all APEC members agreed not to display their national flags. The Chinese and Taiwanese delegates were seated at the oval table in positions where they could avoid eye contact (*China News*, 24 November 1991)! APEC is undoubtedly valuable as a means of improving understanding among politically antagonistic nations, but needless to say little in the way of practical resolutions have so far emerged.

Conclusions and Prospects

Economic inter-dependence in the Asia-Pacific region is strong and growing such that it is incresingly difficult to separate out one nation for scrutiny. Yet at the same time national political awareness remains strong and economic collaboration and cooperation is slow in coming. The nature of the economic inter-relationships helps explain why: they are characterized by hierarchical relationships between the three tiers, and by horizontal competition within the tiers.

What all the countries have in common is an export orientation, and what several have in common is a huge trade surplus with the Western advanced nations. Beyond this the similarities are less easy to identify, and we must distinguish between Japan, the ANICs and the ASEAN4. The hierarchical nature of economic relations between these three tiers is striking. The ANICs are dependent on Japan for technology – i.e. capital equipment and high value componentry – and in Singapore's case also for direct investments. The ASEAN4 are dependent on Japan, and increasingly the ANICs as well, for both technology and direct investment. Among the ANICs there is competition for the same overseas markets in similar sectors, and among the ASEAN4 there is competition both for overseas markets and for direct investments.

The ASEAN4, and more recently also China and Vietnam, are establishing themselves as export platforms for the multinationals, and developing a capacity in the traditional industries. The ANICs on the other hand are shedding their labour intensive operations to the less developed Asian economies and attempting to move up the value chain in the more advanced sectors. And Japan is well on its way to becoming undisputed world leader in a range of the most advanced knowledge intensive industries. These developments have defied the logic of dependency theories, and it would be a brave *dependentista* who would now deny the possibility of further development of the ASEAN4 and the ANICs. But this does not mean we can abandon the necessity of understanding dependencies.

There is quite a gulf between Japan, the ANICs, and the ASEAN4. The questions, 'Can the ASEAN4 become ANICs?', and, 'Can the ANICs become Japan's?', in turn raises the question of, 'What would they have to do to become so?'. A good way to answer this question is to focus on present dependencies and therefore on the obstacles to development. Implicitly, this is exactly what

Asia-Pacific governments have been doing in their attempts to restructure, and Hong Kong apart, they have determined detailed plans to reduce or change their dependencies in favourable ways.

In the chapters which follow we examine the details – which in important ways vary radically – of contemporary economic restructuring in the ANICs. As we shall see, there are some grounds for optimism for Taiwan, Korea and Singapore, but one must be pessimistic about Hong Kong. This examination of changing economic structures forms the basis for the main purpose of the book, which is to explore the roles of, and relationships between, the key economic actors – state, capital and labour. In this first chapter, we have paid scant attention to these actors, whose patterns of behaviour make for unique 'economic cultures' which bear on the prospects for economic futures. More importantly, an examination of the actors in East Asian industrial systems gives us a view of what goes on, to use Frederic Deyo's phrase, 'beneath the miracle'.

Chapter Two: Singapore

Singapore, a tiny island city state with a population of 2.7 million located at the Southern tip of the Malaysian peninsula, attracts great attention from the Western world. No doubt this relates in part to the nation's charismatic and outspoken leader Lee Kuan Yew, whose controversial views extend to world as well as domestic social, political, and economic affairs. Equally important is the fact that Singapore, more than the other ANICs, has based its industrialization (and now bases its attempts to economically restructure) on the attraction of export oriented foreign direct investments. This makes Singapore the archetypal *dependent developer*, and the nation's success in pursuing this mode of development is now aped not just in developing countries, but in regions within the advanced West seeking to regenerate their own ailing economies.

The Singapore government has been clear in the imperatives it identifies for the successful pursuit of this mode of development, and has intervened extensively to create a social, political and economic environment conducive to the attraction of increasingly high quality investments from overseas. Presently, the focus is on the provision of a services infrastructure and human resource base capable of attracting the regional headquarters of multinational corporations with manufacturing facilities in the broader ASEAN region as well as in Singapore, with the aim of making the city state the 'brain centre' of South East Asia.

In the first section of this chapter we examine the development of the economy to a position today where the 'brain centre' ambition sounds almost feasible, and assess the prospects for its achievement. Much of the rest of the chapter focusses on the pervasive role of the state and the ruling party under Lee Kuan Yew, which have attempted to engineer, in part on behalf of multinational capital, an orderly and highly disciplined society. A range of legislative and institutional measures have been taken, and there has been a penetration of the 'grass roots' organizations (including trade unions) which might otherwise have provided a source of organized resistance. While Singapore has been a democracy in the legal sense since independence, and trade unions have been allowed to organize, the reality for workers and for organized labour is an incorporation of the trade union movement and virtually complete managerial prerogatives. How this is achieved is explored in detail.

While for the sake of consistency of presentation with the chapters on Korea, Taiwan and Hong Kong, we have used the subtitles 'state', 'employers' and 'labour', the reader will soon recognize that in the case of Singapore the distinctions between these three actors in the industrial system are rather blurred.

Economic Development and Economic Structure

Following Singapore's separation from the Federation of Malaysia in 1965, the strategy of import substitution, which was being pursued by the federation, was considered untenable for a tiny city state. An export oriented strategy based on the attraction of foreign direct investments, first in labour intensive sectors and later in the more capital intensive, was vigorously pursued, and has continued to be pursued since then. By 1981, foreign enterprises accounted for 58 per cent of manufacturing workers and 72 per cent of manufacturing capital expenditure. Success was reflected in annual average GDP growth rates of nine per cent up to the early 1980s (You and Lim 1984), then following a mini-crisis in 1985 and 1986 (Singapore experienced negative growth in 1985) growth rates again assumed their high levels (see table 2.1 for GNP levels in the late 1980s). Today Singapore is one of the wealthiest nations in Asia.

Table 2.1:   GNP and Per Capita GNP in Singapore, 1970-1990

	GNP (US$ billion)	GNP per capita (US$)
1970	1,894.2	913.1
1980	11,296.7	4,642.5
1988	24,816.8	8,795.6
1989	28,887.9	9,953.8
1990	35,258.0	11,949.0

Source: Ministry of Trade and Industry (1991).

Entrepot trade, which was the original reason for Singapore's existence as a British colony, remains important today: in 1990 re-exports accounted for 34.1 per cent of total exports. But this figure is down from a massive 65 per cent in 1969. The contribution of manufacturing to GDP grew from 11.4 per cent in 1961, to 20.4 per cent in 1970, and to 29.1 per cent in 1980. During the 1980s the percentage contribution of manufacturing to national income stabilized in the upper 20s (K.C. Ho 1991). The growth of importance of export oriented manufacturing is also reflected in the growth of manufacturing employment (table 2.2).

As table 2.2 shows, manufacturing employment as a proportion of total employment has been stable at around 26 per cent throughout the 1980s. The table also shows a tight labour market through the 1980s – an important point to which we shall return.

Table 2.2:   Changes in Employment Structure and Unemployment in Singapore,
1970-1990

	1970	1980	1988	1989	1990
Employed ('000 persons)	644.2	1,073.4	1,238.5	1,277.3	1,324.7
Unemployment rate (%)	6.0	3.0	3.3	2.2	1.7
Manufacturing ('000 persons)*	125.1 (19.4)	287.2 (26.8)	324.9 (26.2)	337.8 (26.4)	352.7 (26.6)

* Figures in parentheses are percentages of employed population.

Source: Ministry of Trade and Industry (1991).

Export Oriented Growth

As in the case of Hong Kong, a useful 'entrepot legacy' was a reasonable if
run down infrastructure, especially port, communications, and financial and other
service facilities, which were to be valuable in developing export markets and
attracting inward investments. To these existing facilities were added key institutions to promote industrial development. The Jurong Town Council was set up
to provide low cost industrial estates; the Development Bank of Singapore was
created to help provide project financing; the Singapore Institute of Standards and
Industrial Research provided technical and consultancy services to industry; and
the most important institution, the Economic Development Board (EDB), was
given the key roles of formulating industrial policies and ensuring those policies
were carried through (Hakam 1983).

Growth in trade was massive, giving Singapore by far the highest export to GNP
ratio among the ANICs. In 1989 the ratio stood at 154.4, and even excluding re-
exports was still 98.1 (see table 1.5, chapter one). Table 2.3 documents Singapore's
trade from 1980 to 1990.

Apart from the continued growth of merchandise trade to and from Singapore
over the past decade, table 2.3 also shows a persistent trade deficit. The doubling
of the deficit in 1990 from 1989 reflected strong domestic demand for imports
combined with a weakening of external demand for re-exports, and the effects of
anti-dumping actions by the EC and the US. However, Singapore's exceptionally
high earnings from services, particularly those related to travel and tourism (the
number of visitors to Singapore grew from 2.5 million in 1980 to nearly five
million in 1989, nearly twice the total population of Singapore) have more than
made up for the shortfall, giving an overall balance of payments surplus in the late
1980s and early 1990s (Ministry of Trade and Industry, Republic of Singapore
1991).

Table 2.3:   Exports and Imports of Singapore, 1980-1990 (US$ million)

	Domestic exports	Re-exports	Imports	Balance
1980	12,051.7	7,307.6	23,979.5	– 4,620.2
1988	24,624.9	14,657.2	43,841.5	– 4,559.4
1989	28,329.8	16,338.4	49,666.1	– 4,997.9
1990	34,623.0	17,904.4	60,582.5	– 8,055.1

Source: Ministry of Trade and Industry (1991).

Unlike the other ANICs, textiles and clothing sectors were never particularly significant in Singapore's export structure (see table 1.8, chapter one), although there was an influx of textiles and garments firms from Hong Kong in 1963 as Hong Kongese companies attempted to avoid British restrictions on exports from the colony (K.C. Ho 1991). Far more important have been petroleum refining, and more recently chemicals and electronics. The structure of Singapore's domestic exports from 1980 to 1990 is shown in table 2.4.

Most striking from table 2.4 is the rapid growth in importance of the electronics and related sectors. In 1990 office machines combined with electronics goods and parts accounted for 39.0 per cent of domestic exports (up from 16.8 per cent in 1980). Exports of mineral fuels declined by a half in value from 1980 to 1990, but still accounted for 27.3 per cent of the total value of exports in 1990. Chemicals and plastics rose from 2.2 to 5.8 per cent, and the rest remained steady. The importance of the electronics sector is also reflected in the structure of manufacturing employment (table 2.5).

Electronics, with 34.4 per cent of the manufacturing work force in 1989, was by far the most important employment generating sector. Reflecting their capital intensity, the chemicals and petroleum refining sectors combined accounted for a mere 3.6 per cent of the manufacturing work force, whereas the clothing (wearing apparel) sector, reflecting its labour intensity, accounted for 8.6 per cent.

This concentration of Singapore's manufacturing and export efforts in the electronics sector is arguably one of the nation's economic structural problems, to which we now turn.

Economic Restructuring: The 1980s

In the late 1970s, with a tight labour market, an unwelcome dependence on foreign labour, and a government hungry for continued high growth and economic success, Singapore ambitiously announced it was to embark on a 'second industrial revolution', whereby the labour intensive aspects of production would be shifted to the neighbouring low wage ASEAN countries, and Singapore would become

Table 2.4: Domestic Exports by Principal Commodity from Singapore, 1980-1990 (US$ million)*

	Re-exports	Food, beverages and tobacco	Mineral fuels	Chemicals and plastics	Office machines**	Other electronic goods and parts	Clothing	Other domestic exports	Total domestic exports
1980	7,307.6	328.4 (2.7)	6,622.5 (55.0)	267.6 (2.2)	123.1 (1.0)	1,903.0 (15.8)	353.6 (2.9)	2,453.5 (20.4)	12,051.7
1988	14,657.2	573.3 (2.3)	5,635.6 (22.9)	1,540.5 (6.3)	4,829.7 (19.6)	4,574.1 (18.6)	885.0 (3.6)	6,586.7 (26.7)	24,624.9
1989	16,338.4	694.5 (2.5)	6,780.4 (23.9)	1,724.7 (6.1)	6,049.7 (21.4)	5,046.0 (17.8)	931.4 (3.3)	7,103.1 (25.1)	28,329.8
1990	17,904.4	741.6 (2.1)	9,454.7 (27.3)	1,996.5 (5.8)	8,010.8 (23.1)	5,513.8 (15.9)	989.2 (2.9)	7,916.4 (22.9)	34,623.0

* Figures in parentheses are percentages of Singapore's total domestic exports.
** Includes automatic data processing machines from 1988.

Source: Calculated from data in Ministry of Trade and Industry (1991).

Table 2.5:   Structure of Manufacturing Employment in Singapore, 1989

	Numbers employed	% of manufacturing workforce
Electronic products	116,080	34.4
Wearing apparel	29,105	8.6
Fabricated metal products	27,085	8.0
Non-electrical machinery	22,606	6.7
Transport equipment	22,396	6.6
Electrical machinery and appliances	22,366	6.6
Printing and publishing	15,299	4.5
Chemical and petroleum products	12,124	3.6
Food	10,391	3.1
Others	60,310	17.9
Total	337,762	

Source: Ministry of Trade and Industry, Republic of Singapore (1991).

the 'brain centre of South East Asia' (Lim Chong Yah 1984). This was attempted through a comprehensive set of policies applied in the early 1980s which cen-tred on attracting companies in new 'high-tech' sectors and persuading existing industries to up-grade through automation. The imperatives placed on companies were reinforced with a high wages policy.

'High-tech' industries were given incentives to invest in Singapore with invest-ment allowances, tax incentives and product development assistance. 'Pioneer status' – which gave among other things zero tax for at least the first five years of operation – was restricted to 'worthy' companies, rather than being offered to any significant foreign investor as in the past. R&D activities were given special attention. In 1978 the government announced a range of incentives for R&D in-vestments and a Science Park, administered jointly by the EDB and the Science Council of Singapore, was set up to encourage interaction between university and company researchers.

R&D as a proportion of GNP remained stubbornly low at just 0.31 per cent in 1982 (up from 0.21 per cent in 1978) and virtually all of this was carried on by educational institutions (Hakam 1983), but as measured by fixed assets per worker, the quality of investment commitments tripled between 1979 and 1981. Tax deductions and cheap loans for mechanization and automation of existing industries also produced some results: from a base line of only a handful of cases of automation in 1981, by 1984 Singapore could boast 564 CNC machine tools, 86 industrial robots, and 220 CAD/CAM stations, and the numbers were increasing rapidly (Wilkinson 1986). The public sector was expected to provide the lead:

the public bureaucracy was put through a massive computerization programme spearheaded by the National Computer Board (NCB), with software developed by Singaporean computer professionals. The NCB also set up its own Software Technology Centre at the new Science Park, hoping to develop software for export as well as domestic use. A few multinationals followed the lead in setting up their own software centres in Singapore.

But the centrepiece of economic restructuring in Singapore was the introduction of a high wages policy from 1979 to 1981 (Chng Meng Kng et al. 1988). Unhappy with the quality of investment commitments in manufacturing during the 1970s, and perceiving the threat of increased competition from the other ASEAN countries and China for the attraction of export-led foreign manufacturing investments as they turned from import substitution to export orientation strategies, the government decided Singapore's balance of advantages lay more in capital intensive sectors which were less sensitive to wage costs. The policy was implemented through the authoritative tripartite National Wages Council (NWC – a key institution whose workings will be discussed later). In terms of real wages the effect was that while the 1970s saw increases of between two and four per cent per year, increases for 1980 to 1983 were between seven and nine per cent. Employers' labour *costs* rose even faster because of increases in labour-related levies. Chng et al. (1988) estimate annual average increases in total labour costs of 1.2 per cent from 1973 to 1978, compared with 10.1 per cent from 1979 to 1984. Potential inflationary effects were controlled by raising the compulsory contributions of employers and employees to the state administered savings and pensions fund (the Central Provident Fund – CPF). This contributed to the rise of Singapore's savings ratio from an already high 28.5 per cent in 1975 to a massive 42.7 per cent in 1985. Lim and Pang (1984) suggested that the high wages policy achieved its objectives by contributing to slowed employment growth, and by raising productivity growth from two to three per cent per year in the 1970s to four per cent per year in the early 1980s.

Arguably, however, the high wages policy was a case of a little too much a little too soon. Singapore's manufacturing labour costs shot ahead of those in the other ANICs (see table 3.10, chapter three). In 1980 Singapore's hourly compensation costs for manufacturing workers were already 99 per cent of Hong Kong's, 149 per cent of Taiwan's, and 154 per cent of Korea's. By 1985 the respective figures were 143 per cent, 165 per cent and 198 per cent. The pushing of wage rates ahead of productivity contributed to reduced company profitability, and this was exacerbated by a decline in some of Singapore's international markets for key sectors. Singapore slid into recession and registered a negative growth of -1.7 per cent in 1985. This was the first negative growth for two decades and it shocked the government into action. The government moved quickly to reduce employers' contributions to the CPF (from 25 per cent down to 10 per cent of wages), to reduce corporate taxes (from 40 per cent down to 33 per cent), and to reduce Statutory Board bills (such as telephone and telex). At the same time the NWC declared a freeze on wages. The result was a reduction in employers' overall wage costs in 1986 (see table 3.10). Even while being implemented, these measures coincided with a recovery in the demand for exports, especially from the US, and hence there was a resurgence of growth (Rigg 1991). Nonetheless the recession brought home to the government the vulnerability of Singapore's exceptionally outward looking economy and its concentration on a small number of sectors, and a thorough review of the nation's economic structure led to another round of economic restructuring from the late 1980s.

Economic Restructuring: The 1990s

The Ministry of Trade and Industry set up an Economic Committee headed by the Prime Minister's son, Lee Hsien Loong, to come up with new directions for the economy, and a report was published in 1986 (Economic Committee 1986). As expected, the report blamed the recession on weak domestic demand, increases in labour costs, and global demand conditions which hit Singapore's oil-related sector especially hard. As well as recommending the short term wages and tax measures described above, and which were implemented in 1986 to 1988, the report put forward ideas on long term restructuring which included economic diversification, further development of the growing R&D base, and the development of Singapore as a centre for the regional operational headquarters of multinational capital. These plans were further refined in the late 1980s to become a coherent economic strategy intended to lead to Singapore's graduation from NIC to developed country status by the year 2000.

Signs of economic diversification so far are hard to find, certainly within manufacturing. Singapore's extreme dependence on the electronics and petrochemicals sectors was demonstrated by data in table 2.4: the two sectors between them accounted for 72.1 per cent of domestic exports in 1990. Table 2.6 shows an intensification of investment commitments in these sectors in the late 1980s and early 1990s. In 1990 they accounted for 72.2 per cent of investment commitments, up from 51 per cent in 1986.

The new investments are, however, in relatively high value areas: the value added per worker of manufacturing investments in 1990 were almost twice the existing manufacturing average. Manufacturing investments have further intensified in the early 1990s, reaching record levels in 1992. More than 40 per cent of these were, however, still in the electronics sector (*Financial Times*, 11 March 1993). The persistent growth in importance of electronics is also reflected in table 2.7, which shows a significant rise in imports of electronic components and parts in the 1980s.

Table 2.7 also shows a heavy rise in imports of machinery and electrical equipment, which reflects both the nation's increased spending on capital goods *and* its

Table 2.6: Investment Commitments in Manufacturing by Sector in Singapore, 1986-1990 (US$ million)*

	Electronic products and components	Petroleum, chemicals and plastics	Machinery and transport equipment	Fabricated metal products	Paper products and printing	Textiles and clothing	Others	Total
1986	180 (27.0)	169 (24.0)	155 (23.2)	38 (5.7)	17 (2.5)	2.6 (0.4)	115 (17.2)	667
1987	356 (40.8)	140 (16.1)	111 (12.7)	52 (6.0)	13 (1.4)	4.9 (0.6)	195 (22.4)	872
1988	431 (41.8)	104 (10.1)	142 (13.8)	57 (5.5)	37 (3.6)	5.2 (0.5)	255 (24.7)	1,031
1989	369 (35.7)	307 (29.7)	111 (10.7)	54 (5.2)	50 (4.8)	1.3 (0.1)	143 (13.8)	1,034
1990	629 (44.2)	399 (28.0)	158 (11.1)	60 (4.2)	44 (3.1)	1.7 (0.1)	132 (9.3)	1,424

* Figures in parentheses are percentages of total manufacturing investments.

Source: Calculated from data in Ministry of Trade and Industry, Republic of Singapore (1991).

Table 2.7:   Structure of Singapore's Imports, 1980-1990 (US$ million)*

	Food, drink and tobacco	Crude materials, fuels and chemicals	Transport equipment	Electronic components and parts	Other machinery and electrical equipment	Others	Total
1980	1,490.5 (6.2)	10,271.7 (42.8)	1,634.8 (6.8)	1,268.5 (5.3)	4,232.0 (17.6)	5,802 (21.2)	23,979.5
1988	2,682.0 (6.1)	11,017.0 (25.1)	1,997.6 (4.6)	4,333.3 (9.9)	12,700.5 (29.0)	11,111.1 (25.3)	43,841.5
1989	2,808.1 (5.7)	12,514.1 (25.2)	3,098.2 (6.2)	4,296.9 (8.7)	14,569.5 (29.3)	12,379.3 (24.9)	49,666.1
1990	3,166.9 (5.2)	15,979.9 (26.4)	3,371.1 (5.6)	4,950.8 (8.2)	18,748.5 (30.9)	14,365.3 (23.7)	60,582.5

* Figures in parentheses are percentages of total imports.

Source: Ministry of Trade and Industry, Republic of Singapore (1991).

dependence on imports of capital equipment. The latter undoubtedly contributed to Singapore's growing negative trade balance in the 1980s.

An overall picture of Singapore's trade-related problems can be completed after considering table 2.8.

This shows that while the US and Europe continue as Singapore's most important export markets, there is a heavy dependence on Japan for imports. As is the case in all the ANICs, these are particularly imports of capital goods (see chapter one). Hence we can characterize Singapore's present economic and trade structure as being highly concentrated in a small number of sectors, with an export dependence on the advanced West and a capital goods import dependence on Japan, and perhaps increasingly the other ANICs.

Diversification is seen as necessary to reduce Singapore's concentration in a small number of sectors and hence reduce the country's vulnerability to sectoral trade fluctuations. The Ministry of Trade and Industry's identification of agro-technology, biotechnology, robotics and automation (in addition to information technology and microelectronics) to be given priority government support (Wu 1991) may help diversification, though with a total work force of only 1.3 million there are clear limits to the extent to which manufacturing diversification can sensibly occur. However, perhaps more important than manufacturing diversification *per se* is Singapore's ambition of greatly strengthening its role as a 'brain centre' and services centre for manufacturing in the whole ASEAN region.

In 1987 R&D expenditures had grown to 0.9 per cent of GNP (virtually all government funded) and there were 1.26 researchers per thousand population (Morris-Suzuki 1992b). These figures are expected to more than double by the mid to late 1990s: the government has already added several specialist research establishments to the existing Science Park, a new technology oriented university has been set up, and foreign talent is now being actively recruited from countries around the world. R&D capability is still very weak compared with that in Korea and Taiwan, but the government appears unwilling to dilute its ambitions, and identifies the provision of R&D services for companies across the ASEAN region as a potential large growth area.

ASEAN figures prominently more generally in Singapore's ambitions to expand its role in service provision. Singapore has long been a switching centre for air and sea cargo traffic in South East Asia, and a regional centre in the provision of financial services (in these regards Singapore's entrepot role within ASEAN has been maintained). These sectors are earmarked for expansion. There will be competition from other major cities in East Asia. Bangkok, for instance, has a serious ambition of becoming the financial hub of the emerging Indo-China economies, and hopes in the longer term to compete as a financial services centre for the whole East and South East Asian region directly with Singapore and Hong Kong (*Far Eastern Economic Review*, 18 March 1993). In the short to medium term, however, Singapore is well placed.

Table 2.8:　Singapore's Exports and Imports by Country of Destination and Origin, 1980-1990 (US$ million)*

	Japan			Malaysia			US			Other ANICs		
	Exports	Imports	Balance	Exports	Imports	Balance	Exports	Imports	Balance	Exports	Imports	Balance
1980	1,159.1 (6.0)	4,279.1 (17.8)	-3,120.0	2,904.0 (15.0)	3,323.2 (13.6)	-419.2	2,462.2 (12.7)	3,380.0 (14.1)	-917.8	2,110.0 (10.9)	1,333.9 (5.6)	771.1
1988	3,392.9 (8.6)	9,622.6 (21.9)	-6,229.7	5,327.5 (13.6)	6,424.5 (14.7)	-1,097.0	9,355.0 (23.8)	6,816.9 (15.5)	2,538.1	4,338.3 (11.0)	4,457.5 (10.2)	-119.2
1989	3,818.7 (8.5)	10,598.1 (21.3)	-6,779.4	6,109.2 (13.7)	6,554.9 (13.2)	-452.7	10,403.9 (23.3)	8,514.2 (17.1)	1,889.7	5,268.7 (11.8)	5,132.6 (10.3)	136.1
1990	4,580.1 (8.7)	12,218.6 (20.2)	-7,638.5	6,868.1 (13.1)	8,255.7 (13.6)	-1,387.6	11,169.9 (21.3)	9,699.6 (16.0)	1,470.3	6,463.9 (12.3)	6,212.8 (10.3)	251.1

	Europe			Others			Total		
	Exports	Imports	Balance	Exports	Imports	Balance	Exports	Imports	Balance
1980	3,097.7 (16.0)	3,278.6 (13.7)	-180.9	7,625.3 (39.4)	8,384.7 (35.0)	-759.4	19,359.3	23,979.5	-4,620.2
1988	6,058.9 (15.4)	6,500.8 (14.8)	-441.9	10,809.5 (27.5)	10,019.2 (22.9)	790.3	39,282.1	43,841.5	-4,559.4
1989	7,081.8 (15.9)	7,643.3 (15.4)	-561.5	11,986.0 (26.8)	11,223.0 (22.6)	763.0	44,668.3	49,666.1	-4,997.8
1990	9,133.3 (17.4)	9,660.8 (15.9)	-527.5	14,312.1 (27.2)	14,535.0 (24.0)	-222.9	52,527.4	60,582.5	-8,055.1

* Figures in parentheses are percentages of total exports and imports.

Source:　Calculated from data in Ministry of Trade and Industry, Republic of Singapore (1991).

Also earmarked for growth is Singapore's role as a location for the regional operational headquarters of multinationals, whereby the city state will provide a sophisticated infrastructure and logistics and R&D support to companies with manufacturing interests across ASEAN (Tokunaga 1992; Wu 1991). Many regional headquarters of the world's corporate giants have already been attracted by the availability of Singapore's highly qualified manpower and the special tax incentives on offer. Started in February 1988, by June 1989 22 companies had already been given the benefits of operational headquarter status. Promotion of the 'growth triangle' (described in chapter one) has further added to the impetus in recent years. Of course, Singapore can in the future be expected to face increased competition from the ASEAN countries themselves, who would expressely prefer to enjoy the benefits of the location of headquarter activities within their own countries rather than serve merely as a cheap labour resource for the lower value manufacturing activities. But in the meantime Singapore appears to have carved out for itself a niche which will see the country improve economically through the 1990s.

Labour Markets

An integral element of economic restructuring since the late 1970s has been strong supply side measures regarding labour. As the government is apt to repeat frequently, 'our only resource is the human resource', and the government invests a great deal of effort in its development and management.

Singapore has an exceptionally highly educated labour force: while education has been given priority since the 1960s, the economic restructuring package of the 1980s included a doubling of the number of graduates between 1980 and 1985, mainly in technology, engineering and management disciplines, so that around 15 per cent of new labour force entrants had a degree. The annual output of graduates from higher education institutions rose from 6,545 in 1981 to 15,052 in 1991, and was still rising (Ministry of Labour, Republic of Singapore 1991). Further, an up-graded Vocational and Industrial Training Board (VITB) and new industry-wide training centres meant that over half of labour force entrants in 1985 were trained as technicians or in a skill. Post-entry training for the employed work force was financed by a Skills Development Fund (SDF) which levies a payroll tax. Introduced in 1979, in 1980 the levy on wages was raised from two to four per cent, but was cut back to two per cent in 1985 in the face of the recession and the fact that there was insufficient demand for the budget. The fund has been used to finance training centres, to re-train retrenched workers, and most importantly to provide up to 70 per cent of the costs of in-company training programmes.

As well as the obvious problem that employers have not advanced into high-tech sectors so quickly as to need such highly educated and trained labour, another problem identified has been the rigidity of the education system with its emphasis on behavioural and psychological conformity (Pang Eng Fong 1982). Wu (1991) comments that measures are now being taken to enhance the creativity of Singaporeans by changing the styles of education.

The tight labour market with which Singapore has had to cope for the best part of two decades has been one of the factors behind the government's continued imperative to up-grade. Another has avowedly been a desire to reduce dependence on large amounts of foreign labour, though the reality has been a careful management of foreign labour in Singapore through the 1980s and into the 1990s. Following Singapore's dependence in 1965, the country continued to engage many workers who were suddenly formally foreigners – i.e. Malaysians. These were defined as a 'traditional source' of foreign labour. But in 1978 the labour market became so tight that the government reluctantly opened Singapore's doors to 'non-traditional sources' (Pang and Lim 1982). Workers arrived in large numbers mostly from Thailand, the Philippines and the Indian sub-continent to take up jobs increasingly considered low status by Singaporeans in textiles, electronics assembly, construction, and domestic service. But already by 1979, as part of the restructuring programme, the government had laid plans to phase out all foreign workers except professionals by 1991, and 'non-traditional source' labour even sooner.

The danger that cheap foreign labour might hold down overall wage levels and encourage factories to continue to operate inefficiently was only one of the reasons given. Others appealed to the fears that guest workers would place a strain on housing provision, medical and recreational services, that the crime rate might increase, and that some would want to marry Singaporeans and settle down (Chew and Chew 1984; Tan Chee Hwat 1984). Stahl (1984) has rebutted these arguments.

But in the mid 1980s the dependence on foreign workers was still strong. In 1985, 150,000 foreigners, around 12 per cent of the total labour force, were employed in Singapore; around half of these worked in the construction industry. The government then announced a flexibility in the phasing out of 'non-traditional source' workers, but at the same time re-emphasized that they were only a temporary expedient by raising the monthly levy charged on their employment and tightening up on the ratios of foreigners to locals permitted at individual work sites. Meanwhile in 1984 the government had announced that workers from Hong Kong, Macao, South Korea and Taiwan would liberally be granted entry and allowed to take up citizenship before the 1991 deadline. Designated 'new traditional source' (sic!) workers, it was claimed that since they were more skilled and more expensive, their presence would not hamper the restructuring programme. Another reason occasionally mooted by government was that 'new traditional source' workers, having a Confucianist cultural milieu in common, might be more easily assimilated with a Singaporean population dominated by ethnic Chinese. As Singapore's then Prime Minister Lee Kuan Yew, speaking on a BBC World Service programme in 1984, put it:

If you get people from, say, Thailand or the Philippines, then you've got a completely different culture. They're a jolly people; they sing, they dance, they like fiestas – particularly the Filipinos – it's unsettling on the local population.

Being dependent on labour exports as a source of foreign income, the governments' of the non-traditional source countries were upset by the new policy, and the Philippines Labour Minister took the trouble to visit Singapore to plead that his country be included in the 'new traditional source' category. He was turned down (*Sunday Times*, 26 August 1984). Since then, few foreign 'new traditional source' workers have entered Singapore to work, and the reliance on 'traditional' and 'non-traditional' sources has continued. K.C. Ho (1991) estimated that around nine per cent of the total work force were foreign workers in the late 1980s. Most work on short term contracts, and there is strong evidence that many suffer poor working conditions, low wages, long hours, and are subject to employment contract rackets in their home countries which can mean they spend at least the first few months of a one or two year spell in Singapore paying off the cost of gaining employment. (For details of the plight of Thai workers in the construction industry in Singapore see Patarapanich et al. 1987; and for a discussion of the problems of female Filipinos employed as domestic servants in Singaporean housholds see Arotcarena et al. 1986).

Today the government varies the number of foreign workers in Singapore according to labour market conditions in specific sectors of the economy – hence giving them the role of buffer for the Singaporean work force in the face of any adverse trading conditions – and ensures any unwanted downward pressure on wages is controlled by varying the levy it charges on their employment.

The government also attempts to intervene in the labour market indirectly through its productivity campaigns intended to change the values and attitudes of the population, and through a eugenics programme aimed at altering patterns of pro-creation. The success (success by the government's definition that is) of these programmes has been limited, but they will be discussed in detail later.

Summary

On the basis of foreign direct manufacturing investment, Singapore developed rapidly from entrepot to major exporter of petro-chemicals and electronics. State-led economic restructuring in the 1980s had a degree of success, but the vulnerability of the economy was brought home by the 1985 recession. The economy came out of recession as quickly as it went in, but the government was now determined to diversify and to become the ASEAN region's 'brain centre' as the location of the operational headquarters of the multinationals who would undertake their labour intensive manufacturing in the surrounding cheaper labour countries. The concept of the 'growth triangle' is a practical and vivid illustration of the regional division of labour within which Singapore is taking a specialized role. While the other ASEAN nations would undoubtedly prefer the activities Singapore is now actively attracting to be located within their own shores, and while there is some doubt over the likelihood that Singapore can really become a centre for R&D, the medium term economic future looks relatively secure.

The State

Comprised of an alliance of left wing labour activists, anti-colonialists and middle class liberals, the Peoples' Action Party (PAP) came into power in Singapore's first general election in 1959. In 1961 the party split: the moderate faction led by Lee Kuan Yew retained the PAP badge, and the left wing re-organized themselves as the *Barisan Sosialis*. Despite the fact that the PAP had lost, in the process, much of its working class support, it managed to win the 1963 elections. Following the separation of Singapore from the Malaysian Federation in 1965, the PAP set about the task of 'nation building', primarily through crushing any serious opposition and attempting to incorporate the mass of the population (for a detailed discussion of the origins and early development of the modern state in Singapore see Clutterbuck 1984). Since then the PAP has become synonymous with government, and the government with Lee Kuan Yew, the world's longest served Prime Minister. Justified by the 'national interest' and 'pragmatism', Lee Kuan Yew's PAP has attempted to dominate almost every aspect of social life such that the only real sense that Singapore can be considered a democracy is the existence of 'one person one vote' (Chua Beng Huat 1985).

Economic Role

With no indigenous bourgeoisie to speak of, and with the government's express ambition to modernize a country with high unemployment and a decaying infrastructure, it was not surprising that the state should in the early years take a lead in economic development. The extent of government intervention in the economy is, nonetheless, quite extraordinarily extensive. As described above, this includes the manipulation of incentives for inward investment, the provision of infrastructure and utilities, work force education and training, and the control of guest workers. The government has also used the National Wages Council (NWC) both to ensure a high company profitability, and to restructure the economy (objectives which have not always gone hand in hand).

The government directly employs around 20 per cent of the working population, in particular in public monopolies which control the utilites and TV and radio broadcasting, though this number might be expected to decline in the near future as plans for the privatization of several government run companies are implemented. The government has also provided low cost housing via the Housing Development

Board (HDB) to the Singaporean work force on public housing estates which accomodate around 87 per cent of the population. Finances for the HDB and other public investments have come in large part from the Central Provident Fund (CPF). In 1988 CPF savings accounted for 24 per cent of gross national savings. In addition the government holds around 75 per cent of all land (Rigg 1991).

Singapore must not, then, be characterized as *laissez faire*, in spite of expressions of admiration for the economy from Margaret Thatcher and Ronald Reagan, among other free market advocates. The economy is probably more open to inward investments and to imports than any of the other ANICs, but even here the types of investment are influenced by the government, and domestic consumption of goods (imported or otherwise) is effectively controlled by varying rates of forced savings via the CPF.

Lee Kuan Yew and the PAP

Singapore's political system has been characterized as a case of 'one party dominance' (Chan Heng Chee 1976). Cambridge educated Prime Minister Lee has overseen a political elite which has extended and consolidated its power since independence through the incorporation of the civil bureaucracy and the leadership of the official trade union movement. Arguably, to understand politics in Singapore means to understand Lee Kuan Yew (Josey 1980). Deriving legitimacy from appeals to the national interest, to 'Asian values', and latterly from economic growth and success, Lee Kuan Yew has sought to engineer an orderly, disciplined society free from the 'Western maladies' of conflict, permissiveness, decadence and individualism. But ideology is not the only means by which the PAP has extended and retained power and control. Equally important has been the control of opposition movements by more or less subtle means. These include censorship of the media, the penetration of 'grass roots' organizations, and where necessary the use of the law.

TV and radio programmes are more or less directly under government control, and national new programmes consist in large part of lengthy quotations from the authorities. TV and radio are also used frequently for government propaganda which tells people how they should behave, and along with books, cinema and other forms of entertainment, programmes are scrutinized for their moral and political content and may be banned or have parts excised (Dhanabalan 1983; Josey 1980). One bizarre case of censorship in 1983 was the removal of inscriptions from the headstone of the grave of a deceased Communist activist who was hanged in Malaysia for the possession of fire arms. The tombstone described Tan Chay Wa as a 'noble revolutionary warrior' and a 'martyr'. His brother, who was responsible for the inscription, was sentenced to a year's imprisonment and the family plastered over the offending words on the advice of the police (*Straits Times*, 12 July 1985).

Newspapers are similarly controlled. The Essential Information Regulations have occasionally been used to prevent public discussion of certain issues such as the abolition of trail by jury for capital offences in 1969 (Amnesty International 1980). George (1973) suggests that the *Nanyang Siang Pau* and the *Eastern Sun* were closed in the early 1970s because their owners were part of the local business elite who at the time were disenchanted with the PAP and threatening to turn their support to opposition political parties. The *Singapore Herald* was also closed in the early 1970s, in this case on the grounds that it was attempting to 'erode the will and attitude of the people' with regard to national service, labour laws and the Internal Security Act, and that it advocated 'with-it-isms' and permissiveness in sex, drugs and styles (Chan Heng Chee and Evers 1978). In 1974 the Newspaper and Printing Presses Act replaced the Printing Presses Ordinance to give the government even wider scope to censor newspapers (Clutterbuck 1984). By the mid 1980s, the monopoly Singapore Press Holdings had virtually complete control over the popular press, and articles critical of the government and government policy had become extremely rare and virtually always contributed by people other than the newspapers' own journalists. Foreign publications have also been dealt with by the government, though not so ruthlessly because of the state's desire to be seen as democratic overseas. Errant foreign journalists have frequently been ousted with a simple refusal to renew work permits (for which reasons do not have to be given), but in 1986 the government took the more radical step of threatening to 'gazette' foreign publications which 'interfere in domestic politics'. Gazetting meant a restriction of sales in Singapore (though the local population would still be free to read the gazetted publication), hence effectively imposing a financial penalty. Among those well known subversive foreign newspapers which have been gazetted are *Time* and the *Asian Wall Street Journal*.

Government infiltration of, and control over, the organizations from which opposition groupings might otherwise be expected to emerge is pervasive, most importantly the trade unions as will be discussed later. Students and academics are also closely watched. The Students Union of the National University is bound by its constitution not to engage in politics or make pronouncements of a political nature, and academics are not allowed a staff association. Pucetti (1972) documents one occasion in 1969 when the Prime Minister gave a personal warning to staff of the departments of philosophy, sociology and political science that he knew what 'twaddle' they were teaching, and that he knew from 'first hand reports' about the 'cracks' they made in class about government slogans. Foreign staff should not engage in politics, they were told: they could be put on a plane within 24 hours. A Suitability Certificate, which was a police guarantee of the student's background, became a prerequisite for entry into university in 1969. This was finally removed in 1978 – it is not known how many potential students were excluded for their political beliefs (Amnesty International 1980).

Also subject to surveillance are the public housing estates: the leaders of Residents' Committees (RCs) were described by Lee Kuan Yew as 'the elders of our modern vertical villages in the sky'. RCs are expected to cooperate with the HDB and the police to, among other things, discourage anti-social behaviour, and detect illegal immigrants and work permit over-stayers. Citizens Consultative Committees (CCCs) on other hand are organized at the constituency level to provide a forum for discussion of government polices and issues of national interest. School children do not escape attention either. The National Police Cadet Corps (NPCC) has over 20,000 police cadets in 120 secondary schools, and the police distribute newsletters to youths and occasionally organize discos and pop concerts.

The PAP's trump card is the Internal Security Act (ISA) which was inherited from the British colonial administration. The extensive powers of arrest without trial and political detention which the ISA lends the government were used widely in the early years of independence to crush Chinese chauvinists and radical politicians, students and trade unionists (George 1973). Since then the ISA has been used selectively against less threatening opposition. For instance in 1987, 20 people accused of a 'Marxist plot' to overthrow the government were detained without trial and, according to Amnesty International, confessions were gained in lengthy interrogations lasting up to 50 hours. The government poo-poohed accusations that torture was used. When public confessions broadcast on TV followed, many Singaporeans were surprised to find that the 'Marxists' were mostly middle class social workers and Catholics with a liberal bent.

While there is clear evidence of a degree of cynicism among Singaporeans towards the PAP and its 'grass roots' activities (Wilkinson 1986) it is also clear that the pervasiveness of PAP influence and control throughout society makes for enormous difficulty in the creation of any credible organized opposition. Serious opposition movements are too easily 'nipped in the bud'. Nonetheless, a small opposition has been allowed, if only to lend credibility to the notion that Singapore is a democracy. The PAP's monopoly on Parliament (the Legislature) was broken after 13 years in 1981 when J.B. Jeyaretnam of the Workers' Party won a famous victory in the Anson constituency. Then in 1985 a second opposition MP, Chiam See Tong, leader of the Social Democratic Party, was elected. Jeyeretnam was jailed and de-barred from becoming an MP for five years for allegedly making inaccurate statments about his Party's finances to the authorites in 1986. Whether or not the charges were 'trumped up' was hotly debated among the local population (but not via the press of course) at the time. Four opposition MPs were elected at the 1991 general election (three from the Social Democrats and one from the Workers' Party), obviating the need for the government to appoint opposition MPs, a measure which was made possible in a new law which was introduced in early 1990.

A more significant development than the stirrings of a growing, albeit small and disorganized, opposition movement in the 1980s was Lee Kuan Yew's announcement that he would retire as Prime Minister at the age of 65. The 'problem of succession' was a key talking point through the mid to late 1980s, and a favourite topic of conversation was whether the Prime Minister's son, Brigadier General Lee Hsien Loong, who had risen rapidly in politics after an army career to become Minister for Trade and Industry by the mid 1980s, would take over and establish a 'Lee dynasty' in Singapore. In fact in 1990 Goh Chok Tong was sworn in as the new Prime Minister, and a couple of years later rumours that Hsien Loong had cancer were officially confirmed. Goh has been associated with a new generation of PAP leaders with a 'softer approach' to the management of *Singapore Inc.* However, Lee Kuan Yew retained a Cabinet seat as Senior Minister without Portfolio, and is still Secretary General of the PAP. Lee commented that 'those who believe that I've gone into permanent retirement really should have their heads examined' and that if Singapore's new generation leaders strayed from the path he had set then if necessary he would return 'even from the grave' (Liu 1990). The emergence of Goh's vision of a 'kinder, gentler Singapore' may, then, be postponed for some time yet.

Social Engineering

... some of the qualities I most admire in (Singaporeans) are qualities which it appears are now to be discouraged and reduced. For instance, their distrust of politicians, their loyalty less towards 'the state' than towards family, small groupings and individuals, and their natural inclination to take people as they find them. These characteristics are not among those which go to make a nation, and the government desires to make a nation (Enright 1969, p.167).

We will be to blame if youngsters ten years from now become hooligans, ruffians and sluts. They can be trained to be otherwise. Even dogs can be trained as proved by the Police Training School where dogs, at a whistle, jump through a hoop, sit down or attack those who need to be attacked (Lee Kuan Yew, cited in George 1973, p.194).

Singapore's agencies of socialization have been pressed into service in what is probably the most extensive experiment of social engineering in the post-war world, with a wide range of measures to promote nationalism and 'Asian' values, and to create an 'orderly' society.

On coming to power the PAP was immediately concerned with establishing a national identity among a citizenry made up of immigrants from various Chinese provinces, from Malaysia, and from the Indian sub-continent (around 75 per cent of the population is ethnic Chinese, 15 per cent Malay, and 6 per cent Tamil). Goh Chok Tong described the nation building programme as a 'marathon' in 1984, and it continues unabated in the 1990s. Moral education at school and national service are justified in terms of 'nation building', as are occasional campaigns such as Total Defence, and Speak Manadarin. The latter campaign is an attempt to persuade the Chinese to speak a common dialect to improve social integration and create a common identity among a population which speaks a variety of dialects.

'Asian' values are frequently contrasted with 'Western' values to legitimate a range of government actions from censorship to the prevention of 'fishbowl government' (see Dhanabalan 1983 for an account by a government minister). Justified by reference to the need to preserve Asian values, the government encourages 'three tier families' through tax incentives and preferential treatment in public housing allocation (Wong 1979), and long ago banned the popular *Cosmopolitan* women's magazine because of its 'immoral' position regarding, for instance, extra-marital and pre-marital sex. 'Western decadence' has also been blamed for 'anti-social' behaviour (hanging around in groups and wearing 'outlandish clothes') among groups of youths such as the 'Centrepoint Kids' (Centrepoint is a shopping centre) and the 'McDonald's Kids'. 'Asian values' also underpin the moral education component of school curricula in the Being and Becoming and Good Citizen programmes.

Perhaps ironically, the PAP had spent its early years in power fighting threats from Chinese educated radicals, trade unionists and secret society leaders, and was representative primarily of the English speaking middle classes (Rosa 1990). It appears that by the 1980s, having reduced the potential threat from the Chinese educated, the government concluded that it could now use Chinese values to justify its policies. In particular, the relevance of neo-Confucian ethics to modern Singapore became a key issue (see Tu Wei Ming 1984 for a discussion), and the Chinese clan associations have been asked to play an active role through working with the government and the grass roots organizations (Kuah Khun Eng 1990). The re-emergence of a Chinese identity is also reflected, as we saw earlier, in the goverment's labour immigration policy which seeks to reduce dependence on the 'jolly' peoples and replace them with the 'new traditional sources' which are all Confucianist.

The existence of orderliness in Singapore is well known to any visitor. Campaigns backed up by heavy penalties have been launched against gambling, spitting, littering, and a range of other minor as well as major misdemeanours. Public video game parlours and dancing in the street (unless a licence from the police has first been gained) were banned in the early 1980s, and volunteer groups have been encouraged to offer youths 'more wholesome activities' (*Sunday Times*, 23 February 1986). Equally remarkable as the *existence* of orderliness, then, is the fact that orderliness, like Asian values and national identity, is *mandated* by the state, rather than springing 'naturally' from the Singaporean population. Indeed, the imperative to follow rules under strict surveillance could, arguably, be reflective of a society in which the cultural values of the population are not given sway.

The most controversial element of Singapore's programme of social engineering must be its eugenics programme. In 1983 Lee Kuan Yew announced that the pattern of pro-creation was lop-sided, and if the less qualified continued to produce more children than the highly educated, then:

for every two graduates, in 25 years time, there will be one graduate, and for every two uneducated workers, there will be three. ... We will be unable to maintain our present standard of living. ... Levels of competence will decline. Our economy will falter, the administration will suffer, and society will decline (*Straits Times*, 15 August 1983).

In the following months various measures were announced, including tax incentives for graduate women to bear more children, priority in school selection for the children of graduate mothers where they had three or more children, reduced state medical provision for the third child of less well educated parents, and financial incentives for less well educated mothers to be sterilized after two children. Most insidiously, a Social Development Unit (SDU) was established to encourage graduates to meet, marry and breed. the SDU organized discos and other activities where it tried to create the atmosphere where romance might blossom, and even organized a 'love boat' which took young well educated Singaporeans to exotic beach resorts in Malaysia. It also attempted to place pressures on the highly educated to marry by persuading employers to give counselling to their bright, single employees (Wilkinson 1986). The package of incentives have since been modified, but still graduate Singaporean women tend to marry late and have relatively few, if any, children. By 1988 the SDU could claim responsibility for only 20 marriages (Wilkinson 1988), and the 1990 census showed that little had changed since 1983: one in four graduate women remained single throughout their lives, and in the 25 to 29 age group, the proportion of unmarried women actually jumped from 59 per cent in 1980 to 64 per cent in 1990 (*Korea Times*, 16 July 1991).

What had, perhaps, changed, was the propensity of young professionals to move out. 4,700 families were reported to have left for Australia and the West in 1988 alone, numbers which Liu (1990) described as reflecting a serious brain drain caused in part by the mid 1980s recession, but more importantly by the increasingly harsh political and social environment.

State-Labour Relations

Of course, work values, like wider family and social values, do not escape the government's attention. In the light of complaints from employers about Singaporean workers' lack of a sense of responsibility and loyalty (the details of which are explored later in the chapter) the government embarked on a productivity campaign in the early 1980s (for details see Wilkinson and Leggett 1985 and Wilkinson 1986). Propaganda reaches its height each November which is designated 'productivity month'. Inspired by the example of Japanese and Korean workers, the Office of the Prime Minister set up a National Productivity Board (NPB) charged with the responsibility of raising productivity consciousness. Songs, films, publications, greetings cards and banners, reinforced by Ministerial speeches and media programmes and articles are used in an attempt to 'create a spirit of infectious enthusiasm and emotional commitment'. The campaign has a mascot in 'Teamy the Bee', chosen because 'bees possess many attributes which are the pre-requisites for higher productivity ... organization, teamwork, industry, good communication and quality output'. In 1980 the Prime Minister's Office also instructed that Human Resource Management (HRM) be made a compulsory subject for all undergraduates at the National University, regardless of their Faculty, as part of an attempt to create a generation of of Singaporean managers who would practice 'people-centred management' to create a 'commitment to common goals'. And between 1980 and 1984 alone the SDF provided training in management and supervision with a human relations emphasis to 44,000 people – around one in 30 of the total labour force. Arguably, however, attempting to create company loyalty and participative management may rub against the grain of traditional Chinese business culture, which is characterized by 'economic familism' (i.e. work and business is for the family, not the enterprise as in Japan), and this may help explain some of the cynicism of Singaporeans towards the government's ambitions (see chapters four and five for a discussion of the Chinese family business in Taiwan and Hong Kong).

Tripartite institutions for ensuring a stability of industrial relations in Singapore include a Skills Development Council which manages the SDF, and the aforementioned NWC, which is the most important body. The NWC is comprised of four government representatives, four from employers' organizations, and four from the National Trades Union Council (NTUC). Since 1972, its recommendations provided a guide for wage increases from which employers varied little, including the during the high wage years of the early 1980s. However, following the mid 1980s recession the NWC gave a little more flexibility by giving broader guidlines on the size of the year-end bonus, which had been frozen at one month of annual salary since 1972, and asking employers to link rises to productivity performance (*Far Eastern Economic Review*, 8 September 1988). Oehlers (1991) gives three reasons as to why, despite the non-binding nature of NWC recommendations, they have almost invariably been followed closely. First, because they are officially tripartite they carry some legitimacy, which is further heightened by Cabinet endorsement. Secondly, the guidelines are fully adhered to in the public sector which sets expectations for the private sector. Thirdly, any disputes arising from wage negotiations are referred to the Ministry of Labour for conciliation, and if necessary to the Industrial Arbitration Court (IAC), which invariably makes judgements in the light of NWC recommendations.

Legislation has also had an important bearing on industrial relations. In 1960 and 1964 the Industrial Relations Ordinance was introduced then strengthened to give the IAC a high degree of authority in conciliation and arbitration. Then in 1968 two pieces of legislation, justified as essential for economic survival, shifted the balance of power decisively in favour of employers. The Employment Act of 1968 altered the conditions of service of employees by increasing standard working hours from 39 to 44; reducing public holidays from 15 to 11 per year; reducing rest days, sick leave and annual paid leave entitlements; and increasing the length of service necessary to receive retrenchment benefits to three years. The Industrial Relations (Ammendment) Act, on the other hand, greatly extended managerial prerogatives by making it illegal for unions to negotiate on issues such as hiring, firing, promotions, transfers, retrenchments, and work assignments. These issues were also put beyond the jurisdiction of the IAC. The Act additionally provided for industrial relations stability by raising the minimum duration of collective agreements from 18 months to three years (Rodan 1989).

As if these measures were not enough, the Trade Union (Ammendment) Act of 1982 redfined trade unionism with a productionist rather than adversarial emphasis. And in 1984 the Employment Act was ammended to increase even further the discretion management could exercise over employment conditions by removing various stipulations. For instance, employers could now adjust work schedules so that even 12 hour shifts would not attract overtime pay, and the minimum interval between rest days was increased from 6 to 12 (Krislov and Leggett 1984; Leggett 1988).

Combined, these laws make for exceptional employer prorogatives and leave employees with little in the way of legal safeguards or bargaining rights. Further, the powers of the IAC mean that a legal strike in Singapore is virtually impossible without the tacit consent of the government: hence workers were apparently allowed to disrupt Aeroflot schedules in a well publicized anti-Soviet protest in 1983, whereas a work-to-rule by the Singapore Airline Pilots Association (SIAPA) in 1980 resulted in the union's de-registration, and public appologies broadcast on TV by several SIAPA officials for initiating illegal industrial action (Leggett 1984).

To understand state-labour relations further demands consideration of the close relationship between the PAP and the NTUC, and this is considered shortly. First, the characteristics of Singapore's employers and their relations with the state and labour will be explored.

Employers

In 1960 the PAP leadership invited a UN mission headed by Albert Winsemius to provide advice on economic and industrial development. The Winsemius report, among other things, advised on how to attract foreign capital in the face of a dearth of local capital and industrial know-how: the state should seduce foreign capital with a range of incentives, and hold wages down. In the early 1960s the report's findings were converted into a four year plan, which was implemented with mixed success (Rodan 1989). However, after the separation from the Malaysian Federation in 1965, labour intensive, export oriented foreign manufacturing direct investments were pursued more vigorously. US capital began to pour in, and the economy began to take off.

Employer-State Relations

The attraction of manufacturing FDI was so successful that by 1981 foreign enterprises accounted for 58 per cent of manufacturing workers and 72 per cent of capital expenditure (You and Lim 1984). In 1990 foreign manufacturers remained dominant, accounting for 89.3 per cent of manufacturing capital expenditure. Table 2.9 shows the amounts and origins of manufacturing investments in Singapore from 1984 to 1990.

Investments from the US (34.8 per cent of total cumulative manufacturing investments from 1984 to 1990) and Japan (27.6 per cent over the same period) have been the most important, with significant investments from Europe as well. These have been concentrated in the electronics, petroleum, chemical and pharmaceutical industries. These figures suggest Singapore's manufacturing industry will continue to be dominated by foreign companies throughout the 1990s.

Local investors were not discriminated against explicitly, but in the early years the EDB did tend to focus on large foreign companies. Further, it was those companies in priority export oriented, labour intensive, industries which were able to invest over US$ 1 million which could claim pioneer status which gave the most favourable terms of investment. This effectively ruled out the majority of local companies which had neither the capital nor the capability in modern manufacturing sectors. In the 1970s the government directly participated in some industries in wholly owned companies or through joint ventures which again meant difficulty in local capitalist participation. And local capital was further handicapped in the early 1980s by the wage rises recommended by the NWC (Deyo 1981; Haggard and Cheng 1987; Lee Shen Yi 1978). Deyo (1981) and Lim and Pang (1984) are not particularly optimistic, either, about opportunities for local firms to supply the multinationals, which in the absence of controls source from a variety of countries and often from other multinationals. The Japanese especially are likely to rely on Japanese subsidiaries or related companies in Singapore. In very recent years, local manufacturing enterprise development has been given more attention by, and assistance from, government (Ministry of Trade and Industry, Republic of Singapore 1991), and the privatization of public companies may increase local participation in business, though it is too early to assess the effects of these changes. Statistics actually show a significant *rise* in the mean size of manufacturing establishments from 82.2 employees in 1981 to 92.5 employees in 1991 (Ministry of Trade and Industry, Republic of Singapore 1991). The contrast with Hong Kong, where small businesses have not been discriminated against, is striking. In Hong Kong the mean size of manufacturing establishments fell from 19.6 in 1980 to 14.9 in 1990, reflecting the growing predominance of locally owned small Chinese family businesses (see chapter five).

The tough labour legislation and corporatist controls established by government obviated the need for employers to develop special management styles to cope with a Singaporean work force, and although there is a dearth of case study

Table 2.9:   Investment Commitments by Country of Origin in Manufacturing in Singapore, 1984-1990 (US$ million)*

	US	Japan	EC 12	Other Europe	Other Foreign	Total Foreign	Local	Total
1984	370.0 (44.1)	76.5 (9.1)	146.4 (17.4)	2.9 (0.3)	17.0 (2.0)	612.8 (73.0)	226.7 (27.0)	839.5
1985	203.0 (38.1)	116.0 (21.8)	85.9 (16.1)	9.5 (1.8)	7.4 (1.4)	421.9 (79.3)	110.4 (20.7)	532.3
1986	203.9 (30.6)	227.0 (34.0)	94.2 (14.1)	6.4 (1.0)	15.9 (2.4)	547.4 (82.1)	119.3 (17.9)	666.7
1987	272.0 (31.2)	300.8 (34.5)	120.6 (13.8)	22.4 (2.6)	8.8 (1.0)	724.5 (83.1)	147.6 (16.9)	872.2
1988	301.4 (29.2)	355.2 (34.4)	177.3 (17.2)	6.7 (0.6)	11.1 (1.1)	851.8 (82.6)	179.6 (17.4)	1,031.4
1989	274.6 (26.6)	285.7 (27.6)	277.3 (26.8)	10.0 (1.0)	10.5 (1.0)	858.0 (83.0)	175.9 (17.0)	1,033.9
1990	604.6 (42.5)	406.0 (28.5)	226.7 (15.9)	22.8 (1.6)	11.0 (0.8)	1,271.1 (89.3)	152.9 (10.7)	1,424.1
Cumulative Total	2,229.5 (34.8)	1,767.2 (27.6)	1,128.4 (17.6)	80.7 (1.3)	81.7 (1.3)	5,287.5 (82.6)	1,112.4 (17.4)	6,400.1

* Figures in parentheses are percentages of total investments commitments.

Source: Calculated from data in Ministry of Trade and Industry, Republic of Singapore (1991).

material which would shed light on employment practices, it seems that Western employers attempted to work in the ways they knew best. As Pang Eng Fong (1981, p.496) puts it:

The main actor in the Singapore industrial relations system is the government and its agencies. Management is given a relatively free hand to maximize profits ... while the labour movement is assigned the role of helping to preserve industrial peace.

Western companies brought to Singapore what, by local standards, were participative styles (Low 1984; Redding and Richardson 1972). However, the employment they generated, especially in the electronics sector, has tended to be low skilled, requiring little training and involvement, and foreign employers have not been slow to retrench workers when market conditions have declined (Deyo 1981). Japanese companies, on the other hand, are reported as having a low trust of local management, and tend to centralize control at headquarters. Singaporeans are largely excluded from *ringi* (bottom-up) decision making, and promotion ceilings for locals have led to frustration (Milton-Smith 1986; Negandhi et al. 1987). Most foreign investors appear to have been exasperated at what they describe as the instrumentality of the Singaporean work force, a point to which we shall return shortly.

Local firms are reported as being managed in an autocratic fashion. Decision making is concentrated in the hands of the owner, the orientation is towards short term profitability, and relations with employees are personalistic and informal (Low 1984; Wee Chow Hou et al. 1989). Even among the larger local Chinese companies (which are particularly noticeable in the financial services and trading sectors) there are few publicly quoted companies, the owning families attempting to retain control. Lee Sheng Yi (1978) comments that these cultural characteristics mean few companies can grow beyond small or medium sized.

The continued preponderance of relatively small firms in the local private sector means a continuation of their relative lack of power *vis à vis* government (see chapter three on Korea for a striking contrast). Lee Sheng Yi (1978) describes an influence which is restricted to the lower levels of Singapore's elite structure. In the late 1970s more than half of Singapore's community centres were run by local businessmen, but businessmen have rarely been trusted to hold key positions which could have an influence on government policy. Multinationals, on the other hand, while having no direct bearing on government policies, have an obvious indirect influence. From the beginning, the PAP government has based its economic and labour policies on creating the right environment for foreign investments, and this continues today.

The 'Labour Problem' and Joint Consultation

Two reports by the EDB and one by the Ministry of Labour in 1979 and 1980 presented lists of complaints from employers which suggested that beneath the veneer of industrial peace lay significant dissatisfaction and distrust on the part of both employers and employees. The 'adverse attributes' of the Singaporean worker included: individualistic and not cooperative; reluctance to work second shifts, overtime and on menial and unpleasant jobs; a refusal to work beyond job specifications; an attrition of managerial authority; and a lack of loyalty. In an extremely tight labour market labour turnover had reached around six to eight per cent per month.

In true Singaporean style the state, with the support of the NTUC, went to work on behalf of foreign capital by publicly chastising 'job hoppers' and 'choosy workers' who would change companies 'for a few dollars more'. In 1981 the work force were told that a scheme was being introduced which made available to employers the CPF records on the employment history of job applicants, so that they could 'check if the prospective employee is guilty of excessive job hopping'. The government also conducted a survey to obtain a demographic profile of the 6,600 persons who had been noted from CPF records to have changed their job three times in the past year. And there was a proposal to set up a special fund in conjunction with the CPF to reward employees who stayed with the same company for a minimum of five years. Cheah Hock Beng (1988) comments that what was intended as a domestic campaign to shame local workers soon began to affect the image of the Singaporean workers in the eyes of potential investors, and partly for this reason negative comments on the work force diminished, and the government focussed instead on attempting to persuade employers to change their approach to labour management.

Less negatively, as well as launching the productivity campaign (described earlier) the government pushed for the adoption of a new set of company based institutions intended to promote new attitudes to work and company loyalty. Many employers did respond, and there was a reasonably widespread, if half-hearted, attempt by companies to change the way they managed during the 1980s.

In fact long before these initiatives there had been an attempt to establish company level joint consultative bodies. As early as 1967 the National Productivity Centre (NPC) was established as a tripartite institution, and it called on all firms employing more than 50 workers to use joint consultation to encourage worker participation for non-collective bargaining issues to improve labour-management rapport, to provide a direct communication link beween top managers and employees, and to encourage worker contributions to productivity improvements. Further impetus was added in 1970 when the NTUC publicly committed itself to joint consultation, and in 1971 when the NPC became a statutory board, the NPB. The NPB intensively campaigned for Works Councils as the means for promoting labour-management cooperation.

However, unlike the cases of Korea and Taiwan (see chapters three and four) workplace-based institutions for worker consultation and involvement were not mandatory, and between 1972 and 1974 only 16 Works Councils were established, and most of these disintegrated soon after (Mok 1980). Partly because of employers' unfavourable perceptions of Works Councils in Europe, in 1975 the Works Council became the Productivity Committee, but by 1978 only 32 Productivity Committees had been formed. In 1978 a further change of title was announced – the Productivity Committee became the Work Excellence Committee (WEC) – and WECs were pushed even more vigorously in the 1980s as a part of the productivity movement and the economic restructuring programme. As Leggett et al. (1983) point out, anticipated rapid technological development added to the perceived imperative to give more serious attention to the social relations of the workplace. By 1984 only 18 WECs were documented.

Joint consultation in singapore was intended as a forum for discussing issues such as safety, social and recreational activites, and productivity – issues subsumed under collective bargaining were ommitted. Labour representatives were to be appointed by the union, with equal numbers representing management, and the chief executive of the company acting as Chairman and having the final say on recommendations. The NPB has gone out of its way to assure employers that 'our Singapore system of joint consultation should not be confused with that of the German (co-determination) or the British (industrial democracy [sic!]) systems' (Ng Kiat Chong 1983, p.24). Yet Mok's (1980, p.305) argument that the prospect of joint consultation raised 'the fear of management that their prerogatives, authority and influence would be undermined' has found support elsewhere. A frustrated WEC promoter commented that the:

greatest problem here, especially among middle management is the fear of losing power or control. ... very few managers would agree to workers' participation in decision making even in areas which directly concern their employees (Yeo Jeu Nam 1984, p.65).

Exasperation at the failure of joint consultation by a government seeking to establish an industrial community (as opposed to a mere industrial society) and by a NTUC elite struggling to justify its existence is clear. However, the rejection of joint consultation by employers who have welcomed the strengthening of their prerogatives should not be wholly surprising.

Employee Involvement

The other main initiatives to encourage a degree of employee involvement and employee identification with the company have been Quality Control Circles (QCCs), Work Improvement Teams (WITs) and Company Welfareism through Employers' Contributions (CoWEC).

QCCs, intended to encourage worker participation in quality and productivity improvements through small group activities, were used by some companies – especially Japanese – in the 1970s. In 1981 the NPB began to actively encourage and provide aid in their adoption more widely. WITs are the QCC equivalent for the public sector, the government's 1981 Committee on Productivity recommending that:

the public sector in Singapore would have to set an example in improving productivity, work attitudes and human management. … QC circle activities should be promoted in the public sector to improve productivity and to encourage worker involvement, participation and bottom-up management (N. Ng 1984, p.23).

By June 1984 1,900 WITs had been formed. Private sector QCCs lagged behind at a total of 900 in an unknown number of organizations, rising to 1,248 by July 1985. Their impact, however, has been superficial. Problems include a lack of commitment by managers who, as in the case of WECs, feel their authority may be under threat; WIT and QCC meetings often become sessions for the airing of grievances; some workers see WITs and QCCs as simply a means of making them work harder; and managers have little belief in the ability or willingness of employees to participate (Cheng Soo May 1986; Wilkinson 1986).

Another workplace-based institution inspired by the example of Japan was CoWEC. CoWEC was aimed at fostering a 'Japanese style' loyalty to the company, and was made possible by an ammendment to the Central Provident Fund (CPF) Act. In the early 1980s employers and employees each had to contribute 25 per cent of salary to the CPF, and this could not be drawn on until retirement. The ammendment enabled employers to reduce their own contribution from 25 to 15 per cent, and to place the remainder in a trust fund, the income from which would be used to finance welfare programmes for employees. Immediately though, employees further confirmed their attitudes towards company loyalty:

one of the thorniest issues has been how the money earned from the investments will be distributed. But the National Productivity Council, which is promoting this concept, is firm that the income should be used for group activities to promote company loyalty (*Straits Times*, 21 June 1984).

It is doubtful whether CoWEC could ever have been wholly successful in promoting company loyalty. The scheme was, after all, a government initiative, and drew on funds which employees quite legitimately saw as their own money. In any case, only 8 companies had introduced CoWEC by 1986, and with the cut in employers' contributions to the CPF from 25 to 10 per cent of wages as part of the response to the recession in the same year, CoWEC became virutally untenable (Cheah Hock Beng 1988). Since 1988 employers' CPF contributions have gradually been increased again, reaching 17.5 per cent in 1991, but CoWEC has not been revived.

Failure of Worker Participation

The avilable evidence suggests a dismal failure in Singapore to create 'Japanese style' worker loyalty; the vision of an industrial *community* appears as far away as ever. Although there are notable exceptions, the general employer disinterest in engaging their work forces in participation schemes and their preference not to develop welfareist practices is clearly a key factor in the elusiveness of worker loyalty. On the other hand, the extent to which instrumental worker values have an influence raises more complex issues. While the government and employers have voiced complaints about the work force, Wimalasiri's (1984) study found an expressed emphasis on non-materialistic values and a desire on the part of workers to more fully engage themselves at work. His conclusion was that managers needed to change their styles and give workers more responsibilities if they wished to prevent job-hopping and the like. Selmer (1987) similarly reports a big gap in multinational (in this case Swedish) employers' perceptions of Singaporeans' values and Singaporeans' own accounts of their values.

Employer and employee attitude surveys, however, have missed two key points. First, the equation between company loyalty and national loyalty which is made in Japan is less feasible in a country which only recently became independent (so national loyalty is less clear cut in the first place) and which relies heavily on foreign-owned corporations: working for Toshiba in Singapore is not likely to have the same meaning for a Singaporean as working for Toshiba in Japan for a Japanese. Secondly, and perhaps most importantly, Chinese and Japanese values, despite a common connection through Confucianism and Buddhism, are not the same. While Japanese values are (arguably) consistent with a devotion to the company, Chinese values are not. As Lee Sheng Yi (1978) made clear, the majority Chinese population in Singapore is primarily loyal to the family as part of a culture of 'economic familism', and the Chinese who are frustrated in their ambitions to run their own businesses are unlikely to become loyal overnight to large anonymous corporations. This is perhaps reflected in Aryee and Wyatt's (1989) examination of the central life interests of Singaporean workers. They found interests outside work, especially family interests, to be more important to Singaporeans than for workers in the US, Britain, Canada and Germany, as well as Japan. In Singapore, where employment for the majority of the population is limited to large companies and the climate for small family businesses not particularly conducive, economic familism may combine with employer disinterest in participation to reinforce instrumental attitudes towards work. Lee Kuan Yew was probably right when he said that:

It may take 15 or 20 years to get Singaporeans as productivity conscious as the average Japanese or Koreans. A change in outlook cannot be achieved in a productivity month. It is only the beginning (cited in Goh 1984, p.35).

Or perhaps Lee was being optimistic.

Labour

Following the PAP-Barisan Sosialis split in 1961, the trade union movement also split into the PAP-loyal Singapore Trades Union Congress (STUC, later to become the NTUC) and the Barisan-loyal Singapore Association of Trade Unions (SATU). Many SATU-affiliated unions were de-registered and their funds sequestrated in the early 1960s (Rosa 1990). 30 Barisan-sympathetic unions remained in 1966, but during this year their leadership was severely repressed, many being imprisoned under the ISA. By the year's end, 'there existed no viable alternative to the NTUC union structure for the handling of worker demands' (Deyo 1989, p.129). With 64 per cent of organized workers in 1963, NTUC affiliates came to represent 95 per cent by 1979 as the PAP sought to broaden the basis of its working class support and embrace the labour movement in its nation building programme (Leggett 1988).

Emergence of Corporatism

The NTUC was increasingly drawn into a close relationship with the PAP during the 1960s, and the role of unions as interest groups involved in collective bargaining was increasingly under pressure. Unions' bargaining power and scope were drastically reduced through the aforementioned employment and industrial relations legislation in 1968, consolidating reliance on conciliation and the legal system for dispute resolution. Then the NTUC, at a widely publicized seminar on trade union 'modernization', made a firm and unambiguous commitment to accepting productionist and socializing roles, and committing labour to compliance with national objectives (National Trades Union Congress 1970). Hence by the end of the 1960s a combination of repression, political incorporation and legislation had created what Deyo (1981) called a 'corporatist' system of industrial relations.

During the 1960s and 1970s the NTUC was financially dependent on government for many of its activities – its headquarters and convention hall were built with government funds. The government also had an influence over NTUC leadership decisions, and overlap between PAP and NTUC personnel grew. By 1970, PAP Members of Parlaiment occupied seven seats of the NTUC Central Committee and led some of the larger affiliate unions as well. PAP guidance of affiliate union activities was effected through the NTUC Research Unit, which played an advisory role in the formulation of union bargaining claims and strategies. Deyo (1981, p.44) concludes that:

By the late 1960s, the NTUC had effectively established its authority over affiliate unions in all questions of policy relating to government, general economic and national matters, union organizational structure, internal discipline, and organizational growth.

Incorporation of the trade union leadership helps explain the acceptance, if not the enthusiastic support, by the leadership of the labour movement of the tough 1968 labour legislation. Among other things, this legislation implied a heightened role for the state in conciliation and dispute arbitration – industrial action was made even more difficult – and indeed the number of IAC hearings and awards increased in the 1970s (Krislov and Leggett 1985). However, the enthusiasm of the NTUC leadership for the curtailment of the trade union role in collective bargaining did not appear to be shared by the membership. Between 1962 and 1970, despite a rapidly growing working population, the number of trade union members fell from 189,032 to 112,458, just 17.3 per cent of the total employed work force (Deyo 1989).

PAP-NTUC Symbiosis

The special PAP-NTUC relationship came to characterized as a 'symbiosis' at the NTUC seminar on *The Modernization of the Labour Movement* in 1969. The seminar overtly endorsed the commitment of the NTUC to abandoning the pursuit of sectional interests and focussing on the inculcation of productionist and cooperative attitudes among the work force in pursuit of national economic objectives. The promise of involvement in joint consultation machinery and productivity councils, together with the NTUC decision to embark on producer cooperative ventures (some of which continue to be successful today) helped turn the tide of membership decline, as did the credibility given the NTUC by its participation in the NWC from 1972. Between 1972 and 1979 NTUC affiliates' total membership grew by an average 15,000 per year (Leggett 1988).

The NTUC-PAP symbiosis became so complete during the 1970s that it became increasingly difficult to distinguish between the political and labour elite. Civil servants and MPs took senior positions among cooperative societies, and according to Rosa (1990), in the late 1980s 59 unionists represented the labour movement in 29 public institutions, 20 civil servants and 63 private sector excutives sat on the boards of 10 labour organizations, and 8 out of the 20 members of the Executive Committee of the NTUC were also PAP MPs. Other PAP MPs held key positions among NTUC affiliates.

A major problem of such close relations is inevitably legitimacy. The NTUC leadership openly publicizes the symbiotic relationship and claims the ability to strongly influence government policy in a way which is favourable to labour. According to NTUC deputy secretary general Lim Boon Heng (cited in Rosa 1990, p.493), 'when members and the public do not see what has been done, they may be left with the mistaken impression that unions are weak'. The invisibility of trade union leadership influence was undoubtedly made progressively worse in the 1970s and 1980s as the 'old guard' unionists were giving way to University educated technocrats with little grass roots organizing experience (Leggett 1988).

Failure of the Japanese Model

In the early 1980s, the interest in the Japanese model which informed the productivity movement, WECs and CoWEC, also informed the NTUC's decision
to promote enterprise unions. The Singapore National Employers' Federation
(SNEF) also expressed support for enterprise unions following a SDF-subsidized
study mission to Japan in 1983. SNEF felt 'the house union would be better able to
promote the bond and cooperation between the employee and his company', and
advised that supervisors, as in Japan, should be encouraged to join house unions
so they could play the dual role of supervisor and union leader (*Straits Times*,
30 April 1984). The NTUC 'persuaded' several affiliates to dissolve themselves
and re-form as house unions, and around 30, mostly in the public sector, had
been formed by 1985. Ong Teng Cheong, then NTUC secretary general, in a vein
remarkably similar to SNEF, explained that:

in a house union, the workers are better able to identify themselves with the company, and
to see clearly the nexus between their own well being and the success of the enterprise
(cited in Rodan 1989, p.158).

Since then, however, the structure of trade unions has changed little. Despite the
comments of SNEF, private sector employers showed little enthusiasm in practice
to shift rapidly to house unions.

During the 1980s, the NTUC had to show its support for ammendments to the
new Employment Act (discussed earlier) which extended management prerogatives, and for the NWC's recommendation of a pay freeze and a big reduction in
employers' contributions to CPF during the recession. In the meantime employers
were reported to be at best luke warm, and at worst antagonistic to, unionization
(Rosa 1990). As table 2.10 shows, union density again fell in the 1980s.

Industrial Conflict

The problem of the 'invisibility' of the negotiating skills of the leadership of
the NTUC and its affiliates have no doubt been compounded by the fact that no
industrial stoppage has occurred since 1977 (table 2.11).

But the end of *overt* industrial conflict in Singapore does not necessarily
mean industrial harmony. Strikes were curtailed simply because the government
clamped down with legislation and showed a willingness to use its powers to
refer disputes to mediation and arbitration. A strike is illegal once a dispute has
been referred, and imprisonment of union leaders may follow if the instruction
is ignored. The services of the IAC, as table 2.11 shows, were called upon more
frequently in the years following the end of strike activity, though the increase
was not dramatic, and reduced in the second half of the 1980s. In part this is
because employers and unions have been aware that the IAC will make awards

Table 2.10:   Union Membership in Singapore, 1975-1991

	No. of trade unions	Total membership	Union members as % of total employed work-force
1975	89	208,561	25.0
1979	85	249,710	24.5
1984	86	192,394	16.4
1989	83	212,874	15.3
1990	83	212,204	14.4
1991	83	217,086	14.2

Source: Ministry of Labour, Republic of Singapore, *Singapore Yearbook of Labour Statistics,* various issues.

in line with existing employment legislation or, in the case of wages disputes, NWC recommendations. It may also relate to the fact that the NTUC views appeals to the government's mediation and arbitration services as a sign of failure in management-labour relations which it would prefer to avoid. The number of trade disputes referred to Ministry of Labour for conciliation actually declined at the end of the 1970s, then held steady at around 300 to 350 during the 1980s and early 1990s. 'Individual' disputes, however, rose significantly in the second half of the 1980s, and jumped upwards significantly in 1990 and 1991, perhaps reflecting the failure of the trade union movement to represent the interests of workers who have increasingly had to rely on individual appeals to the state to gain redress for employer injustices.

The PAP-NTUC elite showed its awareness of the crisis of trade union membership and credibility in the late 1980s. In 1989 the NTUC called on affiliates to engage in more aggressive marketing strategies to reverse the membership slide, and on employers to publicly declare their support for tripartism. SNEF issued a statement that its approach to industrial relations had always been based on tripartism (Rosa 1990). The number of union members picked up in 1991, but only slightly. No doubt, further measures will be taken to attempt to revive interest in the official labour movement.

Prospects for Labour

Table 2.12 shows a relatively high union density in the 'transport, storage and communications' category, and large numbers of union members in the 'services and other' category, which includes large numbers of public sector employees.

Table 2.11:   Industrial Disputes in Singapore, 1974-1991

	Industrial stoppages	Man-days lost due to industrial stoppages	IAC awards*	Trade disputes**	'Individual' disputes***
1974	10	5,380	89	1,091	855
1975	7	4,853	73	709	1,991
1976	4	3,193	57	694	2,465
1977	1	1,011	33	640	2,228
1978	0	0	35	548	2,000
1979	0	0	73	577	1,635
1980	0	0	94	484	1,332
1981	0	0	100	392	1,335
1982	0	0	82	311	1,588
1983	0	0	59	353	1,466
1984	0	0	48	338	1,400
1985	0	0	35	340	2,185
1986	0	0	74	317	2,730
1987	0	0	39	275	2,960
1988	0	0	22	366	2,818
1989	0	0	38	353	2,516
1990	0	0	46	303	3,835
1991	0	0	31	323	4,197

*   The Industrial Arbitration Court hears and determines the outcome of referred trade disputes.

**   'Trade disputes' refer to industrial disputes which have been referred to the unionised disputes section of the Ministry of Labour for conciliation.

***   'Individual disputes' arc registered when a dispute between an individual and an employer is referred to the individual disputes section of the Ministry of Labour.

Source: Ministry of Labour, Republic of Singapore, *Singapore Yearbook of Labour Statistics*, various issues.

    The low level of unionization in construction is explained in large part by the predominance of foreign workers in this sector. The manufacturing sector, on the other hand, has a density of only 15.5 per cent of the work force. Yet it is in exactly this sector, characterized as it is by large numbers of blue collar workers in relatively large establishments, that one would expect a high density. One explanation for the weak organization in manufacturing is the large numbers of female employees and high labour turnover – especially in the export oriented electronics sectors (Deyo 1989). Another must be the continued indifference, and sometimes hostility, of the foreign employers who dominate the manufacturing sector to trade unions.

Table 2.12:   Unionization by Industry in Singapore, 1991

	No. of employees	No. of trade union members	Union members as % of employed
Manufacturing	429,612	66,570	15.5
Commerce	345,339	17,075	4.9
Transport, storage and communications	152,931	46,206	30.2
Construction	98,981	671	0.7
Services and others	497,451	86,564	17.4
Total	1,524,315	217,086	14.2

Source: Ministry of Labour, Republic of Singapore, S*ingapore Yearbook of Labour Statistics 1991.*

In spite of government and NTUC success in creating the conditions under which trade union involvement is non-threatening, and potentially could contribute to productivity, employers have instead preferred to keep trade unions at arms length. Where trade unions *are* recognized, there has been a reluctance to engage in the activities the government believes would create the sort of industrial community which exists in Japan. CoWEC, WITS, WECs, QCCs, house unions and the like have had little impact, even among the Japanese multinationals – less than half of them had adopted QCCs in the mid 1980s (Milton-Smith 1986). Deyo (1981, p.14) suggests that 'if community is to emerge at all it will have to be a creation of the state'. But apparently the very legislation the government has laid down to encourage the development of work place-based communities has been either ignored by employers, or used by employers to extend their prerogatives and maintain distanced relationships with employees. Hence the 'incompatible goals of social mobilization and control' are still pursued by the state with regard to labour, and as yet there is little sign of the state escaping its dilemma. Neither is there much sign, in spite of the rhetoric of a softer approach under the new Prime Minister Goh, of the state giving up in its determination to maintain the order which prevents the contradictions turning into overt conflicts. The prospects for labour's collective organizations, then, appears to be more of the same.

Conclusions and Prospects

The Singaporean economy is unique among the ANICs in its almost complete dependence on foreign direct manufacturing investments for industrialization. It is also the most dependent of the ANIC economies on domestic exports. And it is at least *as* dependent as the others on imports of technology, increasingly from

Japan. No one could question the remarkable success of Singapore's economy: the country has advanced hugely in the space of 30 years, and has, arguably, restructured far more successfully than Hong Kong (see chapter five) which was the nearest economic equivalent to Singapore in the early years of industrialization. But Singapore remains an export platform, albeit an export platform *par excellence* which attracts higher quality investments than its competitors in South East Asia (and probably higher quality than in some regions in Europe which also compete for foreign investments). Being dependent on another for the things one values means the other can exert power – through the imposition of barriers to exports, or the withdrawal of direct investments, for instance.

Fully aware of this relationship beween dependence and power, the ruling elite under the leadership of Lee Kuan Yew has made, and continues to make, an economic, political and social environment on the island of Singapore which meets the perceived needs of international capital, in return for economic advance. So successful has the government been in its pursuit of the imperatives it has identified that in 1981, when insults levelled against the 'instrumentality' of the Singaporean work force were at their height, the influential Business Environment Risk Information (BERI) concluded that Singapore had the best labour force out of 45 countries studied from the viewpoint of the international investor, with a high rating for 'worker attitude', and the top rating for 'relative productivity in manufacturing' (Rodan 1989).

In the late 1980s and early 1990s, Singapore has begun to spread its risks by taking on the role of regional base and logistics and services centre for the ASEAN and wider South East Asian region, and is attempting to make Singapore the regional R&D base for multinational organizations increasingly interested the potential of South East Asia as a market. But while these roles may guarantee Singapore economic growth through the 1990s, the country's dependence on foreign capital and international markets, and therefore its vulnerability to exogenous factors, will remain.

The relationship between state and (foreign) employers might best be characterized as love-hate. FDI has undeniably brought Singapore full employment, and increasingly high quality employment, if not quite so rapidly as the ambitious state would prefer. On the other hand, the reluctance of employers to engage in the joint consultation, company welfareism, etc., which the state sees as necessary for the creation of an industrial community as a part of nation building, has frustrated the government. While employers maintain a distant relationship with their work forces, the PAP-NTUC elite is left with the responsibility of maintaining industrial order, a responsibility which continues to tax the leadership and which depends on a continued renewal of propaganda, campaigns and initiatives, backed up by occasional use of the extraordinary powers of the state under the provisions of the Internal Security Act.

Chapter Three: Korea

As the largest *and* the most recent industrializer among the ANICs, Korea has deservedly attracted significant attention from political economists. An indication of Korean success is the fact that lessons are now being drawn not just for other would-be NICs, but for 'advanced' Western nations with an ambition to *re*-industrialize. Amsden (1989) celebrates Korea's transformation from 'learner' to 'teacher', and expresses optimism that the economy will continue to thrive in the post-1987 democratic-political era.

After half a century of Japanese colonial rule, followed by World War II then the Korean War, Korea's industrialization-proper began only in the 1960s, and in spite of the burden of a continuously massive defence spend (mostly it has represented around six per cent of GNP) the nation had advanced to a stage in the 1980s where it could compete successfully in a range of sectors in world markets. Throughout this period, growth was led by large indigenous private organizations subject to close guidance by the state and benefitting from state support in various forms. Unlike Singapore, foreign direct investment never played the central role in economic development, though first US aid, then foreign loans to indigenous companies underwritten by the government, were essential.

In the late 1980s and early 1990s, however, Korea ran into serious problems. Some of these relate to changes in the rules of the game in international trade; others are domestic problems regarding the crisis of relationships between state, labour and capital. The future of the Korean economy, we will argue, depends in part on international economic developments, and particularly the extent to which the US and Europe become even more aggressive in their stance on trade relations. A discussion of trade relations takes up most of the first part of this chapter. Korea's economic future also depends on state, capital and labour reaching some sort of accord which supports, or at least allows, the pursuit of national economic objectives. This will be no easy task – the antagonisms resulting from three decades of authoritarian rule will not easily transform themselves into cooperation.

Economic Performance and Economic Structure

The beginnings of Korea's rapid economic growth are usually traced to the 1961 military coup which led to the replacement of President Rhee by the authoritarian Park regime. Authoritarian government was justified as essential for the economic resurgence which was to be based on the attraction of foreign investment and the expansion of exports (Caiden and Jung 1985). Growth rates have averaged nearly 10 per cent per year since the 1960s, and although they show signs of steadying in the 1990s (see table 3.1), they appear set to remain exceptionally high relative to Western levels.

Table 3.1:   GNP and Per Capita GNP in Korea, 1970-1990

	GNP (US$ billion)	GNP per capita (US$)
1970	8.1	252
1975	20.9	594
1980	60.5	1,592
1985	89.7	2,194
1987	128.9	3,110
1989	211.2	4,994
1990	244.0	5,659

Source: Korea Labour Institute (1992).

Rapid growth has been associated with a rapid urbanization and rural migration to the cities – Seoul, with a population of over 15 million, is now one of the largest cities in the world – and with a massive growth of the manufacturing work force. As a proportion of the total work force, manufacturing peaked in the late 1980s, and has marginally declined since then (table 3.2), leading to the suggestion that in the space of 30 years Korea has evolved from a rural to an industrial to a post-industrial society. Unemployment has declined to such low levels that the associated problems are to do less with the economic and social costs, and more with a chronic labour shortage. The decline of unemployment in the 1980s is all the more remarkable for the fact that the number of Koreans working overseas (mostly in construction) declined from 225,000 in 1983 to 45,000 in 1990, mainly because of the improved job opportunities and wages at home (*Korea Times*, 20 October 1991).

Export Oriented Growth

With manufactured goods for export as the engine of growth, Korea rapidly developed as a trading nation. Total trade rose from less than US$ 0.5 billion in 1962 to US$ 47.4 billion in 1981 (Cha Dong Se 1988), and has continued to expand since then. Table 3.3 shows the expansion of Korean trade during the 1980s.

Korea's first trade surplus since industrialization-proper got under way was achieved only in 1986. This was taken as an opportunity to reduce dependence on the foreign debt which had fuelled the nation's manufacturing growth, and which stood at a massive US$ 46.7 billion at the end of 1985 (*Far Eastern Economic Review*, 11 February 1988). Coinciding with the new trade surplus was a growth

Table 3.2:   Changes in Employment Structure and Unemployment in Korea, 1963-1990

	1963	1970	1975	1980	1985	1988	1990
Economically active ('000 persons)	8,230	10,062	12,193	14,431	15,592	17,305	18,487
Unemployed (%)	8.2	4.5	4.1	5.2	4.0	2.5	2.4
Agriculture, Forestry and Fishing (% of employed population)	63.1	50.5	45.9	34.0	24.9	20.7	18.3
Mining and Manufacturing (% of employed population)	8.7	14.3	19.1	22.6	24.5	28.5	27.3
Services and others (% of employed population)	28.2	35.2	35.0	43.4	50.6	50.8	54.4

Sources: Economic Planning Board, *Annual Report on the Economically Active Population Survey,* various issues; Ministry of Labour, Republic of Korea, *Yearbook of Labour Statistics 1991.*

in the domestic savings rate which exceeded the nation's investment rate for the first time in 1986 (table 3.4).

Combined, these two factors enabled Korea to reduce dependence on foreign borrowings, and the country rapidly moved towards becoming a net foreign creditor. Korean government economists are well aware of the problems caused by huge foreign debts to countries like Mexico and Brazil, and it is not surprising that the reduction of foreign debt dependence was seen as the overcoming of a major obstacle to economic maturity.

A new set of obstacles which at the time few would have foreseen, however, were looming on the horizon.

Trade Friction

Korea's surplus sounded warning bells in the United States. The US was taking around one third of Korea's total exports, and since the early part of the 1980s had found its own traditionally positive balance with Korea turn negative. Korea's new overall trade surplus was taken as an opportunity by many American politicians

Table 3.3:   Exports and Imports of Korea, 1980-1990 (US$ million)

	Exports	Change (%)	Imports	Change (%)	Balance
1980	17,504.9	16.3	22,291.7	9.6	– 4,786.8
1981	21,253.8	21.4	26,131.4	17.2	– 4,877.6
1982	21,853.4	2.8	24,250.8	– 7.2	– 2,397.4
1983	24,445.1	11.9	26,192.2	8.0	– 1,747.1
1984	29,244.9	19.6	30,631.4	16.9	– 1,386.5
1985	30,283.1	3.6	31,135.7	1.6	– 852.6
1986	34,714.5	14.6	31,583.9	1.4	+ 3,130.6
1987	47,280.9	36.2	41,019.8	29.9	+ 6,261.1
1988	60,696.4	28.4	51,810.6	26.3	+ 8,885.8
1989	62,377.2	2.8	61,464.8	18.6	+ 912.4
1990	65,015.7	4.2	69,843.7	13.6	– 4,828.0
1991*	50,883.7		60,513.5		– 9,629.8

* 1991 figures for first three quarters only.

Source: Bank of Korea, *Monthly Balance of Payments*, various issues.

Table 3.4:   Savings and Investment Ratios in Korea, 1975-1991 (%)

	Investment Ratio	Savings Ratio
1975	28.9	18.2
1980	32.0	23.1
1985	29.9	29.1
1986	28.9	32.8
1987	29.6	36.2
1988	30.7	38.1
1989	33.5	35.3
1990	37.1	36.0
1991	39.3	36.1

Source: Bank of Korea, *Monthly Statistical Bulletin*, various issues.

to declare Korea 'another Japan', and immediately the US stepped up pressure on Korea to adopt free trade policies. Korea was reluctant to open itself to a flood of imports while large foreign debts were still outstanding, insisting that a trade surplus was a short-run necessity and that Korea was not 'like Japan'. Fallows (1988, p.32) cites Koo Bon Ho, then President of the Korea Development Institute, as saying:

In our forty year history we have had exactly one year of surplus, and Americans instantly conclude that we're behaving like Japan. ... We have *no* intention of running a permanent surplus. We need to reduce our debt – it's fifty four per cent of GNP, which is too high for any country. So we need about US$ 5 billion surplus for the next few years. After that we want balance, not any surplus at all. ... (Japan's) per capita income is the highest in the world, but to us they live like ants. ... If you ignore housing, roads, recreation, public facilities, you can get a big surplus – but so what? We have no intention of following that model.

In a similar vein (and with similar apparent upset towards any suggestion that Korea might be like Japan) Presidential Adviser Park Yung Chul (cited in Clifford 1988, p.56) said:

We will never be a second Japan. ... I find it repugnant to run a huge surplus. It's inefficient and it does not help economic welfare. Running a surplus cannot be our economic objective. The objective is to make life healthier and more pleasant.

The US was unconvinced, or at least behaved as if it was unconvinced: with the American deficit with Korea ballooning from US$ 4.3 billion in 1985 to a peak of US$ 9.6 billion in 1987, the US placed great pressure on Korea to reduce tariff barriers quickly. Europe added to the pressure as the EC deficit with Korea jumped upwards in 1986 and peaked at over US$ 2 billion in 1988 (table 3.5).

The pressures brought to bear on Korea included Won appreciation (though Korea did not suffer in this regard so much as Taiwan – see table 1.7), and the insistence that tariff barriers be reduced. Tariffs were reduced, though many still exist and the government has remained willing to raise or impose tariffs when this is seen as strategically necessary. The US announced the end of GSP status for Korea in 1989, and the EC removed Korea from its GSP beneficiary list in 1988. The EC later restored Korea's GSP status after the government made promises to protect European intellectual property rights (Economic Planning Board, Republic of Korea, *Economic Bulletin*, October 1991) but soon after announced the removal of Korea along with the other ANICs from 1994. The US has also frequently attacked a Korean 'frugality campaign' which hurts Western luxury imports. In 1990 pressure from Washington forced Seoul to abandon the drive and to replace the Trade-Industry Minister who was accused of leading the campaign. However, Korean private organizations and the mass media have continued the drive, and the US has accused the government of orchestration of the campaign. The inevitable reduction in surpluses with the US and Europe in the late 1980s contributed to the return of Korea to an overall trade deficit in 1990 (table 3.3).

Such international political pressures and actions have coincided with rising labour costs (explored below) leading to slowed export growth. An added worry for Korea is the recent emergence of *Japan-Asia* (see chapter one) which is claimed to be damaging Korean exports to Japan in cheap consumer goods by combining Japanese technology with cheap South East Asian labour (*Korea Times*, 8 October 1991).

Table 3.5:   Korea's Exports and Imports by Area of Destination and Origin, 1980-1990 (US$ million)

	Japan			US			EC 12		
	Exports	Imports	Balance	Exports	Imports	Balance	Exports	Imports	Balance
1980	3,039.4	5,857.8	-2,818.4	4,606.6	4,890.2	-283.6	2,619.5	1,583.8	1,035.7
1985	4,543.4	7,560.4	-3,017.0	10,754.1	6,489.3	4,264.8	3,160.0	2,991.3	168.7
1986	5,425.7	10,869.3	-5,443.6	13,880.1	6,544.8	7,335.3	4,304.8	3,214.6	1,090.2
1987	8,436.8	13,656.6	-5,219.8	18,310.8	8,758.2	9,552.6	6,596.6	4,613.4	1,983.2
1988	12,004.1	15,928.8	-3,924.7	21,404.1	12,756.7	8,647.4	8,131.8	6,042.0	2,089.5
1989	13,456.8	17,448.6	-3,991.8	20,639.0	15,910.7	4,728.3	7,393.6	6,492.2	901.4
1990	12,637.9	18,573.9	-5,936.0	19,360.0	16,942.5	2,417.5	8,843.6	8,410.3	433.3

	South-East Asia			Other		
	Exports	Imports	Balance	Exports	Imports	Balance
1980	2,255.8	1,895.9	359.9	4,983.6	8,064.0	-3,080.4
1985	3,435.9	3,540.3	-104.4	8,389.7	10,554.4	-2,164.7
1986	3,506.5	2,903.1	603.4	7,597.4	8,025.1	-454.7
1987	4,913.1	4,027.1	886.0	9,023.6	9,964.5	-940.9
1988	7,770.1	5,064.9	2,705.2	11,386.3	12,018.2	-631.9
1989	8,892.2	6,062.1	2,830.1	11,995.4	15,551.0	-3,555.6
1990	10,404.6	7,157.2	3,247.4	13,769.6	18,759.8	-4,990.2

Source: Bank of Korea, *Monthly Balance of Payments*, various years.

It is in the face of unabating political pressure, the threat of trade bloc formation, and the certainty that a renewed export drive would lead to further trade friction, that Korean companies have increasingly established export platforms in ASEAN, or directly within the EC or NAFTA. At the same time the government has urged Korean companies to improve their product innovativeness through increasing their spending on R&D, and has turned attention to the domestic problems associated with labour unrest which followed democratization in 1987. These issues are taken up below. First, it is worth pin-pointing Korea's structural economic problems by examining import and export structures in more detail.

Structural Problems and Economic Restructuring

The imbalances in Korea's import and export structures are suggested in table 3.5 which shows large positive balances with the US and Europe (and recently South East Asia) set against a persistent trade deficit with Japan. But if expanding direct exports of mass produced consumer goods to the West cannot be the solution to Korea's trade problems, attacking the deficit with Japan may prove equally difficult. On the one hand the Japanese market is no easier for Korea to penetrate than it is for the US and Europe; on the other Korea's imports from Japan are primarily of capital goods which cannot be easily or quickly substituted. In 1980 47.2 per cent of Korea's imports from Japan were of capital goods, and this figure gradually increased to 58.0 per cent in 1990, or a massive US$ 10.8 billion out of US$ 18.6 billion.

The structure of Korea's total imports is shown in table 3.6. As is readily apparent, foreign capital goods imports have been on the increase in the 1980s, representing 38.9 per cent or US$ 18.4 billion of total imports for domestic use in 1990.

The increased reliance on capital goods imports – over half of which come from Japan – reflects the nation's attempt to automate and therefore reduce overall labour costs in the face of rising unit labour costs in a tight labour market, and to up-grade production to higher value activities. Automation appears to have taken place on a large scale in small as well as large companies. According to a report by the Korea Federation of Small Businesses, per-company investment for factory automation in a sample of 300 small and medium sized enterprises rose from Won 180 million in 1988 to Won 310 million in 1990 (*Korea Times*, 6 August 1991). Restructuring is also indicated in table 3.7 which shows rises in the proportion of total exports of electronics, autos, machine tools and engines, and office equipment, and declines in the proportion of total exports in the traditional areas of steel, shipbuilding and textiles.

The effect is further apparent in table 3.8 which focusses on the crucially important electronics sector. Here there is a rise in the export of integrated circuits and micro-assemblies faster than that of finished electronic consumer goods,

Table 3.6:   Structure of Korea's Imports, 1980-1990 (US$ million)*

	Goods for re-export	Goods for domestic use			Total
		Food and consumer goods	Industrial materials and fuels	Capital goods	
1980	5,786.8	1,926.3 (11.7)	10,600.1 (64.2)	3,978.5 (24.1)	22,291.7
1985	13,494.5	2,041.2 (11.6)	10,444.5 (59.2)	5,155.4 (29.2)	31.583.9
1990	21,082.4	5,568.1 (11.7)	23,415.6 (49.4)	18,418.4 (38.9)	69,843.7

* Figures in parentheses are percentages of domestic imports only.

Source: Bank of Korea, *Monthly Balance of Payments*, various issues.

which are increasingly likely to be assembled by Korean companies located in the cheaper labour South East Asian economies or within NAFTA and the EC. Korea is now third behind only the US and Japan in the production of semiconductors. The problem is that Korea is finding difficulty in developing its own capacity in capital goods production and high value component manufacture quickly enough to meet the demands of the changing domestic economy. Even in semiconductors, where export volumes rose to US$ 5.7 billion in 1991, there were problems. Most exports were high volume memory chips, whereas high value custom designed chips were mostly imported – at a cost of US$ 4.8 billion in the same year (*Far Eastern Economic Review* 10 September 1992).

Korea had already 'restructured' during the 1980s by creating an indigenous capacity to compete in world markets in several manufacturing sectors, and most notably in consumer electronics. The government now demands further restructuring in the face of rising labour costs, trade frictions with America and Europe, and an over-dependence on Japanese technology. The Korea Development Institute (1991, 10 (3), p.29) has argued that:

a strategy … of developing products largely by imitating Japanese products and trying to compensate for low product quality and function with the advantage of lower prices on the international market has reached its limit,

and that the new strategy must be one of 'closing the technological gap with its competitors in new, advanced products'. Korea's R&D spend in fact grew from 0.86 per cent of GNP in 1980 to 1.99 per cent in 1986 (table 3.9).

Over the same period R&D workers per 1,000 of the population grew from 0.48 to 1.13, the vast majority working in applied technology and experimental

Table 3.7:   Exports by Principal Commodity from Korea, 1980-1990 (US$ million)*

	Textiles and wearing apparel	Footwear	Vessels and floating structures	Metal goods (incl. iron and steel)	Chemicals and plastics	Motor vehicles
1980	4,938.7 (28.2)	870.5 (5.0)	617.6 (3.5)	2,425.9 (13.9)	290.3 (1.7)	93.6 (0.5)
1985	6,627.1 (21.9)	1,524.9 (5.0)	5,040.0 (16.6)	3,327.8 (11.0)	574.5 (1.9)	538.6 (1.8)
1990	13,938.2 (21.4)	4,023.5 (6.2)	2,800.6 (4.3)	5,662.5 (8.7)	1,743.1 (2.7)	2,157.4 (3.3)

	Machine tools and engines	Electronic products	Office machinery	Others	Total
1980	268.9 (1.5)	1,771.1 (10.1)	87.3 (0.5)	6,141.0 (35.1)	17,504.9 (100.0)
1985	565.9 (1.9)	3,251.3 (10.7)	581.6 (1.9)	8,251.4 (27.2)	30,283.1 (100.0)
1990	2,229.3 (3.4)	11,642.8 (17.9)	2,658.0 (4.1)	18,160.3 (27.9)	65,015.7 (100.0)

* Figures in parentheses are percentages of total exports.

Source: Calculated from Bank of Korea, *Monthly Balance of Payments*, various issues.

development (Lee Dae Chang 1990). But more investment, both public and private, is being encouraged, with the aim of reaching Japanese and US levels of more than three R&D workers per 1,000 of the population (Wang Yen Kyun 1990). Such a target may appear ambitious, but the nation is starting from a base of a relatively highly developed education system.

Korea's electronics manufacturers are a special target. Although world number two in consumer electronics and number three in semiconductors, the government wants a better performance. In 1991 the Korean electronics industry invested 5.2 per cent of turnover in R&D (the Japanese figure was 9.4 per cent in 1989): the government has set a target of eight per cent by 1996 (*Korea Times*, 19 October 1991). The government also wants to see the local content ratio in electronics improved from 67 per cent in 1991 to 75 per cent in 1996, and is willing to force manufacturers in this direction. For instance in 1991 large cathode ray tubes

Table 3.8:   Electronics Exports from Korea, 1980-1990 (US$ million)*

	TV sets, Hi-fi and VCRs	Communications apparatus	Integrated circuits and micro-assemblies	Others	Total
1980	834.3 (47.1)	242.0 (13.7)	354.0 (20.0)	340.8 (19.2)	1,771.1 (100.0)
1985	1,432.9 (44.1)	483.4 (14.9)	817.1 (25.1)	517.9 (15.9)	3,251.3 (100.0)
1990	4,282.6 (36.8)	1,414.0 (12.1)	4,262.1 (36.6)	1,680.1 (14.4)	11,642.8 (100.0)

* Figures in parentheses are percentages of total electronics exports.

Source: Calculated from Bank of Korea, *Monthly Balance of Payments*, various issues.

Table 3.9:   Trends in R&D Investment in Korea, 1980-1986 (Won billion)*

	1980	1982	1984	1986
Government R&D spend	215 (0.58)	233 (0.56)	227 (0.45)	307 (0.52)
Private R&D spend	102 (0.28)	218 (0.53)	494 (0.99)	872 (1.47)
Total R&D spend	317 (0.86)	451 (1.09)	721 (1.44)	1,178 (1.99)

* Figures in parentheses are ratio of GNP.

Source: Presidential Commission on Economic Restructuring (1988).

(CRTs, an important high value component in TV sets and computer monitors) were designated an 'import source diversification' category, which means a virtual ban on imports. This will force Korean manufacturers to produce their own large CRTs rather than continue to purchase them from Hitachi and Toshiba in Japan (*Korea Economic Weekly*, 18 November 1991). Another special target is small and medium sized companies, which the state wants to see take on a more important role. Plans are to increase R&D investments by SMEs from 0.2 per cent of turnover in 1989 to 1 per cent in 1996, and the government has earmarked over US$ 1 billion to help small companies achieve this ambitious target (*Korea Times*, 25 August 1991). Such measures are considered necessary for the achievement of the goals laid out in the latest five year economic plan, which aims for an average growth rate of 7.5 per cent to 1996 based on a virtual doubling of exports (*Korea*

Economic Weekly, 13 November 1991). With 'dumping' charges increasingly laid against standardized mass produced goods exported to the West, including standardized mass produced chips, future export growth is sought in high value areas and unique products which have been developed indigenously.

The Labour Problem

While Korea's economic structural problems and challenges are similar in many respects to those of the other ANICs, the labour problem is exceptional. Korea has faced not just a tight labour market, but a surge of work force militancy since 1987 which has pushed up labour costs for Korea faster than for the others. While Korea's per capita GNP is still the lowest among the ANICs by a significant margin (see table 1.2, chapter one), manufacturing labour costs have risen so dramatically since 1987 that by 1990 they were virtually the same as those for Singapore and Taiwan, and much higher than Kong Kong's (table 3.10).

The problem is that since 1987 the costs of wage increases have been far outstripping the savings from productivity increases, leading to a dramatic increase in unit labour costs. Table 3.11 compares the situation in Korea with that of its two most important competitors, Japan and Taiwan.

As table 3.11 shows, Japan's productivity performance has been remarkable, accounting for the nation's continued international competitiveness in the face of *endaka* (the high Yen crisis in the mid 1980s). Taiwan has also performed well: large wage increases and a rapidly appreciated new Taiwan dollar have been countered with a 37.3 per cent productivity improvement since 1986, and this is reflected in the country's recent healthy trade balance and export performance. Korea, on the other hand, has faced massive wage increases *and* failed to improve productivity to a sufficiently great extent, leading to a rise in unit labour costs by 67.8 per cent between 1986 and 1990, compared with only 15.1 per cent for Taiwan and a decrease of 8 per cent for Japan. The situation appears even worse when taking into account the appreciation of the Korean won against the US Dollar and other major export destination countries' currencies (but not Japan's) between 1986 and 1989: in Dollar terms Korea's manufacturing unit labour costs rose 108.9 per cent between 1986 and 1990. (The appreciation of the Won against the US Dollar was reversed in 1990, but not sufficiently to prevent a trade imbalance crisis in 1991.) The Korea Development Institute (1991, 10 (3)) attributes a 36.9 per cent increase in export prices between 1986 and 1990 directly to these rising unit labour costs.

Exactly why productivity has not increased at as fast a rate as in Taiwan remains open to question. Perhaps more could be done regarding automation and shifting to higher value activities (though Korea has possibly done more in the late 1980s and early 1990s than Taiwan according to the available evidence – see chapter four), but one also suspects a failure on the part of employers to mobilize workers in

Table 3.10:   Hourly Compensation Costs of Production Workers in Manufacturing in
Selected Countries, 1975-1990 (US$)*

	US	Japan	Korea	Hong Kong	Singapore	Taiwan
1975	6.36	3.05	0.33	0.76	0.84	0.40
	(100)	(48)	(5)	(12)	(13)	(6)
1980	9.87	5.61	0.97	1.51	1.49	1.00
	(100)	(57)	(10)	(15)	(15)	(10)
1985	13.01	6.43	1.25	1.73	2.47	1.50
	(100)	(49)	(10)	(13)	(19)	(12)
1986	13.25	9.31	1.34	1.88	2.23	1.73
	(100)	(70)	(10)	(14)	(17)	(13)
1987	13.52	10.83	1.65	2.09	2.31	2.26
	(100)	(80)	(12)	(15)	(17)	(17)
1988	13.91	12.80	2.30	2.40	2.67	2.82
	(100)	(92)	(17)	(17)	(19)	(20)
1989	14.31	12.63	3.29	2.79	3.15	3.53
	(100)	(88)	(23)	(19)	(22)	(25)
1990	14.77	12.64	3.82	3.20	3.78	3.95
	(100)	(86)	(26)	(22)	(26)	(27)

* Figures in parentheses indicate the proportion of the US wage standard.

Source: Bureau of Labour Statistics, Department of Labour (1991).

productivity campaigns or otherwise to extract a greater effort. Any conclusion in
this regard would depend on serious research which has not yet been undertaken,
but certainly the relation between labour and capital in Korea appears to tend
more towards antagonism than cooperation, and since 1987 the Korean labour
movement has been successful in eliminating some of the worst exploitation
by employers, which, arguably, underpinned strong economic performance until
recently.

   Given this context it is not surprising that attention in Korea has come to be
sharply focussed on the 'labour problem'. The state and employers are searching
for a model of industrial relations and a new accord between state, capital and
labour which will serve national economic needs in the new democracy. This is a
key issue to which we shall return throughout the rest of the chapter.

Table 3.11: Unit Labour Costs in Manufacturing in Korea, Japan and Taiwan, 1985-
            1990 (index: 1986 = 100)

	1985	1986	1987	1988	1989	1990
Korea						
Nominal wages	91.6	100	111.6	133.5	166.9	200.6
Labour productivity	92.3	100	102.9	110.4	110.4	119.6
Unit labour costs	99.2	100	108.5	120.9	151.2	167.8
Japan						
Nominal wages	98.1	100	102.6	104.4	110.2	115.3
Labour productivity	102.1	100	108.8	116.4	121.4	125.3
Unit labour costs	96.0	100	94.3	89.6	90.8	92.0
Taiwan						
Nominal wages	90.8	100	109.9	121.9	139.7	158.5
Labour productivity	90.1	100	110.5	116.4	127.0	137.7
Unit labour costs	100.8	100	99.5	104.7	110.0	115.1

Source: Korea Development Institute (1991), 10 (3).

Summary

Korea's remarkable economic performance since the 1960s has been the result of the successful pursuit of an export oriented industrialization strategy. Today the nation is among the world's leaders in the production of goods in several sectors, most notably in consumer electronics, and increasingly in higher value areas. Korea has shed its chronic foreign debt dependence, and is now a net capital exporter. By some measures, then, it could be argued that Korea has already joined the league of the advanced industrial nations.

However, the structure of Korea's trade with the world has increasingly posed problems. Korea depends heavily on imports of capital goods and technology, especially from Japan. And at the same time the country depends on the mass consumer markets of the US and Europe. Expanding direct exports has become increasingly difficult due to trade frictions with an increasingly defensive West and the new competition from *Japan-Asia* for Western *and* Japanese markets. And at the same time as export growth has slowed, import growth, especially in capital goods, has continued to rise rapidly in the late 1980s and early 1990s. Hence as the country has attempted to improve labour productivity through automation and to produce higher value goods which depend on more sophisticated componentry, its subordinate relationship with technology-rich Japan has deepened.

The government has installed a new, ambitious five year plan and has developed a set of economic policies, some of which have been described above, which represent attempts to overcome present structural problems. Since the 1960s, the targets set out in five year plans have mostly been exceeded, but this was in the context of a favourable world economic situation, and a domestic situation characterized by virtually complete state-capital control over labour. The new world economic context, with growing trade friction and the threat of economic blocs looming, and the new domestic context of democracy and relative trade union freedom which limit the extent of labour exploitation, present a new and very different set of obstacles to be overcome if Korea is to continue to progress into the ranks of the most advanced industrial economies.

The State

Economic Role

The key role of the state in Korea's spectacular economic growth – a case of 'directed development' according to some scholars – has been well documented (e.g. Amsden 1989; Woronoff 1983). Following the end of Japanese colonial rule, the Korean War and a long spell of political and economic turbulence, the Park regime, established in 1961 following a military coup, set the scene for Korean-style rapid economic growth. Korea was bequeathed a significant infrastructure and a relatively highly educated population by its Japanese colonial master, but the tragic events of the 1940s and 1950s left the nation in a poor state of economic health, with more in common with the ASEAN4 than the other ANICs.

At the same time as entrepreneurialism was encouraged, the new Park government directed the economy along strategic paths identified via a talented Economic Planning Board with the help of Western economists. For the first decade or so massive US aid helped the rebuilding of the economy. A wide range of measures directed investments to targetted industries with an emphasis on exports. Publicly owned enterprises were developed where the indigenous private sector was incapable of taking the lead, and foreign loans, if necessary underwritten by government, were generally preferred to foreign direct investment for industrial development. Between 1962 (the first case of FDI in the post-war period) and 1981, cumulative FDI totalled US$ 1.25 billion compared with total investment of US$ 22.7 billion, and the FDI which was approved had to be export oriented (Westphal et al. 1984). FDI has not been insignificant, but foreign companies have accounted for less than 20 per cent of exports, which is a small proportion compared with that for Singapore (Henderson 1989). For those private sector organizations willing and capable of developing the economy along the lines laid down in economic plans there were a whole range of incentives and privileged treatments such as favourable bank loans (often from foreign banks but underwritten by the Korean government) and generous investment and export incentives (Caiden and Jung 1985; Woronoff 1983).

The government provided protection of the domestic market with quotas, tariffs, and lists of prohibited goods, and industry was largely freed from the burden of controlling the rapidly growing working class as the state ruthlessly suppressed representative workers' institutions, just as it suppressed most organized opposition, on the grounds that political stability was a prerequisite for economic growth (Irwan 1989). Between 1972 and 1980 all organized union activities were simply banned (Park Young Ki 1992). Ambitious-looking five year Economic Development Plans and economic growth targets have typically been exceeded since 1961, and the rapid economic restructuring which took place under the Park regime is indicated by the massive changes documented above.

Apart from these direct roles, the government oversees a significant economic information dissemination service to the business world and indeed to the whole population: when export or other targets are surpassed, honours are awarded to the best performing companies, and newspapers report the accompanying national celebrations. The government also orchestrates national productivity and quality management initiatives and campaigns through a range of institutions, especially the Korea Productivity Centre and the Industrial Advancement Administration.

Transition to Democracy

Following Park's assassination in 1979, army general and former director of the Korean Central Intelligence Agency Chun Doo Hwan became the new President in September 1980 (Lo Shiu Hing 1990). His economic policies were much the same, though he fast developed a reputation for a style of government considered authoritarian and repressive even by Korean standards. The Chun regime held power until 1987 when, in spite of severe repression, popular opposition became too strong.

Opposition and democratic movements, with students usually the first to act, have traditionally been vocal in Korea. Their strength is attributed by Chu Yin Wah (1992a) and Deyo (1989) to three main factors. First, a large firm bias restricts mobility through entrepreunership and therefore limits opportunities for economic betterment for large segments of a highly educated and ambitious population. Secondly, the state has failed to incorporate trade unions, religious and community groups which have had little choice but to engage in 'dissident' activities in order to air their opinions. Thirdly, a geographical concentration of large factories has made the recruitment and mobilization of the new working class by trade unions far easier than would otherwise have been the case. A broadly-based democratic movement which included church groups and students as well as workers' organizations and opposition political parties finally brought about Chun's downfall in 1987.

Repudiating authoritarianism and introducing a wide-ranging 'democratization package' which included direct Presidential elections, press liberalization and the release of political prisoners, the new President Roh Tae Woo was able, with some justification, to present Korea as a modern economic democracy in time for the 1988 Olympic Games when the world's eyes were fixed on Seoul. The first fully democratic regime was finally established in 1992. Roh's Democratic Liberal Party (DLP) won under the new leadership of Kim Young Sam, whose mandate was further strengthened at the Presidential election later the same year. Kim Dae Jung, leader of the opposition Democratic Party (DP) resigned following the Presidential elections, avowedly because of the 'dirty tricks' campaign of the DLP. The dirty tricks included pinning the old 'North Korea menace' label to the DP with the slogan 'a vote for Kim Dae Jung is a vote for Kim Il Sung' (*Far Eastern Economic Review*, 7 January 1993). In consequence something of a political vacuum has been left among opposition political groups. These have on the whole acted independently of student, church and trade union organizations, and an interesting question is the extent to which the opposition may in future attempt to ground their activities in a more active way with such pressure groups.

Legitimacy

While spectacular economic success laid the basis for state legitimacy, corruption among government ministers and government officials has been a recurring if not constant factor undermining that legitimacy. Roh probably made modest advances in this regard, but the new Kim government will have to do a great deal more work to establish the sort of trust among the electorate and among groups such as students and the church it so clearly desires.

It is difficult to distinguish between sanctions on government officials for genuine corruption, and those sanctions meted out on the rhetorical grounds of corruption but in reality for political reasons (which thereby mean a sort of corruption on the part of government itself). But the evidence of corruption at various levels of the state apparatus has been more than sufficient to cause public exasperation over a long period of time. The Park regime sacked, reprimanded and sanctioned thousands of officials during the 1970s, and one of the first acts of the Chun regime which emerged following Park's assassination in 1979 was the purging of 4,760 public employees and the dismissal of 232 top public executives, including a cabinet minister and six vice-ministers, as part of its avowed ambition to 'purify' public services (Jun Jong Sup 1985).

During the rapid shift towards democratic forms of representation and government from 1987, the facts about the corruption of Chun's own regime were widely disseminated by the media, including through televized public hearings by the National Assembly. However, the Roh administration has had to continue to battle against public mistrust of government, with Roh's own officials still appearing reluctant to act within the law. Between July 1990 and June 1991 alone 967 public servants were punished for various 'infractions' (*Korea Times*, 4 September 1991). Roh also tried to 'clean up the image' of government with threats to make public the names of those politicians, top government officials and local council members guilty of 'conspicuous consumption' and 'leading an extravagant life', which were identified as 'a major element causing a relaxation of social discipline by alienating people in low income brackets' (*Korea Times*, 30 August 1991).

The crisis of legitimacy of the state which has continued despite constitutional and other major reforms has made for difficulty in asserting power and influence over both employers and trade unions, whose reform and re-direction are seen as necessary for the continuance of economic growth. The election results of 1992 will undoubtedly boost the confidence of the government to assert its power, but it seems unlikely that they will be taken as a mandate to revert to purely repressive measures: the democracy movement remains strong, and as we will see later in the chapter, both employers and trade unions can in their own ways swing public opinion such that the state has to continue to tread warily.

With regard to both employers and trade unions, the most obvious change by the state in 1987 was a shift from an unambiguous role of controlling labour on behalf of capital to one of 'hands off in industrial relations' (Taigi Kim 1990). The result, which is described in detail below, was a massive growth in trade union activity and an outburst of strikes. Park Duk Je (1992) characterizes the mood of the labour movement at the time as one of 'strike first, negotiate next'; many of the strikes took place before the expiration of existing wage agreements, and most were illegal in one way or another. With some public support, the government has since then managed to reassert its authority so that the number of strikes has been reduced and those which do occur are mostly within the law. Table 3.12 shows recent trends in strike activity.

Arrests of labour leaders and trade unionists engaging in action deemed illegal have still nonetheless been commonplace. Kim Young Rae (1991) documents 377 such arrests between January and July 1991 alone. Such government action is often justified by the government on the grounds of the threat from Communist North Korea, and specifically entails the use of the National Security Law (NSL), which gives the state extensive powers similar to those derived from the Internal Security Act in Singapore (see chapter two). The NSL bans revolutionary organization and 'dissident' activity (*Korea Times*, 27 August 1991). Critics of the government deny any connection between North Korean communists and all but a tiny minority of radical activists, and complain of 'trumped up charges' used to re-generate a fear among the public of legal and legitimate trade union activity.

Table 3.12:   Labour Disputes in Korea, 1965-1991

Year	No. of labour disputes	Working days lost ('000)
1965	113	
1970	88	
1975	133	
1980	407	
1985	265	64
1986	276	72
1987	3,617	6,947
1988	1,873	5,401
1989	1,616	6,351
1990	322	4,487
1991 (Jan-Sep)	214	3,258

Source: Ministry of Labour, Republic of Korea, various years; Korea Labour Institute, *Quarterly Review*, VIII-II, 1992.

New State-Labour Relations

Post-1987 labour legislation has resulted in a relaxation of various restrictions on trade union organization and activity (Cho Woo Hyun 1990; Park Young Ki 1990). However, remaining restrictions such as the illegality of third party intervention in industrial disputes, the ban on participation in politics by trade unions, the ban on strikes over re-instatement issues, and the restrictions on union organization and strike activity in most public sector and 'public interest' organizations, have been subject to continued bitter state-union dispute (Cho Woo Hyun 1990). A recent concession by the government was a promise to lift the ban on trade union political participation (though the extent to which participation will be allowed in practice is not yet clear). Also in 1991 the government, under heavy pressure from the labour movement, withdrew plans to lengthen the validity of collective bargaining agreements from one year to two or three years, and to introduce an annual salary format which would constrain wage negotiations at individual enterprises (*Korea Times*, 31 October 1991).

While the state and trade unions have continued to challenge each others' legitimacy and power, the state has in the meantime attempted to introduce a degree of industrial relations order through the strengthening of dispute resolution mechanisms and the encouragement of labour-management consultation. The main dispute resolution mechanism, with committees at national and local levels, is the tripartite Labour Relations Commission (LRC) which attempts mediation, conciliation and arbitration. Although many cases have been put to the LRC, it has in fact been rare for disputes to be resolved by the Commission, which neither unions nor employers tend to trust (Bai Moo Ki 1990; Taigi Kim 1990). Labour-management consultation on the other hand has been forced on enterprises with over 100 employees since 1980, and enterprises with over 50 employees since 1987. Labour Management Councils are intended among other things to foster a degree of cooperation and mutual understanding between employer and employee, though the general consensus appears to be that in most cases trade unions are sceptical of such institutions except where they can turn them into a bargaining forum, and that employers participate only reluctantly and in the case of non-union companies fear they could lead to collective awareness and demands for union recognition.

The failure of the state in bringing employers and unions together, and in its tentative attempts to establish authoritative tripartite institutions, was also reflected in its failure to establish a Singapore-style National Wages Committee in 1989. Such an institution was to bring together representative organizations of labour and employers to establish guidelines for wage increases across the whole economy. Employers have been ambiguous towards such an institution; trade unions have been hostile (Taigi Kim 1990).

While the government might just take some credit through its attempts to create cooperative institutions for the decline in the number of industrial disputes in 1990 and 1991, in the light of the discussion so far it seems more likely that the reassertion of government action against militant trade unionists, the swing of public opinion against excessive strike activity, and a general awareness of the economic problems suddenly facing Korea, are the more important factors. Recent dispute figures may also be subject to error: in 1991 provincial labour administrations were reported (*Korea Times*, 27 September 1991) as having extensively issued documents falsifying the number of disputes at particular companies in order to enhance companies' credit ratings from banks. Officials are thought to take bribes for under- or non-reporting.

Employers and trade unions may have learned a little about how to bargain hard without resorting to strikes or lock-outs which can be costly in terms of production, income or public opinion, but their relationship remains essentially antagonistic. In order to understand this antagonism further we will turn attention first to employers, then to labour unions.

Employers

Korea is famous for its huge conglomerates which have been primarily responsible for the growth of manufactured exports, though during the 1980s the fastest growing employing organizations were the very large *and* the very small (see Douglass and DiGregorio 1991 for a detailed analysis). In 1990, 5.1 million were self-employed, 2.1 million 'family workers', and 1.5 million 'daily workers' out of the 18 million total workforce. Data on employment by size of firm in Korea are poor, though table 3.13, which shows employment by size of firm for a large section of the workforce (5.4 million out of the 9 million not accounted for above) shows a significant concentration of employment in large organizations. Table 3.14 shows that the employees of large organizations (as is the case in Japan and Taiwan) are relatively privileged with significantly higher wages.

Table 3.13:   Employment by Size of Establishment in Korea, 1990

Establishment size	No. of employees	%*
5 – 9	321,742	6.0
10 – 15	289,163	5.4
16 – 29	526,457	9.8
30 – 49	570,579	10.6
50 – 99	745,446	13.9
100 – 199	672,661	12.5
200 – 299	382,419	7.1
300 – 499	393,981	7.3
500 – 999	486,522	9.1
1,000 plus	976,643	18.2
Total in sample	5,365,613	

* Figures are percentages of employees working in establishments of a particular size for the sample only. Sample excludes government employees, army, police, public education, and firms employing less than five and self-employed.

Source: Ministry of Labour, Republic of Korea, *Yearbook of Labour Statistics 1991.*

Table 3.14:   Monthly Earnings by Size of Establishment in Korea, 1990*

Size of firm	No. of workers working 160 hours or more	% of workers with monthly earnings of Won			
		< 200,000	200,000 – 400,000	> 400,000 – 699,000	> 700,000
10 – 29	744,105	4.6	65.6	18.1	11.5
30 – 99	1,221,013	4.0	44.5	38.0	13.5
100 – 299	1,001,373	3.0	42.0	39.9	15.1
300 – 499	355,606	2.0	37.7	39.6	20.6
500 +	1,352,075	1.2	32.7	42.3	23.8

* Sample as in table 3.13, but also excludes organizations employing 5-9 persons, and all workers working less than 160 hours per month.

Source: Calculated from data in Ministry of Labour, Republic of Korea, Y*earbook of Labour Statistics 1991.*

The future of Korea's large organizations is uncertain, but undoubtedly for the past three decades or so Korea's most important employers who have been responsible for the bulk of growth in export-oriented manufacturing have been the large *chaebol*. As we shall see, in many respects these huge conglomerates still behave as if they were small firms.

The Chaebol

The *chaebol* are unique among the four East Asian NICs. Singapore is heavily dependent on large numbers of foreign direct investors. Hong Kong and Taiwan's recent growth on the other hand has largely been a result of indigenous but typically very small, highly networked companies, albeit in the case of Taiwan with the ability to establish joint-ventures with multinational giants where strategically useful. Korea, like Taiwan, has developed a highly successful indigenous bourgeoisie, but its activities are centred on huge, highly diversified conglomerates supported by the state. Such conglomerates are often compared with Japan's *zaibatsu*, and indeed the Chinese characters for Korea's conglomerates, *chaebol*, are the same. As Korean economists and business experts are keen to tell any foreign visitor, *zaibatsu* and *chaebol* both mean something like 'finance clique' or 'business group'. They are also keen, however, to point out important differences between the *zaibatsu* and the *chaebol*. *Zaibatsu* are characterized by diffused ownership within the group and diffused shareholdings across companies. In the *chaebol*, firms are under the head of the family's centralized control. Rivalry between *chaebol* firms is so intense they sometimes refuse to buy components from each other; inter-*chaebol* cooperation is uncommon (Biggart 1990). Also unlike the *zaibatsu*, which surround themselves with sub-contractors known as *keiretsu* groups, the *chaebol* tend to restrict sub-contracting and keep as much production as possible in-house (Clifford 1988; Whitley 1992).

The *chaebol* had humble beginnings in the 1950s as small family businesses, but grew rapidly from the 1960s onwards as they took advantage of the incentives offered by government for targetted industries. Some of these growing businesses were spectacularly successful, and the concentration of economic power grew rapidly. As they grew in size they became increasingly capable of, and succesful in, competing for favourable loans and government credit, and concentration continued to increase through the 1970s and into the 1980s (Zeile 1990). By 1984 Korea's top five *chaebol* ranked in the top 60 in *Fortune International's 500* ranking (Hamilton et al. 1987). The enormous contribution of the *chaebol* to Korea's growth is not disputed. They have given Korea the ability to compete head-on in a variety of export markets with the world's largest corporations – arguably a feat which would not have been achieved without the economies of scale and technological capabilities made possible by large firm size. *Chaebol* success meant Korea became the world's second largest manufacturer and exporter of electronic consumer goods in 1987, producing 12.9 per cent of global output and taking 11.6 per cent of the world market in 1990; in semiconductors, another *chaebol* speciality, Korea lagged behind only Japan and the US in 1990, commanding 15.9 per cent of global trade. By the late 1980s Korea had risen to a position of around twelfth in the world league table of exporters (Tank 1992). However, although the *chaebol* have undeniably been central in Korea's success as an export oriented economy, concerns have increasingly been raised about the dysfunctions of too much economic concentration, about the potential drawbacks of a combination of business ownership and management control, and about *chaebol* misuse of power.

Various figures are put forward to demonstrate the extent of economic concentration in Korea, and these often appear contradictory due to different bases of calculation. Amsden's (1989) claim that in 1984 the three largest *chaebol* accounted for 36 per cent of GNP has been criticized by Zeile (1990) as misleading for assuming an incorrect definition of GNP and using only sales data. His own more sober and detailed analysis based on value-added measures shows the top 50 *chaebol* in the mid 1980s accounting for nearly 20 per cent of GNP; within manufacturing they accounted for 23 per cent of employment, 28 per cent of value-added, and over 40 per cent of sales. These figures still indicate a significantly higher degree of concentration than in the US, as do figures put forward by Cho Woo Hyun (1990) which indicate far higher concentration ratios than in the economically advanced countries of Germany and the UK as well as the US. A Presidential Commission on Economic Restructuring (1988) cites the 30 largest conglomerates as representing 40.2 per cent of the total value of shipments, 17.6 per cent of employment (Hyundai alone employs 160,000), and 41.3 per cent of exports in manufacturing in 1985; the top five conglomerates alone accounted for 23 per cent of shipments, 9.7 per cent of employment, and 27 per cent of exports. A final figure worth citing to give the reader a feel for economic concentration in Korea is that in 1990 Hyundai's group of 41 corporations had a combined annual turnover of US$ 37 billion. This was roughly the size of Korea's fiscal budget for 1991 (*Korea Times*, 8 September 1991).

Employer-State Relations

The state has frequently demonstrated that it recognizes a dependence on *chaebol* when lending a hand in times of financial difficulty – for instance through providing new loans or facilitating debt rescheduling when companies have been on the verge of bankruptcy (Clifford 1988). As Eckert (1990, p.24) puts it: 'the *chaebol* have become too important to the economy for the state to ignore their needs and demands'. The political patronage of *chaebol* leaders has also been welcomed by government leaders on some occasions, and many Korean critics believe an exchange of economic favours for political contributions has continued after 1987.

However, the government has at the same time been highly critical of many aspects of *chaebol* activities. The Presidential Commission on Economic Restructuring (1988) reiterated views which had frequently been expressed in the past in identifying problems in the hindrance of competition due to the *chaebol*'s superior bargaining power, excessive monopolistic profits, and the development of unhealthily close ties between the leaders of conglomerates, government and the military. Developing the latter point, Choi Jong Pyo and his colleagues (1991) have documented marriages between family members of the top politicians, *chaebol* leaders, and military leaders, and suggest Korea might be witnessing over the last 10 years the emergence of a new homogeneous upper class. However, any such development does not appear to have arrived in time to resolve the current acute problems: the occasional outbursts of conflict which characterized state-employer relations since the 1960s have again reared their head since 1987. The underlying problem appears to be the conflict between the state's national long term objective of joining the ranks of the advanced nations, and *chaebol* goals of short-term profit-maximization.

In recent years *chaebol* leaders have demanded less government interference and direction (Eckert 1990). The Federation of Korean Industries (FKI), which acts as the public voice of many *chaebol*, has publicly attacked 'excessive restraints' such as the forced disposal of non-business purpose real estate, restraints on imports by businesses of various categories of foreign made products, and the compulsory selection of main business lines (*Korea Economic Weekly*, 18 November 1991). The government on the other hand has been expressing clear ideas about the neglect of R&D (despite the fact that national R&D spending grew four-fold, mostly within the private sector, to over two per cent of GNP between 1980 and 1988) and the failure to up-grade technology (in spite of massive investments during the late 1980s). According to one report embarrassing to *chaebol* leaders, entertainment expenses of Korean companies exceed R&D expenditures by a factor of four (Clifford 1988).

Some of the most recent attacks by the government on *chaebol* have focussed on the wealth of business leaders, whose declared incomes alone (many are suspected of having massive undeclared incomes) are typically counted in the millions of Dollars per year, and in particular on the manner in which wealth is kept within the family through avoidance of inheritance and donation taxes. In the last few months of 1991 Hyundai and its ageing leader Chung Ju Yung were given special attention and the case was subject to massive media coverage. Chung, whose personal shareholdings are worth hundreds of millions of dollars, was accused of illegally passing on around US$ 20 million-worth of shares to his children in order to avoid 56 per cent inheritance taxes (*Korea Times*, 3 October 1991). Hyundai disputed the charges, but eventually apologized and paid up US$ 180 million in penalty taxes. A (temporarily) humbled Chung publicly commented:

I will devote the remainder of my life to the nation and society, and the democracy on earth. I have lived only for my family. I will live from now on as if I were reborn (*Korea Times*, 10 October 1991).

In November 1991 the Office of National Tax Administration (ONTA) spread its net to investigate 10 more *chaebol* on suspicion of illegal changes of stock ownership to avoid inheritance taxes (*China News*, 24 November 1991).

Some opposition MPs claimed the investigations by ONTA (which had been suspected in the past of being used as a tool by government to punish employers who stepped out of line) might have been caused by Roh's displeasure at the recent attempt by the *chaebol*, led by Hyundai, to sponsor the development of a new political party which served their interests. But whatever the real reason for the burst in ONTA activities, the blow against Hyundai was no more than a softener compared with the announcement in November 1991 of plans to disperse concentration and separate ownership and control. As part of the Seventh Five Year Socioeconomic Development Plan, the government announced the detailed objectives of reducing the equity ownership ratio of large business groups from the present 46.9 per cent to 30 per cent, and greatly increasing the average public offering ratio of only 28.7 per cent by the 30 largest *chaebol*. Land and real estate speculation – particulary unpopular *chaebol* side-businesses – are to be curbed, and ceilings on non-voting shares are to be reduced from the present 50 to 25 per cent (*Korea Economic Weekly*, 18 November 1991). Business groups manufacturing goods which can be made by small and medium sized enterprises will be persuaded to hand them over to the latter, who will receive special help from government to improve their technological capabilities to the necessary standard (*Korea Times*, 25 August 1991).

Table 3.15 demonstrates the extent to which the ownership of the *chaebol* is concentrated in the hands of family members.

For all the top ten *chaebol* less than half the member firms of the business group are listed on the stock market. Family members may control stock either directly through each member company, or indirectly through the 'core' company which in turn owns shares in the subsidiary companies (Biggart 1990). Family member plus family firm shares of paid-in capital among the top ten range from 23.6 per cent at Lotte, to 67.8 per cent at Hyundai, and these figures are not untypical of ownership patterns among the rest. As well as indicating the great wealth of the owning families, these figures make clear how single owning families (should they so desire, and they do as we shall discuss below) have the power to exert virtually complete control over the individual member firms.

Events following the government's attack on Chung Ju Yung and on the *chaebol* more generally in 1990 and 1991 were quite remarkable. In 1992 Hyundai's 're-born' President Chung Ju Yung led the new United People's Party (UPP) into the national elections, though without the (overt) support of other *chaebol* leaders who had gone on the defensive. The UPP was defeated (though the UPP gained 31

Table 3.15:   Ownership of the Top Ten Chaebol, as at 1 April 1991

	Paid-in capital (Won million)	Share of family members (%)	Share of family firms (%)	No. of member firms	No. of firms listed on stock market
Hyundai	2,236,000	27.5	40.3	42	15
Daewoo	3,132,174	9.8	40.6	24	8
Samsung	1,249,756	8.5	44.7	48	13
Lucky-Goldstar	2,062,558	7.6	30.6	52	18
Ssanyong	734,127	7.6	34.4	22	10
Hanjin	504,622	27.7	24.3	22	8
Sunkyung	583,387	21.5	29.1	26	3
Korea Explosives	541,174	10.5	30.8	27	9
Daelim	291,690	7.6	31.6	14	4
Lotte	1,199,445	3.6	20.0	32	4

Source: Korea Fair Trade Commission.

out of 229 parliamentary seats and Chung did manage to get a 16.1 per cent share of the vote in the December Presidential election), and the new President Kim took the opportunity to re-affirm the government's determination to rein in the *chaebol*. Chung vowed to continue in politics, leaving his younger brother Chung Se Yung to apologize to the government on Hyundai's behalf for the company's use of its own money and personnel to support the UPP campaign. Hyundai, like the other *chaebol*, relies heavily on the government directly for contracts (especially for major construction projects) and indirectly for favours. Hence Chung Se Yung's statement to President Kim that Hyundai 'will cooperate two hundred per cent with your government in the future' (*Far Eastern Economic Review*, 9 April 1992, 14 January 1993).

The *chaebol* may have been powerful enough to resist or ignore previous attempts to break their strength, but if the balance of power tilted towards the *chaebol* in the 1980s (Biggart 1990) it has certainly shifted back to the state in the 1990s in the context of economic crisis and widespread public awareness of *chaebol* misdemeanours. Certainly the state gives the appearance of a strong determination to break the power of the *chaebol* family leaders as part of its attempt to restructure Korean industry under the imperative of economic renewal.

Management Styles

If relations between capital and the state can be characterized by dependency *and* antagonism, so too can those between capital and labour. But before assessing the extent of antagonism and its consequences, we will explore the management style characteristic of Korean industry.

Most private companies in Korea, regardless of size, are owned and controlled by the founding father or his children (Clifford 1988; Park Duk Je 1992) and the style of management is typically described as 'paternalistic' and 'authoritarian' (Deyo 1985; Rhee 1985). Woronoff (1983) claimed that Korea's economic growth was dependent on 'shedding much of its Confucian heritage', but it is popular now to attribute the Korean management style (and therefore economic success) precisely to that heritage. Kim Byun Hwan (1992) relates paternalistic management to neo-Confucian traditions, with their stress on hierarchical and reciprocal human relationships as the basis of social order. In particular Kim attempts an explanation of the predominance of seniority wages systems in Korean organizations in terms of the neo-Confucian ideologies and behaviours inherited from pre-modern times and today carried by Korean employers and managers. There are serious problems with this argument (explored fully in the final chapter of this book), not least of which are the lack of explanation of historical link between pre-modern and modern institutions, and the importance of Christianity generally and Catholicism in particular in modern Korea. Fallows (1988) explains that Catholicism was embraced by large segments of the Korean population because of the anti-colonialist stance taken by the church, and today something like a quarter of the population would describe itself as Catholic.

Biggart (1990) provides a more careful historical account linking pre-modern Korean institutions to modern management practices. Rather than make a simple causal connection between neo-Confucian ideology and management style, Biggart distinguishes the Korean from Japanese and Chinese histories, and describes a unique Korean 'patrimonialism' and 'personalism' which stresses the importance in social relations of family connections, regional origins and alumni ties as well as Confucian hierarchy. A regional and clan consciousness which derives historically from the importance of regionally based *yangban* elites which competed for the favour of the royal Patriarch helps explain fierce inter-*chaebol* competition and political patronage in Korea. *Chaebol* family owners (like their *yangban* elite predecessors) tend to identify themselves with a particular region, and to fill the top ranks of management from the same region. Again in line with tradition, the head of the group (*haejang*) appoints sons, or if necessary brothers or sons-in-law, to top positions in group firms. The *haejang* surrounds himself with a centralized personal staff in the core company and a tight control is attempted over group firms (just as the *yangban* elites attempted control over their regions).

The *haejang* and his personal staff control strategic planning, finance and investment for all the member firms, and set detailed targets for performance on a range of criteria. Performance against targets is closely monitored and is subject to rigorous reviews. Sometimes management selection and management development is also undertaken at the core company in an attempt to ensure a loyalty to the group and the *haejang* rather than the business unit. Employee pay and promotion prospects are then determined more by educational background, sex, loyalty, and length of service than performance considerations (Park Se Il 1988 describes in detail how this occurs in four case studies), and the personal relationship of the employee with the superior assumes great importance. Often large bonuses account for more of the monthly wage of managers than base pay, and nepotism and favouritism are assumed to be important in determining levels of bonus and promotion prospects in many firms.

There do appear, then, to be parallels between pre-modern forms of social organization and modern management styles, and although further specific historical research into the origins of *haejang* values and styles would be useful, it seems likely that authoritarian and paternalistic styles do owe something to a historical legacy. However, it should *not* be assumed that an ancient culture simply translates into an organization structure and a management style through some sort of cultural programming of the minds of the population. Such an argument might help legitimate a particular regime, but contributes little to our understanding of history.

The predominance of the *chaebol* with their paternalistic and authoritarian styles was made possible only with the support of the modern state, and in particular with a ruthless state suppression of workers' organizations which had rather different views about appropriate styles of management. The latter point is crucial, for the *culturist* perspective generally neglects consideration of the different interests and values of different actors or groups within a society or an organization. In the Korean case, it is important to recognize that the style of management, whatever its historical source, might reflect the values, and certainly has served the interests, of the *chaebol* elite, but not necessarily anyone else, and that the maintenance of such a style has depended on the assertion of their power. This raises questions for discussion later. What is important here is to point out that the authoritarianism of Korean employers rubs against the grain of popular demands for democracy and participation – hardly Confucian values!

Employer-Labour Relations

To continue the historical analogy, just as *yangban* (ruling class) suppression and exploitation of *sangmin* (ruled class) was characterized by conflict and resistance in pre-modern Korea (Bai Moo Ki 1990), *chaebol* exploitation and resistance by workers has characterized modern Korea. Eckert (1990, p.31) argues that:

the bourgeoisie has evinced little capacity or willingness to look beyond its own narrowly defined class interests and envision a capitalist system that genuinely embraces and accomodates the working class.

In the light of rigid state controls over labour on behalf of capital this is perhaps unsurprising – the bourgeoisie has only recently been forced to look beyond its own interests.

The responses of employers to the assertion of trade union strength since democratization and the liberalization of labour laws since 1987 have been varied, but fighting workers head on – and frequently losing – has tended to be the option favoured over more accomodative means. Dismissals of union activists have been commonplace, though it is impossible to estimate the number. There is some protection for such workers under the law, and between January 1988 and August 1991 Labour Committee rulings forced 278 industrial companies to re-instate a total of 570 workers dismissed for union activity (*Korea Times*, 28 September 1991). The law is still not, however, wholly on the workers' side: strikes over re-instatement issues are illegal, and in 1991 the government threatened to send in troops to break a strike by 18,000 workers at Hyundai Heavy Industries. Workers were demanding the re-hiring of 34 colleagues dismissed in 1987, and were unhappy with Hyundai's offer to re-instate only 14 after a four month 're-orientation' period. The mobilization of 'save the company squads' has been widespread (Kim Hwang Joe 1990) as has the use of secret recruitment blacklists, generated and circulated by the government among employers according to some critics (*Korea Times*, 18 September 1991, 4 October 1991).

Employers, with the backing of the state, have also resorted to ideological attacks on workers. These include overt threats to relocate production overseas. H.S. Corp.'s director J.H. Jeong, for instance, said:

The labour unions seem to dislike it but the fact is that because of the growing strength of South Korean labour unions there will be more factories built out of South Korea. That is their fault. They can ask for 20 per cent or 30 per cent wage rises, but they will be killing themselves. More jobs will be leaving South Korea.

As we documented in chapter one, many factories have been built out of Korea, but it is difficult to distinguish rhetoric from genuine threat: there are pressures beyond the assertion of labour strength informing production relocation decisions.

As well as the not unexpected attacks on labour militancy, popular conservative opinion in Korea occasionally blames a 'decline in work values' for the recent economic malaise. Deputy Editor of the *Korea Times* (issue 22 October 1991) Park Chang Seok recently let rip as follows:

The rampancy of easy money has led the people into shunning the so-called 3-Ds (dirty, difficult and dangerous work) and to subsequently indulge in a gay life. … social discipline and the moral integrity of the people have been rapidly rupturing … .

Quantifying any such 'rapid rupturing of moral integrity' (even if it could be agreed such a characterization is appropriate) is of course highly problematic, though the Korea Chamber of Commerce and Industry (reported in *Korea Times*, 26 September 1991) recently attempted to measure changes in attitudes in a survey of around 5,000 workers from 650 companies. Over the previous 10 years the number of workers who said they 'obeyed their bosses faithfully most of the time' had declined from 85 to 65 per cent, and the number who considered their companies to be a 'second home' declined from 94 to 59 per cent. That Korean workers are beginning to consume in favour of working and saving was indicated in table 3.4, which demonstrates a decline in the savings ratio in Korea from 1988 (38.1) to 1991 (36.1). In response the government has re-emphasized its nation-wide savings campaign (*Korea Times*, 30 October 1991).

There are, however, problems with the effectiveness of appeals to values by government and employers, who have, compared with their counterparts in Singapore, been restrained in their attacks on the moral integrity of the work force. Clearly they know such attacks would be seen as a case of the pot calling the kettle black. Indeed, Korean public opinion, if it is against union militancy and 'over-consumption', is at least equally concerned with the 'morality' of employers and government.

A problem for employers, which is no surprise in the light of the above discussion, has been the difficulty of putting up a united front against trade union demands. For instance while some employers have called for a united application of a 'no work no pay' principle, more than 80 per cent of strikes in 1989 ended with full or partial payment for the period of the strike (Taigi Kim 1990). The principle was reported to be taking root in 1990 (Korea Employers' Federation, *Quarterly Review* 1990, IX-III), but an authoritative combined employer voice on wage guidelines and the handling of disputes is still absent.

More sophisticated means of improving industrial relations appear to be used only in exceptional *chaebol* such as Samsung (considered locally as the 'IBM' of Korean companies), and the Korea Employers' Federation continues to fight an up-hill battle to persuade companies to take Labour Management Councils more seriously, to introduce carefully designed performance-related pay, personnel evaluation, etc. systems, and generally to change the decision-making styles and increase levels of consultation and communication.

Labour

Trade Union Organization

The Korean trade union movement has a complex history (Kim Hwang Joe 1990) but the position before democratization was an emphasis on enterprise level organization as stipulated in 1980 changes to labour law. Revisions to labour law in 1987 mean unions are allowed to organize at the level they choose, but so far bargaining has tended to remain firmly at enterprise level. Korean enterprise unions must be distinguished from their celebrated Japanese counterparts. Although in both countries enterprise unions assumed importance in the context of state suppression of radical national level union organizations, in Japan enterprise unions were carefully incorporated by employers to serve a socialization role. Today supervisors and middle managers are often also union representatives, and the union can serve as a career route into middle management positions (Moore 1987; Whitehill and Takezawa 1986). Recent translations of the work of Japanese labour historians and sociologists demonstrate the seriousness which employers attached to enterprise based trade union organization, and the extents to which they have been willing to go to ensure the full incorporation of local union officials and activists (see for instance Kumazawa forthcoming 1994; Tabata 1989 and Yamamoto 1990). In Korea, enterprise unions were widely considered ineffectual organizations until 1987, but when the outburst of disputes came, most were led by these unions. Clearly, most employers had failed to take union relations seriously, let alone attempt their incorporation, until it was too late.

For obvious reasons, union leaders tend to be young and inexperienced. It is in this context that during labour disputes in 1987 and 1988 the union leader organizing the dispute was replaced in around *50 per cent* of cases. This says something about the spontaneity of industrial action and lack of organization at the time (Taigi Kim 1990).

The only legally recognized nation-wide organization is the Federation of Korea Trade Unions (FKTU), with 21 affiliated industrial unions which in turn oversee over 7,000 enterprise unions. The FKTU, which traditionally has been closely aligned to the ruling party, was ineffectual before democratization and was generally considered a puppet of the government. Since 1987 the federation has not played any significant direct role in industrial disputes, trade union power being concentrated at the enterprise level. Indeed, the union leaders in large enterprises have been reluctant to move towards industry-level bargaining because of distrust of the FKTU leadership, for fear of loss of their own influence and power, and in a situation where they might justifiably claim they can make better gains with the present set up (Park Duk Je 1992).

In 1987 the underground leaders of the radical trade union movement appeared in public. The FKTU, which had little authority anyway, was further undermined, being branded a 'yellow union organization' and a 'puppet' of the government. Radical trade unionists established an alternative national federation on 22 January 1990 – *Chonnohyop*, or the National Federation of Trade Unions (NFTU) – despite the fact that it was banned a few days before its official founding (Park Young Ki 1992). *Chonnohyop* began with a membership of around 200,000 in 450 organizations. However, being declared illegal from the start (though its member unions are not), its activities have been subject to close surveillance, and many of its leaders have been arrested. Soon after its foundation, *Chonnohyop's* membership was reduced to 150,000. Nonetheless, it continues to have a strong voice at national level, it can easily attract tens of thousands to its occasional demonstrations and rallies, and it can claim some credit for the shift in the position of the FKTU from one of extreme conservatism to one where it is, on some issues, willing to challenge government policies. The comment of a journalist who had studied the Korean labour movement closely (in an interview with the author in 1991) probably still holds true: '*Chonnohyop* and other dissident trade union organizations have legitimacy but no organization; the FKTU has organization but no legitimacy'.

Industrial Disputes

In 1987, democratization inevitably meant the lid was taken off industrial relations, and Korea witnessed an unprecedented explosion of strikes and industrial unrest. As table 3.12 (above) shows, the number of labour disputes rose 13-fold and the number of working days lost rose almost 100-fold between 1986 and 1987. More recent figures, particularly those for 1990, suggest some sort of 'cooling off' or 'readjustment' – the number of disputes declined dramatically – though working days lost due to labour disputes were still massive compared with their pre-democratization levels, and figures for the first nine months of 1991 suggested they might be increasing again (Korea Development Institute 1991). Surveys by the Korea Employers' Federation (*Quarterly Review* 1992, VIII-II) suggest a continuing antagonism and distrust between unions and employers.

Table 3.16 shows that trade union membership virtually doubled since 'democratization'. Equally importantly, table 3.17 demonstrates a dramatic increase in the number of organizations with trade unions in manufacturing industry.

Table 3.16:   Union Membership and Union Density in Korea, 1985-1990

	Union Membership	Union Density (%)
1985	1,004,398	*
1986	1,035,890	*
1987	1,267,475	11.7
1988	1,707,465	15.9
1989	1,932,415	18.0
1990	1,886,884	17.4

* Figures not available because of changes in methods of data collection in Korea.

Sources: Ministry of Labour, Republic of Korea, *Yearbook of Labour Statistics*, 1991; Korea Labour Institute, *Quarterly Review*, various issues.

The union density figures in table 3.16 underestimate the support for the labour movement. Bai Moo Ki (1990) estimates that the proportion of organized to organizable workers (excluding casuals and those prohibited from trade union membership such as teachers) had reached around 22 per cent in 1990, and trade union recognition in companies employing more than 500 workers grew from less than half of companies in 1986 to over 80 per cent in 1990 (table 3.17).

Table 3.17:   Establishments with Trade Unions in Korea, 1986-1990 (%)

Size of establishment (No. of employees)	1986	1989	1990
10 – 29	1.4	2.0	1.4
30 – 99	2.5	7.7	11.1
100 – 299	11.0	30.6	40.8
300 – 499	25.9	59.4	54.2
500 – 999	45.9	77.0	} 81.7
Over 1,000	51.6	79.2	
All establishments	4.9	20.3	

* N. B. data for 1990 gives one figure (81.7) for establishments with over 500 employees.

Source: Bai Moo Ki (1990).

The immediate consequences of the surge in workforce militancy are at least partially quantifiable. For capital and the state there are crises in both competitiveness and legitimacy, which were arguably in any case coming but undoubtedly have been accelerated by labour gains. For labour there have been gains in wages and working conditions.

Labour Gains

The most obvious and often-cited gain for labour has been on wages. Table 3.18 shows nominal and real wage increases during the 1980s.

Table 3.18:   Nominal and Real Wage Increase Rates in Korea, 1982-1991 (%)

Increase	Nominal wage		Real wage
	All industries	Manufacturing	All industries
1982-86*	10.6	10.8	6.7
1987	10.1	11.6	6.9
1988	15.5	19.6	7.8
1989	21.1	25.1	14.5
1990	18.8	20.2	10.2
1991	17.5	16.9	5.9

* Average

Sources: Bai Moo Ki (1990); Korea Employers' Federation (1990); Korea Employers' Federation (1991); Korea Development Institute (1992), 11 (1).

Wage increases since 1987 were particularly high in manufacturing where most trade union organization is concentrated. Wages also increased markedly compared with the other three East Asian NICs, with Korea moving from a clear bottom position to second between 1987 and 1989 (table 3.10). It is of course difficult to separate out trade union strength from labour market and consumer price effects on wage rates, but there is no doubt that the exertion of trade union power in the larger of Korea's unionized organizations has led to substantially improved wages.

The assertion of union strength has also contributed to an accelerated reduction in wage differentials related to sex, education, seniority and occupation (Bai Moo Ki 1990; Lee Won Duck 1989; Korea Employers' Federation 1990). There is no equal opportunities legislation as yet, but this is on the agenda of trade unions and opposition groups and seems likely in the near future (Lee Won Duck 1989). But differentials between large and small firms increased from 1986 to 1989 due to the concentration of trade unions in large companies (Park Duk Je 1992). This was because in 1987, while less than 1 per cent of companies with less than 50 employees experienced a dispute, nearly 70 per cent of companies employing over 1,000 were faced with disputes (Park Young Ki 1992). However, in 1990 the size differential trend was reversed as small and medium-sized companies were forced to 'catch up' in the context of an extremely tight labour market (Korea Employers' Federation, *Quarterly Review* 1990, IX-III).

Minimum wages law was passed at the end of 1986 when the government judged that the Korean economy had developed to a level where its effects would not be of great detriment. The Minimum Wage Council, made up of employer, trade union and 'public interest' representatives, made its first recommendation in 1987 and this was implemented for 1988. Since then both the coverage of employees and minimum wage levels have increased, in part because of the strength of and support for the labour movement. Table 3.19 shows the increases in minimum wages up to 1992.

The year-on-year increase in minimum wages has consistently been above the rate of inflation *and* (apart from 1990) above increases in average earnings. From the start legal minimum wage decisions were hotly debated – employees' representatives boycotted the 1987 final vote and employers the 1988 vote. Employers' organizations unsuccessfully pressured the government to reconsider the 'excessive' increase voted in 1990 (for 1991) on the grounds that too many workers would benefit (390,000) causing serious problems for many employers, and that unions might take the 16.4 per cent increase as a barometer in wage negotiations (*KEF Quarterly Review* 1991, XII-II). The government, however, stood by the recommendation, and a further large rise was voted in and accepted for 1992.

Higher wages have not been the only gain labour has struggled to achieve since 1987. Arguably an equally important development has been the rapid reduction in working hours. As table 3.20 shows, Korean manufacturing workers have for the whole of the 1980s worked longer hours than their notoriously hard working

Table 3.19:   Scope of Application and Levels of Legal Minimum Wages in Korea,
              1988-1992

	1988	1989	1990	1991	1992
Scope of application	Manufacturers with > 10 employees	Manufacturing, mining and construction companies with > 10 employees	All industries with >10 employees		
Minimum wage rate					
(Won) (hourly)	462.5	600	690	820	925
(Won) (daily)	3,700	4,800	5,520	6,560	7,400
Rate of increase (%)	—	29.7	15	16.4	12.8

Sources: Korea Employers' Federation (1990); Korea Employers' Federation, *Quarterly Review*, XII-II, 1991; *Korea Times*, 12 October 1991.

East Asian counterparts – at least according to official figures – but the length of the working day is now rapidly declining.

Table 3.20:   Weekly Hours of Work in Manufacturing in Selected Countries, 1980-1991

	Korea	Taiwan	Singapore	Japan	US
1980-85*	53.8	48.8	47.6	48.6	39.9
1986	54.7	48.2	47.7	48.1	40.7
1987	54.0	48.3	48.4	48.1	41.0
1988	52.6	47.6	47.4	47.6	41.1
1989	51.1	47.0	48.6	47.1	41.0
1990	49.8		48.5		40.8
1991	45.2		48.7		

* Average.

Sources: Kim Choong Soo (1991); Ministry of Labour, Republic of Korea, *Yearbook of Labour Statistics 1991*; Korea Labour Institute, *Quarterly Review*, VIII-II, 1992; Republic of China (1990); Ministry of Labour, Republic of Singapore, *Singapore Yearbook of Labour Statistics 1991*.

The government was perhaps tacitly accepting trade union arguments for more leisure time when the Transportation Ministry announced locomotive engineers' monthly working hours would be reduced from 245 to 224 following a strike in July 1988 (*Korea Times*, 1 September 1988). In March 1989 legal standard working hours in Korea were reduced from 48 per week to 46 per week, and further down to 44 per week from October 1990 (Bai Moo Ki 1990). Six day working is still typical in Korea, but small numbers of companies have been reported to have begun implementing five day work weeks (Korea Employers' Federation, *Quarterly Review* 1989, X-III).

Other concessions to labour by the state and employers are numerous. Bai Moo Ki (1990) documents minor improvements in pension, medical and social security provisions, and improvements in physical working conditions, health and safety, holidays, recreational facilities, workers dormitories, etc. – often following strikes – are widely documented.

But while the number of labour disputes, the rapid growth of membership, and significant labour gains reflect the newly-found power of the trade union movement, this power resides mostly at the grass roots level. At national level trade unions are remarkably weak and lacking in organization, and it is likely to take some time before the trade union voice at that level can become a united one based on a clearly articulated ideology. We have documented the important gains made by trade unions since 1987, but there are also serious remaining problems. One of the most important is the restriction on trade union membership and activity among public servants and other groups. A lifting of these restrictions could give a further boost to trade union membership, power, and probably legitimacy, but the government is extremely reluctant to give way, and hundreds of teachers have been sacked or imprisoned since 1988 for membership of and activity in their illegal union organization (Kim Hwang Joe 1990).

Conclusions And Prospects

The leaders of both state and employers in Korea have seen their authoritarian regimes challenged by the democratic movement and the labour movement in particular. Yet so far they have failed to reconcile their own differences of interest, let alone embrace labour with a vision of a new socio-economic order. Labour on the other hand has problems of leadership and organization such that its challenge, though strong, is uncoordinated and without a clear rationale – or at least without a single rationale agreed upon by the different factions of the movement.

While open conflict between the three parties continues, the nation faces serious economic problems. The trade deficit is a reflection of deeper structural problems in the economy which, arguably, can be resolved only with a new set of relations between capital, labour and the state. Korea's remarkable growth to the end of the 1980s was based on giant conglomerates with an export orientation directed by the state and able to make use of an abundant, cheap and largely compliant labour force. Arguably, however, it is Korea's very success which has led it to the point where the labour surplus has dried up, and where a highly educated workforce with high expectations and ambitions have become capable of challenging the old order. That a revolution has not occurred may owe more to the fragmentation and problems of organization of the democratic and labour movements (and perhaps to the world crisis of Socialism) than to any legitimacy the Korean elite can command.

If Korea is to advance as an industrial nation, then it must cope with the new challenge of the rapidly rising second-tier NICs such as Thailand and Malaysia which can increasingly compete in some of the same markets as Korea, but with far cheaper labour. It must also compete with Japanese transplants in poorer South East Asian countries (known by local economists as 'Japan-Asia') which export back to Japan as well as across the world. This is well recognized by the state which is currently attempting to implement a radical up-grading of the economy.

Regardless of its desirability in the eyes of some employers, a return to the days of cheap labour seems an unlikely option. However, to pursue the strategy of 'closing the technological gap with its competitors in new, advanced products', as advocated by the KDI, will mean a radical shift in companies' strategies and structures, and therefore on state, capital and labour reaching some sort of accord. Japanese enterprises, with which Korea's enterprises increasingly have to compete directly, and especially in electronics, responded to *endaka* with impressive productivity gains and a successful restructuring of operations with the cooperation of labour and the state. Taiwan, too, appears to have responded to its own structural problems more quickly than Korea, *and* has the great advantage of massive foreign exchange reserves which are being used in a huge government spending programme to bolster economic growth in the 1990s (see chapter four). Korean enterprises, faced now with their own crisis of competitiveness, appear relatively slow to respond *and* lack the confidence of both the state and labour.

In raising labour costs and reducing the extent of labour exploitation, the Korea labour 'problem' has brought on – arguably brought forward – a crisis of national competitiveness. While the state has identified the restructuring it sees as necessary for economic renewal, employers are relatively slow to respond and find themselves being attacked from both sides. In the absence of an over-arching ideology and a set of workable institutions which accomodate the interests and ambitions of all three parties, and with the end of authoritarian state control, it is difficult to see how Korea can implement an economic strategy not subject to serious state-capital, state-labour, and capital-labour conflict. If Korea fails to develop the conditions in which such a strategy is workable the economic consequences could be severe. If on the other hand Korea *does* manage to overcome its present problems and begin the transition to a new industrial order (and the author would not see this as an impossible task) it may look back and thank the labour movement for precipitating a crisis which was easier to handle earlier rather than later. The labour 'problem' may yet turn out to be a progressive force.

Chapter Four: Taiwan

Taiwan (earlier Formosa), like Korea, was a Japanese colony prior to World War II. Following liberation, the island was taken back by the Chinese, but immediately the Communist revolution was taking place on the mainland. The Kuomintang and loyalist troops fled to Taiwan, where they liquidated any opposition, to establish a provisional government and to await the opportunity to return to the mainland and take up what they saw as their rightful place at the seat of power. In the meantime the US Seventh Fleet patrolled the waters to protect the nationalists and, as in Korea, provided huge amounts of aid as an 'economic' defence against the rising tide of Socialism in the region. As it became apparent that the mainland Communists were not going to collapse, the ambitions of the KMT were effectively restricted to Taiwan, and it was here that the philosophies of Sun Yat Sen were put into practical effect in the modern world. Today the native Taiwanese retain a distinctive identity: the mainlanders control government and the public sector; the Taiwanese run private business.

After a decade of import substitution, export oriented industrialization got under way in the 1960s, and by the end of the 1970s Taiwan had developed an indigenous capacity in a range of industries, heavy and light, capital intensive and labour intensive. The state took control of the strategically important capital intensive heavy industries (many of which are still publicly owned today) while small businesses in the private sector were allowed to develop the lighter industries – first textiles and clothing and other traditional industries, later the more advanced such as electronics and machine tools. Indigenous industry was heavily protected by the state. Foreign capital was encouraged (Taiwan is famous for its pioneering of the concept of Export Processing Zones, EPZs) and accounts in part for Taiwan's acquisition of a significant technological capability, but the foreign owned sector never became dominant as a source of employment or exports. In the 1990s the state continues to lead industrialization through both direct ownership and control and through guidance of the private sector, which is made up of mainly small businesses.

Industrialization and economic development has been underpinned by a ruthless repression of radicals and dissidents, together with the creation of a state controlled and enterprise based trade union organization. Welfare responsibilities were forced onto employers, with trade union involvement in their administration. In recent years state hegemony has been challenged as an alternative labour movement arose following the lifting of martial law in 1987. However, the KMT remains dominant and the opposition labour movement fragmented.

As in Korea, labour militancy has added to Taiwan's recent economic problems, which relate to a tight labour market and rapidly rising wages, increased pressure

from the West to act more 'responsibly' in trade relations, and the need to up-
grade production and move into the more R&D intensive sectors rapidly. The
Taiwanese government is, however, in at least one respect in a better position
to respond to the new challenges than the Korean government. Taiwan has been
consistently registering big trade surpluses, and has massive foreign reserves.
These are now being drawn upon in a US$ 300 billion state led infrastructural
development programme which at the least is likely to maintain high growth rates
through the mid 1990s, and if entirely successful would push Taiwan further up
the ladder of the league of advanced industrial nations. There are still serious
problems to be overcome, but there are probably more grounds for optimism for
Taiwan's economic future than for any of the other ANICs.

Economic Performance and Economic Structure

China ceded Taiwan (then 'Formosa') to the Japanese in 1895 following defeat
in the Sino-Japanese War. China re-acquired the island following World War
II, then in 1948 the Chinese nationalists were forced by the Communists to
flee the mainland, and they set up what they believed would be a 'temporary'
government in Taiwan, awaiting the opportunity to return to the mainland and
establish themselves as the legitimate rulers of China. In the meantime they
established authoritarian rule over the Taiwanese. The US Seventh Fleet protected
the nationalists, who also benefited from substantial US aid in the 1950s. Although
the rhetoric of Chinese nationalism continues even in the 1990s, and Taiwan is
still officially the 'Republic of China', the Taiwanese government long ago made
its focus of attention the economic performance of the island.

Under Japanese rule Taiwan was largely an 'agricultural appendage' to the
Japanese economy, though something of an infrastructure had been developed,
and a small industrial base, especially for food processing, had been established
(Haggard and Cheng 1987; Rabushka 1987). An import substitution strategy financed largely by American aid was successfully pursued during the 1950s, with
a focus on traditional industries such as textiles and rubber goods. However, this
strategy eventually led to the problems of market saturation, a high import dependence, and balance of payments problems (Rabushka 1987). With the Americans
seeking to cut their aid commitments in the latter part of the 1950s (they were in
fact terminated in the mid 1960s) the need to earn foreign exchange grew, and
at the turn of the decade economic reforms shifted the structure of incentives
in a more outward looking direction (Haggard and Cheng 1987). There was no
looking back. Export oriented manufacturing, as in the other ANICs, worked,
and the economy grew more rapidly than the mainland Communists would have
believed possible. Growth rates from 1960 to 1991 are indicated in table 4.1.

Full employment was a national priority from the early 1950s, and as table 4.2
shows unemployment has been kept under control. Recently, and again as in each

Table 4.1: GNP and Per Capita GNP in Taiwan, 1960-1991

	GNP (US$ billion)	GNP per capita (US$)
1960	1.7	154
1965	2.8	217
1970	5.7	389
1975	15.4	964
1980	41.4	2,344
1985	63.1	3,297
1988	125.3	6,333
1989	150.3	7,512
1990	160.9	7,954
1991	180.3	8,815

Source: Council for Economic Planning and Development, Republic of China, *Taiwan Statistical Data Book 1992.*

of the other ANICs, an acute labour shortage has developed and manufacturers have faced increasing difficulties in recruiting.

In 1960 the manufacturing workforce, at 14.8 per cent of the total working population, was already significant (Korea's manufacturing and mining workforce combined was only 8.7 per cent in 1963 – see table 3.2, chapter three), but grew steadily through the 1960s and 1970s, peaking at 34.5 per cent in 1988 (table 4.2).

Manufacturing's percentage contribution to national income is similarly high, growing from 12.9 per cent of GDP in 1952, to 22 per cent in 1963, and peaking at 39.7 per cent in 1986 (in 1991 the figure was 34.2 per cent).

Export Oriented Growth

Taiwan's real growth averaged around eight per cent per year throughout the 1980s, and while growth is expected to slow in the 1990s under a host of pressures, growth rates of around seven per cent have been registered for 1991 and 1992 after a dip to about five per cent in 1990. Of course, the growth engine is the manufacture of goods for export. Taiwan's total trade with the world only grew from US$ 0.3 billion to US$ 0.5 billion between 1952 and 1962 (the import substitution phase) but reached US$ 5.5 billion by 1972, and ballooned to US$ 39.5 billion in 1980. Trade expansion has continued unabated since then, and table 4.3 shows the growth of exports and imports from 1980 to 1991.

Taiwan began to develop trade surpluses back in the early 1970s, and the last recorded trade deficit was as long ago as 1975 (deficits in 1974 and 1975 were due to the oil shock). The largest surplus – a huge US$ 18.7 billion – was recorded in 1987. But while various international pressures have since then attacked the

Table 4.2:   Changes in Employment Structure and Unemployment in Taiwan, 1960-1991

	1960	1970	1975	1980	1985	1988	1990	1991
Economically active ('000 persons)	3,617	4,654	5,656	6,629	7,651	8,247	8,423	8,569
Unemployed (%)	4.0	1.7	2.4	1.2	2.9	1.7	1.7	1.5
Primary industry (% of employed population)	50.2	36.7	30.4	19.5	17.5	13.7	12.9	12.9
Manufacturing (% of employed population)	14.8	20.9	27.5	32.6	33.5	34.5	32.0	31.0
Mining, construction and utilities (% of employed population)	5.7	7.1	7.4	9.8	7.9	8.1	8.8	9.1
Services and others (% of employed population)	29.3	35.3	34.7	38.1	41.1	43.7	46.3	47.0

Source: Council for Economic Planning and Development, Republic of China, *Taiwan Statistical Data Book 1992.*

surplus, it has remained stubbornly large into the early 1990s. The combination of trade surpluses with high domestic savings (see table 4.4) has meant Taiwan has not suffered the problem of foreign debt which plagued Korea for most of the 1970s and 1980s.

Domestic savings have, for the most part, exceeded investment since the 1970s, and Taiwan has been a net foreign creditor for the best part of two decades, and for virtually the whole of the 1980s. In 1992 Taiwan had the largest central bank foreign exchange reserves in the world – more than US$ 88 billion (*Financial Times*, 9 October 1992). (The relatively low investment ratio is a problem to which we shall return.)

As with all the ANICs, export success has brought foreign criticism, and measures have been taken by Western countries, especially the US, in an attempt to reduce their trade deficits with Taiwan. Table 4.5 shows that in 1987 Taiwan's exports to the US exceeded imports by a huge US$ 16 billion.

The withdrawal of preferential treatment from Taiwan, along with the other AN-ICs, by the US and EC was described in chapter one. Another area where Taiwan

Table 4.3: Exports and Imports of Taiwan, 1980-1991 (US$ million)

	Exports	Imports	Balance
1980	19,811	19,733	77
1981	22,611	21,200	1,412
1982	22,204	18,888	3,316
1983	25,123	20,287	4,836
1984	30,456	21,959	8,497
1985	30,726	20,102	10,624
1986	39,862	24,181	15,680
1987	53,679	34,983	18,695
1988	60,667	49,673	10,995
1989	66,304	52,265	14,039
1990	67,214	54,716	12,498
1991	76,178	62,861	13,318

Source: Council for Economic Planning and Development, Republic of China, *Taiwan Statistical Data Book 1992*.

Table 4.4: Savings and Investment Ratios in Taiwan, 1980-1991

	Gross capital formation (% of GNP)	Gross national savings (% of GNP)
1980	33.8	32.3
1985	18.7	33.6
1986	17.1	38.5
1987	20.1	38.5
1988	22.8	34.5
1989	22.3	30.8
1990	21.9	29.2
1991	22.4	29.9

Source: Calculated from data in Council for Economic Planning and Development, Republic of China, *Taiwan Statistical Data Book 1992*.

might suffer is that of intellectual property rights. For instance the US threatened heavy punitive duties on Taiwan's electronics exports (of which US$ 3.8 billion went to the US in 1991) unless software counterfeiting was brought under control. In June 1992 Taiwan signed a sweeping agreement on intellectual property rights, with promises of better law enforcement and stiffer penalties for pirates. The US will undertake quarterly reviews of the situation (*Far Eastern Economic Review*, 8 October 1992). However, Taiwan was hit most severely by the forced appreciation of The New Taiwan Dollar, which rose from 39.8 to the US Dollar in 1985 to 26.9 in 1990 (see table 1.7, chapter one) and to 25.1 in 1992. Since 1987 exports to the

Table 4.5: Taiwan's Exports and Imports by Country of Destination and Origin, 1980-1991 (US$ million)

	Japan			US			UK, France and Germany		
	Exports	Imports	Balance	Exports	Imports	Balance	Exports	Imports	Balance
1980	2,173	5,353	-3,180	6,760	4,673	2,087	1,814	1,129	685
1985	3,461	5,549	-2,088	14,773	4,746	10,027	1,683	1,360	324
1987	6,986	11,841	-4,855	23,685	7,648	16,037	4,309	2,900	1,409
1989	9,065	16,031	-6,966	24,036	12,003	12,033	5,753	4,316	1,437
1990	8,338	15,998	-7,661	21,746	12,612	9,134	6,294	4,954	1,342
1991	9,189	18,858	-9,669	22,321	14,114	8,207	7,293	5,277	2,015

	Hong Kong			Others		
	Exports	Imports	Balance	Exports	Imports	Balance
1980	1,551	250	1,301	7,513	8,328	-815
1985	2,540	320	2,220	8,269	8,127	142
1987	4,123	754	3,370	14,576	11,840	2,736
1989	7,042	2,205	4,837	20,408	17,710	2,698
1990	8,556	1,446	7,110	22,280	19,706	2,574
1991	12,430	1,947	10,484	24,945	22,665	2,280

Source: Council for Economic Planning and Development, Republic of China, Taiwan Statistical Data Book 1992.

US have more or less stopped increasing, and the surplus with the US was cut by almost a half between 1987 and 1991 (table 4.5). The proportion of total exports destined for the US declined from 48.1 per cent in 1985 to 29.3 per cent in 1991. Taiwan's surplus with the UK, France and Germany has increased by a quarter over the same period, though the European market remains far less important than the American. The primary source of continued export growth since 1987 is in fact the new trade with mainland China. For political reasons this is conducted indirectly, and principally via Hong Kong. The five-fold growth in exports to Hong Kong between 1985 and 1991 (table 4.5) are in fact mostly destined for the mainland. This is confirmed on examination of table 5.9 (chapter five): in 1989, 49.1 per cent of Hong Kong's imports from Taiwan were for straight re-export, and an unknown quantity of the rest would be exported on from Hong Kong after some sort of further manufacturing activity had been performed on them within the colony.

Taiwan's growth and export success has, then, continued into the 1990s, but there are potential problems on the horizon, to which we shall return shortly.

Industrial and Export Structures

Taiwan became famous for its three Export Processing Zones (EPZs) which it developed in the 1960s and which have provided a model which many developing countries across the world have followed. The intention was to attract capital, and especially foreign direct investments, with various incentives and duty free imports allowed into the zones. Patterns of investment in the zones in 1991 are indicated in table 4.6.

The EPZs provide a whole range of support facilities to ease the process of inward investments, including a recruitment service for employers. Banking and other services are also available to employees. Their success in attracting foreign capital – particularly in the form of joint ventures which can be valuable avenues for technology transfer, should not be underestimated. Neither, however, should their real importance be overstated. In 1988, when EPZ exports peaked, EPZ companies employed 90,876 workers and accounted for US$ 3,766 million of Taiwan's exports – i.e. only 3.2 per cent of Taiwan's total number of manufacturing employees, and 6.2 per cent of total exports. Their most important contribution has been in the electronics sector – around 70 per cent of investments and 64 per cent of employment created in the EPZs have been in electronics.

In spite of EPZs and a generally favourable climate for foreign direct investments, FDI has not assumed very high levels, accounting for only around 5 per cent of employment and 15 per cent of exports in the early 1980s (Castells 1992; Henderson 1989). Japan and the United States accounted for 32.7 per cent and 30.2 per cent, respectively, of the total cumulative FDI of US$ 12.8 billion between 1952 and 1991 (excluding overseas Chinese investment) and Europe accounted

Table 4.6:   Investment Patterns in Taiwan's Export Processing Zones, as at 1991

	No. of export enterprises	No. of employees	Amount of investment (US$ million)	% of investment by local capital	% of investment by foreign capital	% of investment by joint venture capital
Kaohsiung EPZ	90	21,931	218.0	27.7	44.8	27.5
Nantze EPZ	103	33,195	496.1	16.4	34.1	49.5
Taichung EPZ	46	12,091	155.2	14.4	46.1	39.5
3 EPZs total	239	67,217	869.3	18.9	39.0	42.1

Source: Export Processing Zone Administration, *Export Processing Zone Concentrates*, various issues.

for 17.4 per cent. The biggest area for foreign investment has been electronics and electrical products, attracting 32.5 per cent of the non-services total, followed by chemicals with 25.1 per cent. The government, through the Investment Commission, has consistently channelled foreign investments into export oriented sectors or those sectors considered strategically important for technology transfer. Joint ventures have been given special encouragement. Foreign investments aimed at servicing the local market, on the other hand, have effectively been discouraged or faced high local equity participation requirements (Haggard and Cheng 1987).

Unlike Korea, manufacturing investment in Taiwan is dispersed throughout the country, often in small towns in rural areas, this being the result of a deliberate strategy by the government, which wanted to avoid concentration in the cities (Deyo 1989). Another notable feature in Taiwan, contrary to popular perceptions, has been the willingness of government, where necessary, to directly invest in areas considered strategically important. Wade (1990) documents state ownership – sometimes temporary before being handed to the private sector – in synthetic fibres, plastics, electronics, steel, and other areas – and characterizes Taiwan's economy as 'state-led industrialization'. The present diversity of goods manufactured in Taiwan owes much to the leading role of the state. The diversity is indicated in table 4.7, which shows the structure of Taiwan's exports by commodity.

For a recently developed small country with a population of around only 20 million, the diversity of Taiwan's industry is quite remarkable. Taiwan has sig-

Table 4.7: Exports by Principal Commodity from Taiwan, 1981–1991 (US$ million)*

	Machinery and electrical equipment	Textile products	Electronic products	Metals and metal articles	Information and communications products	Transport equipment	Footwear	Garments
1981	1,492.0 (5.6)	2,218.5 (9.8)	2,940.3 (13.0)	1,532.8 (6.8)	159.8 (0.7)	841.3 (3.7)	1,503.7 (6.6)	2,557.5 (11.3)
1985	2,272.1 (7.4)	2,849.6 (9.3)	3,038.3 (9.9)	2,353.8 (7.7)	1,317.6 (4.3)	1,241.2 (4.0)	2,349.0 (7.6)	3,151.2 (10.3)
1989	6,859.5 (10.3)	6,408.7 (9.7)	8,138.2 (12.3)	5,192.2 (7.8)	4,423.9 (6.7)	3,020.2 (4.6)	3,799.5 (5.7)	3,946.9 (6.0)
1991	9,333.3 (12.3)	8,478.6 (11.1)	8,183.3 (10.7)	5,805.9 (7.6)	5,558.8 (7.3)	3,929.3 (5.2)	3,810.8 (5.0)	3,518.6 (4.6)

	Plastic and rubber products	Toys, games and sports equipment	Precision instruments	Furniture	Chemicals	Household electrical appliances	Other	Total
1981	721.7 (3.2)	1,331.3 (5.9)	531.6 (2.4)	406.7 (1.8)	294.5 (1.3)	286.9 (1.3)	5,792.4 (25.6)	22,611
1985	1,230.1 (4.0)	1,784.1 (5.8)	614.5 (2.0)	768.4 (2.5)	424.8 (1.4)	586.8 (1.9)	6,744.5 (22.0)	30,726
1989	3,003.4 (4.5)	3,037.7 (4.6)	1,681.2 (2.5)	1,634.2 (2.5)	1,058.3 (1.6)	1,096.1 (1.7)	13,004.0 (19.6)	66,304
1991	3,297.2 (4.3)	3,044.0 (4.0)	2,034.7 (2.7)	1,659.3 (2.2)	1,569.8 (2.1)	1,006.0 (1.3)	14,948.4 (19.6)	76,178

* Figures in parentheses in %.

Source: Council for Economic Planning and Development, Republic of China, Taiwan Statistical Data Book 1992.

nificant capacities in areas such as chemicals, automobiles, and machine tools, as well as electronic products, and has maintained capacity in the more traditional sectors of textiles, garments and footwear. Table 4.7 also shows changes in export structure between 1981 and 1991. Notable here is the rapid decline of the importance of the garments (clothing) sector, though the footwear and toys sectors have declined less rapidly. The other main 'traditional' sector is textiles, though textiles manufacture is more capital intensive than the others. Here, there has actually been a significant increase in recent years. This seems to indicate (though systematic research is needed) that Taiwan's textile manufacturers have expanded along with an expanded Taiwanese-owned clothing sector, which increasingly has been relocated in China and the ASEAN countries. Automobile production, which makes up the bulk of the transport equipment sector, has grown, with export growth from 3.7 per cent to 5.1 per cent of total exports in 1991. But this growth has been less than Taiwan would have hoped, and presumably less than the multinationals which (exceptionally) dominate this sector would have wished. Electronics exports have been up and down, but obviously remain important at 10.7 per cent in 1991: note however that information and communications products, which includes computers, software and computer peripherals, is listed separately. This new sector has grown from virtually nothing to an export value of US$ 5.6 billion in the space of ten years. The other sector which has shown remarkably rapid growth, and which includes machine tools and other capital goods, is the machinery and electrical equipment category.

Taken together, changes in export structure over the decade to 1991 suggest significant industrial advance, and this would appear to be confirmed in table 3.11 (chapter three), which documents an improvement in labour productivity of 37.7 per cent between 1985 and 1990 – almost twice the improvement recorded for Taiwan's most important competitor nation, Korea. And when we consider industrial restructuring, continued high export performance, and foreign credit all together, Taiwan has much to celebrate. But not wishing to be a party-pooper, these healthy economic indicators hide certain structural problems which potentially could become extremely serious.

Structural Problems

Potential problems on the horizon can clearly be seen when we examine the trends in Taiwan's imports. These are documented for 1982 to 1991 in table 4.8.

Unfortunately, the data is not broken into definite capital, consumer and raw material goods categories, but we can gain a good impression of developments from the figures. The two categories of imports which have risen most significantly are machinery and electrical equipment, and electronic components. What seems to be behind these figures, as for the other ANICs, is again an increasing dependence on imported capital equipment and high value (especially electronic)

Table 4.8:   Structure of Taiwan's Imports, 1982-1991 (US$ million)*

	Soyabeans, wheat, maize and cotton	Crude oil and chemicals**	Base metals and metal articles	Transport equipment
1982	1,242.6 (6.6)	6,185.3 (32.7)	1,799.0 (9.5)	1,506.9 (8.0)
1985	1,307.1 (6.5)	6,302.6 (31.4)	2,011.6 (10.0)	1,146.0 (5.7)
1989	1,750.3 (3.3)	8,405.4 (16.1)	6,776.6 (13.0)	3,956.1 (7.6)
1991	1,948.3 (3.1)	10,331.8 (16.4)	8,078.4 (12.9)	3,964.1 (6.3)

	Machinery and electrical equipment	Electronic components	Others	Total
1982	3,777.2 (20.0)	725.4 (3.8)	3,651.6 (19.3)	18,888
1985	4,476.3 (22.3)	1,063.1 (5.3)	3,795.3 (18.9)	20,102
1989	14,949.3 (28.6)	3,510.1 (6.7)	12,917.2 (24.7)	52,265
1991	18,568.9 (29.5)	5,241.7 (8.3)	14,727.8 (23.4)	62,861

*   Figures in parentheses are percentages of total imports.
** The basis of classification of 'chemicals' changed in 1989. Some 'chemicals' appear in the 'Other' category for 1989 and 1991.

Source: Council for Economic Planning and Development, Republic of China, *Taiwan Statistical Data Book 1992.*

componentry. One half of machinery and electrical imports in 1991, unsurprisingly, came from Japan. This would be confirmed by Wade's (1990) observations of the machine tool and personal computer sectors. In the machine tool sector, the largest Taiwanese firm (Leadwell) has about 2.5 per cent of the world export market, but even this company imports the most technologically advanced component, the numerical controller, from Japan. The government has provided subsidized design help to machine tool manufacturers, and also given protection to domestic sales by raising barriers to imports, but further development of the industry will be necessary before Taiwanese manufacturers compete with Japan and Germany in the highest value, high precision, segments. In electronics Wade shows how Taiwanese (and Korean) firms have tended to move into the 'price-elastic' (read standardized mass produced goods) markets abandoned by the Japanese in favour of more highly differentiated, price-inelastic and higher value markets. Multi-national electronics firms in Taiwan use the country largely for labour intensive aspects of production, and the relatively small Taiwanese producers have had difficulties in developing a capability to compete directly with the best Japanese and American producers.

However, the 'imitation lag' between the production of a new personal computer product in the US and the marketing of a machine with similar functions by Taiwanese companies is now only around six to nine months. The Taiwanese leader in PCs is Acer, which has three per cent of the world market in IBM-compatible PCs. The company is only a matter of months behind 'state of the art': it had 4,800 employees in 1987, 15 per cent of them dedicated to R&D, and is rapidly diversifying into other computer-related sectors (Wade 1990). Making the shift to innovator from mimic is clearly not complete – about half of personal computer components are imported – though the government is putting great effort into developing the conditions under which indigenous innovations are more forthcoming, and under which the highest value componentry can be made locally.

Another (potential) problem which is becoming apparent is a declining savings ratio (table 4.4), which is down nearly 10 percentage points from 38.5 per cent in 1987 to 29.2 per cent in 1990. Relatedly, there has been an increase in consumer spending, especially on foreign goods. This accounts for the bulk of the near doubling of the value of imports from the US between 1987 and 1991, and for an unknown but probably significant part of the increase in imports from Japan and Europe over the same period. Of course, Taiwan has significant 'breathing space', and heightened consumer spending could be seen as a healthy sign, but as the Korean case demonstrates, trends can quickly become landslides.

Two further developments which, if left unchecked, could contribute further to economic problems are first, renewed pressure on the New Taiwan Dollar: in 1992 and 1993 the US was making it clear that it felt there was room for further strengthening of the currency, and Europe was in agreement: this could cause problems for exports across the board. Secondly, although not so quickly as in Korea, wages have been rising rapidly since 1987 – up an average 10 per cent per year in manufacturing, and 15 per cent per year in services between 1987 and 1992 (*Financial Times*, 9 October 1992). Looking back again at table 3.11 (chapter three) we see that although labour productivity is recorded as increasing by 37.7 per cent between 1987 and 1990, manufacturing wages have increased by 58.5 per cent, the net result being a 15.1 per cent increase in unit labour costs. Combined with a strengthened New Taiwan Dollar, the indication is of something of a mini-crisis for Taiwanese manufacturing. It is in the light of these problems that a further restructuring of Taiwan's manufacturing industry is taking place.

Further Restructuring

Some readers will have noticed a peculiarity in table 4.4 which has not yet been commented upon: this is the low (by East Asian standards) investment ratio which has characterized Taiwan in the 1980s. In fact, the investment ratio – measured as gross capital formation as a percentage of GNP – was well over 25 per cent throughout the 1970s, reached a peak at 33.8 per cent in 1980, then gradually declined to its low of 17.1 per cent in 1986. It had recovered only slightly to 22.4 per cent in 1991. The large positive discrepancy between savings and investment helps explain Taiwan's healthy balance of payments and foreign reserves situations, but the relatively low ratios of investment (compare Taiwan's 22.4 per cent in 1991 with Korea's 39.3 per cent) raise questions about the ability of Taiwanese industry to up-grade its manufacturing industries. Lin Ching Yuang (1988) blames the relative decline of investments on a squeeze on the private manufacturing sector's profit margins, a conservative government attitude towards private investment abroad and foreign currency holding at home, and the increased political uncertainty stemming from popular demands for democracy at home and a slowness in responding politically to China's opening up from 1977. But whatever the real reason, a persistently low investment ratio is not likely to contribute to a lifting of Taiwan's structural problems.

Perhaps in recognition of this, and certainly in response to international and domestic pressures, the Taiwanese government has renewed its restructuring efforts very recently through liberalizing investment outflows and inflows, increasing spending on R&D, and most importantly taking the lead in investment via a massive infrastructure development programme as part of the present economic plan.

Investment liberalization occurred in 1987. Taiwan had welcomed inward investments, especially in key sectors considered strategically important, since the 1960s, but now eased restrictions in 310 finely-defined industrial sectors, mostly high technology areas such as industrial robots and laser machine tools. Companies in these sectors would now be allowed to repatriate capital and profits from day one of the operation, and exchange controls would no longer apply to inward investors. Inward investment did increase substantially from 1987 (Hong Kong and Shanghai Bank 1988) though this was undoubtedly also spurred by the lifting of martial law (discussed later in this chapter) in 1987. The bulk of investments went into the electronics and the newly liberalized financial services sector, and the majority of investments came from Japan (US$ 2,824 million or 34.6 per cent of the cumulative total of private foreign investments between 1987 and 1991) and the US (US$ 2,020 million or 24.7 per cent over the same period).

More remarkable in 1987 was the government's encouragement of outflows of private direct investment, which had been negligible up to then. At the same time as offering a regional aid programme worth US$ 3 billion to South East Asian countries, the government announced low interest loans and tax incentives to businessmen willing to set up export industries in the ASEAN4 countries of the Philippines, Indonesia, Thailand and Malaysia (Hong Kong and Shanghai Bank 1988). Loan and tax incentives were probably not necessary, other than their role in signalling that the government was serious about liberalizing investment outflows. The Taiwanese government officially recorded US$ 4,518 million in approved direct investment outflows between 1986 and 1991. Spurred on by a strengthened New Taiwan Dollar, and by rising labour costs and labour scarcity at home, approved investment outflows were recorded at much higher levels by the *Far Eastern Economic Review* (9 April 1992).

Cumulative totals of Taiwanese FDI between 1986 and mid 1991 were US$ 5 billion to Malaysia alone, and another US$ 3.4 billion went to Thailand and US$ 2.8 billion to Indonesia. The Philippines was the destination for a further US$ 400 million, and by May 1992 US$ 743 million was recorded as destined for Vietnam (*Far Eastern Economic Review*, 28 May 1992). Massive additional (but officially unrecorded) amounts of Taiwanese direct investments have found their way to mainland China, which became more popular than Malaysia as an FDI destination for Taiwanese capital in the early 1990s – the *Far Eastern Economic Review* (18 March 1993) cites an estimated 7,000 companies setting up operations with investments totalling US$ 6 billion to 1992. And of course some of the larger Taiwanese companies have already set up significant production capacity within the EC and NAFTA (McDermott 1992). The Taiwan government recorded US$ 794 million destined for Europe and US$ 1,475 million for the US between 1986 and 1991.

Attempts to develop Taiwan's R&D capability in fact go back to the early stages of the country's economic development, but these accelerated in the mid to late 1980s. A landmark was the opening of the Hsinchu Science Park in 1980, which represents Taiwan's closest equivalent to a 'Silicon Valley'. Foreign and domestic high technology firms operate in close proximity to one another, and the government is willing to take up to 49 per cent equity in each venture. Hsinchu represents one of the attempts to reduce Taiwan's dependence on technology transfer from abroad (Wade 1990). R&D spending, heavily focussed on applied research and experimental development, boomed in the late 1980s, as shown in table 4.9.

As table 4.9 shows, there has been a massive increase in non-defence national R&D expenditure between 1985 and 1990, though the government intends that this be increased further to catch up with levels in the advanced countries. Extra money will come directly from government and via a private sector offered generous government support. Foreign R&D amounted to only 0.2 per cent of the total non-defence R&D spend in 1990.

Table 4.9: Non-defence National R&D Expenditure in Taiwan, 1980-1990 (US$ million)

	Government	Private	Total	% GNP	R&D manpower per 1,000 population
1980	177.3	116.4	293.7	0.7	0.8
1985	384.3	253.8	638.1	1.0	1.3
1990	1,209.3	1,430.8	2,640.1	1.5	2.3

Source: Calculated from Council for Economic Planning and Development, Republic of China, *Taiwan Statistical Data Book 1992*.

The ambitions of the government were set out in the *Six Year National Development Plan* (Council for Economic Planning and Development 1992), whose overall goal is to raise per capita GNP from under US$ 8,000 in 1990 to US$ 14,000 in 1996, and which would place Taiwan an estimated twentieth on the list of the world's high income nations. This would depend on an annual average per capita income growth of around 7.5 per cent. Ten major industries, mainly information and electronics related but also advanced materials, chemicals, automated machinery and (most ambitiously) aerospace, are targeted for development, as are eight key industrial technologies, including biotechnology and advanced sensing technology, as well as electronics and computer-related applications. The government's determination to enter the aerospace sector received a set-back when a joint venture between McDonnell Douglass, China Steel Corporation and Taiwan Aerospace Corporation worth US$ 2 billion fell through. The project was to have led to US$ 5 billion annual aerospace production in 1995 compared with US$ 500 million in 1990 (*China News*, 23 November 1991). More recently there was a proposal for a US$ 250 million deal with British Aerospace, but still no definite plans (*Far Eastern Economic Review*, 8 October 1992).

Perhaps the most significant aspect of planned restructuring is the infrastructural development to which the government has committed itself. The *Six Year National Development Plan* involves spending a huge US$ 303 billion on developing an infrastructure which has lagged behind Taiwan's rapid development. Money is earmarked for the conversion of agricultural land to housing and industrial usage, to improve water and energy supplies, to improve the quality of education and vocational training, and to strengthen transportation and telecommunications networks. The latter includes the construction of high speed railways and roads between population centres, and new mass rapid transit systems within them, which will help maintain Taiwan's geographically dispersed development, the development of Taiwan as a telecommunications 'switching centre' for Asia, and the development of harbours, transport management systems and shipping fleets to make the island a 'transportation hub for the Western Pacific'. To help finance the plan a budget deficit (the first in nearly 20 years) of US$ 10 billion was run in 1991, rising to US$ 15 billion in 1992, and the government has expressed a willingness to carry even higher deficits should the private sector fail to participate as actively as is desired (*Financial Times*, 9 October 1992). The government's share of gross fixed capital formation reached around 30 per cent in 1992, up from 17 per cent in 1987. Of course, huge foreign reserves means the government can, at least in the short term, afford such levels of spending.

As well as indicating Taiwan's recognition of the need for serious economic restructuring, the massive spending plan suggests two further important points. First, the plan is an explicit acknowledgement of the limitations of the small business sector (which predominates) in its ability to restructure independently and to shift activities into the highest value sectors. Secondly, those who remained unconvinced of Wade's (1990) detailed critique of the notion that Taiwan is a shining example of a *laissez faire* economy must surely now accept his arguments and acknowledge that Taiwan is indeed a case of 'state-led industrialization'.

Labour Markets

Taiwan's labour force was not particularly well educated when the KMT fled to the island from China in the late 1940s, but the adult literacy rate grew from 54 per cent in 1960 to 82 per cent in 1977, and the establishment of free and compulsory schooling led to a high school enrolment rate of 80 per cent by 1980. Vocational training, and especially engineering, was given greatest emphasis by the government, and by 1980 around half of post-high school graduates were engineers, giving Taiwan an exceptionally high per capita engineering population (Wade 1990). Large numbers of students from the 1960s received their education overseas, especially in the US, and especially in the science and engineering disciplines. Out of around 7,000 Taiwanese students studying overseas in 1988, over 2,400 were studying natural sciences or engineering. In very recent years the old problem of students not returning to Taiwan, which represented something of a brain drain, may have reversed – many highly qualified Taiwanese engineers with overseas education and experience are now reported to be returning to Taiwan to take advantage of the new opportunities associated with the recent restructuring. A well qualified labour force, and a national culture which reveres engineers, stands Taiwan in good stead for the future.

The main labour market problem in the early 1990s, in spite of the relocation of significant manufacturing capacity overseas, is the generally extremely tight labour market. Unemployment has been consistently below two per cent since 1988, and the problem for manufacturing companies is exacerbated by what the Council of Labour Affairs (CLA) calls a 'boss mentality'. A recent CLA survey (reported in *The Free China Journal*, 6 March 1992) identifies the boss mentality as being strongest among the younger generation and the less well educated. These groups have been leaving manufacturing employment to set up their own small businesses in the rapidly growing private services sectors, which are dominated by small businesses and the self-employed. The under-30s population in the service sector grew by 70 per cent between 1986 and 1991.

Illegal immigrants have helped manufacturing employers plug the gap. Clifford and Moore (1989) estimated that in 1989 between 12,000 and 30,000 illegal workers were filling the jobs the Taiwanese were no longer willing to do, and *Newsweek* (10 December 1990) suggested an estimated 50,000 mainlanders – most from Fujian province – were living illegally in Taiwan in 1990. Fujian province is where the bulk of Taiwanese investment in China has been located, and Taiwanese radio and television is broadcast in the area, exposing the mainland population to the capitalist riches to be found on the island. Taiwanese entrepreneurs have been accused of running rackets in which mainlanders are promised jobs in Taiwan, but are asked to pay an overnight boat ride at a cost of US$ 500 to US$ 1,000 – a sum which would take the average Chinese worker at least several years to save. They are treated harshly in Taiwan, with meagre wages and cramped dormitories, and threatened that the police will be informed of their presence if they complain. However, while the government insists it will still take a tough line on illegal immigrants, it recently gave in to employer demands for foreign labour imports. In 1992 the government approved the importation of 50,000 contract workers – not from China but from the ASEAN4 countries (*Far Eastern Economic Review*, 16 April 1992; *Financial Times*, 9 October 1992). Employers say this is not enough, and it seems unlikely that illegal immigration will be curtailed.

There is, finally, a set of developments which could potentially cause labour market problems, and certainly which change the rules of the game for employer-employee relations. These relate to the new-found strength and relative independence of the labour movement, and new labour legislation, which have both emerged in the late 1980s as part of Taiwan's democratic reforms. As mentioned above, manufacturing wages and manufacturing unit labour costs in Taiwan have been rising rapidly since the late 1980s (see tables 3.10 and 3.11 in chapter three) and although it is impossible to separate out 'democratization' effects from the simple effects of a tight labour market, there can be no doubt that wage gains attributable to trade union demands, and reduced exploitation due to both trade union strength and labour legislation, have made a contribution. The changes to state-capital-labour relations consequent upon democratization will be explored in detail below.

Summary

Taiwan's export oriented industrialization, which followed a decade of US aid-dependent import substitution, has been remarkably successful, and in the 1980s Taiwan's indigenous manufacturers were close on the heels of the world's best in a range of sectors. Small and medium sized companies dominate, but these have consistently been protected, supported, subsidized and led by a state which has taken a detailed interest in their activities and their contribution to the country's strategic aims. One indication of Taiwan's relative economic maturity and industrial capability is the increasing competition among development agencies in Europe and America for Taiwanese direct investments.

In the late 1980s and early 1990s a number of factors have, nonetheless, combined to pose problems for Taiwan's further development. These are primarily: Western protectionism and trade measures which make the export climate more difficult; a forced appreciation of the New Taiwan Dollar; a heightened dependence, on Japan in particular, for the import of high value componentry and capital goods; a chronically low investment ratio; a tight labour market which has contributed to rapidly rising wage costs; and a new climate of industrial relations which reduces some of the worst exploitation, at the same time as adding further pressure on wages.

The economic situation is, then, in many respects similar to that in Korea. But there is one crucial difference. This is vast foreign currency reserves which have built up in the Central Bank. The state has decided to use these savings in the 1990s in a huge development programme which makes nonsense of any notion that the country has a *laissez faire* economy. As well as developing transport, utilities and communications infrastructure, capital will be targetted at human resources development, technological up-grading and the enhancement of R&D capacity, in an attempt to make the decisive leap from mimic to innovator. The package of measures as set out in the current *Six Year National Development Plan* are aimed at taking Taiwan into the ranks of the advanced industrial nations by the end of the century. Such an ambition would have appeared implausible to most observers even just 10 years ago; although one should not underestimate the problems which still have to be overcome, today few would doubt the enormous potential of the island.

The State

Economic Role

Enough has already been said to demonstrate a key role of the state in economic development, but it is worth summarizing and adding a few more details. As well as taking the usual responsibilities of infrastructure development and educational provision, the state has been extremely active in the areas of export promotion, manufacturing investment incentives, local market protection, and leadership in high technology sectors through public enterprises and through a range of government institutions.

Export promotion was pursued from the early 1960s with a set of economic reforms enshrined in the third *Four Year Plan* (1961-1964). The exchange rate was deliberately stabilized at NT$ 40 to the US Dollar (which held all the way through to the mid 1980s), and a range of tax incentives and investment allowances favoured export oriented manufacturers (Rabushka 1987). The scope of the Statute for Encouragement of Investment was expanded in 1965, which was the same year the creation of the duty free EPZs was authorized. Duty paid on imported raw materials and capital equipment, if not available locally, was refundable to export oriented firms, and various taxes were held low. At the Hsinchu Science-based Industrial Park (established 1979) tax incentives were even more favourable, and some companies were offered, in addition, exemption from land rentals for five years, low cost loans, and government equity participation to reduce initial investor outlays.

Where the private sector has been unwilling or unable to invest in areas considered strategically important, the government has persisted in its willingness to establish public companies to provide the lead. Government-employed workers constituted 12 per cent of Taiwan's working population, and 3.3 per cent of all manufacturing employees, in 1990; in the same year 10.7 per cent of manufacturing value added came from the public sector. But these figures understate the importance of the publicly owned sector, which tends to dominate heavy industry and the more capital intensive sectors. In fact, public enterprises have consistently been central to Taiwan's economy, contributing a massive amount of total gross fixed capital formation (table 4.10).

In the 1970s Taiwan had one of the largest public enterprise sectors outside Africa and the Communist countries (Wade 1990). Table 4.10 shows a significant decline in public sector importance during the early to mid 1980s, but note the sudden decline of the private sector share from 1988. The private sector's share of gross fixed capital formation increased significantly from the mid 1970s (45.8 per cent in 1975) through the 1980s (up to a 62.9 per cent peak in 1988) but has declined in 1989 and 1990 to hit its lowest level since the mid 1970s. The public enterprise share has grown again, and most noticeably the government share hit its highest recorded level at 26.7 per cent in 1991, reflecting the beginnings of the massive infrastructural development programme for the 1990s.

Apart from public enterprises, the state has also helped direct the activities of the important privately owned small and medium sized manufacturing companies. Very important here is the lead provided by the Industrial Technology Research Institute (ITRI). Set up in 1973, the ITRI had a staff of 4,500 by 1987 devoted to the development of product and process technologies and the transfer of innovations from overseas to local companies in key industrial sectors. The ITRI and other quasi-government organizations have played a lead in licensing foreign technologies and undertaking reverse engineering on foreign products, then encouraging and overseeing the diffusion of the technologies through the private sector (Wade 1990). But the most important government institution is the Industrial Development Bureau (IDB) which translates broad policy guidelines into detailed trade and other measures in specific sectors. A recent example is the IDB's response to the broad policy goal of reducing Taiwanese reliance on

Table 4.10:   Composition of Gross Fixed Capital Formation in Taiwan by Owner,
              1955-1991 (%)

	Government share	Public enterprises share	Private sector share
1955	16.2	37.8	46.0
1960	13.9	33.5	52.6
1965	12.6	20.9	66.5
1970	13.4	29.4	57.2
1975	13.9	40.3	45.8
1980	14.7	34.2	51.1
1981	15.3	32.7	52.0
1982	17.2	33.8	49.0
1983	16.3	31.1	52.6
1984	16.7	25.4	57.9
1985	19.0	24.0	57.0
1986	19.0	23.8	57.2
1987	17.2	22.0	60.8
1988	18.3	18.8	62.9
1989	19.8	19.4	60.8
1990	23.5	24.6	51.9
1991	26.7	24.4	48.9

Source: Council for Economic Planning and Development, Republic of China, *Taiwan
            Statistical Data Book 1992.*

Japanese industrial technology. In order to enable local manufacturers to develop
an indigenous competence in the production of the highest value products (e.g.
high definition TV), the IDB has identified 66 core industrial parts and components, a competency in the production of which will be systematically developed
in Taiwanese laboratories, then diffused throughout industry (*China Post*, 22
November 1991).

    Finally, it is worth mentioning government protection of home markets against
imports. Tariff and non-tariff barriers have been widely used to protect key economic sectors, especially during developmental phases, against foreign competition. Recently, attention has been turned to the activities of the estimated 300
Japanese trading companies in Taiwan, whose sales of imported consumer goods
have contributed to Taiwan's deficit with Japan. The Taiwan government has
threatened an outright rejection of Japanese business applications to open companies in Taiwan unless they can demonstrate an export orientation (*Korea Times*,
16 July 1991). However, domestic market protection has become increasingly
difficult due to growing Western pressures for market liberalization.

Authoritarian Rule

Following World War II and the end of Japanese colonial rule over Taiwan, the nationalist Kuomintang (KMT) arrived from China to establish control. Rabushka (1987, p.106) comments that:

The Nationalists (KMT) imposed their rule over an unfriendly local population, who were treated more as conquered enemies than as liberated compatriots by governors that Chiang (Kai Shek) sent to take over from Japan in late 1945.

On 28 February 1947, an assault by a soldier on a woman for selling imported cigarettes sparked riots which were quelled by troops under a KMT general. Troops shot people indiscriminately in the streets and rounded up and summarily executed large numbers of rioters. Estimates of the dead in this single incident range from 5,000 to 50,000 (*China News*, 21 November 1991). The KMT took total control over Taiwanese society between 1947 and 1950, strengthened by the arrival of the bulk of the KMT leadership from the mainland during the Communist revolution. Both Formosan nationalists and Communist sympathizers were liquidated, exiled or silenced, and martial law was established (Haggard and Cheng 1987). Not surprisingly, then, the KMT's legitimacy has been under question from the beginning. Even today, the KMT massacre in February 1947, known as the 'two-twenty eight' incident, is remembered, and associations made up of the families of victims are still demanding that the government apologize for the killings, and that two senior KMT politicians should make their apology in public (*China News*, 21 November 1991).

The KMT did attempt to establish itself as legitimate through a formal constitution with a division of powers between executive, legislature and judiciary, and elections have regularly been held for members of the legislature and local government offices. However, the extensive powers lent government through the exercise of martial law have frequently been used to quell any serious opposition, and the ruling KMT has routinely mobilized various groups to instruct the electorate on how they should vote. Lo Shiu Hing (1990) mentions for instance the use of boy scout troops to campaign on their behalf, and teachers in public schools have been instructed by the KMT to visit students' homes to tell their parents to vote for KMT candidates.

Opposition candidates at elections finally organized themselves, albeit loosely, into the *dangwai* (which means 'outside the ruling party') in the 1970s. As well as acting as a quasi-political party the *dangwai* organized various protests in the late 1970s and 1980s, in particular against martial law, but these were usually met decisively by police and/or troops with arrests and often political imprisonment. In 1986 the *dangwai* formed the Democratic Progressive Party (DPP), attempting to put together alternative policies rather than acting as a mere anti-government protest organization. The opposition movement is mainly a middle class Taiwanese national movement which draws support from the indigenous small and medium sized business sector and nationalists who would seek formal independence from mainland China (the KMT's official line remains that it is still the legitimate government for the whole of China). Historically, the mainlanders (who constitute around 15 per cent of the population today) have run the government and the public sector, and the Taiwanese have run small and medium sized businesses. A 'Taiwanese' consciousness based on this division has remained throughout (Chu Yin Wah 1992a). Calls for independence are, in fact, considered seditious and are a criminal offence, and the government has frequently used the law to imprison Taiwanese who have called for 'local' rule. Since 1986, however, the KMT has had to tread more warily, and was forced to end martial law in 1987.

Democratic Transition

A number of factors led to the lifting of martial law and other democratic reforms. The US had been putting pressure on the Taiwan government since 1979, and the Taiwanese opposition were spurred on in their own campaigns following the success of Filipino 'people power' in the mid 1980s. A series of scandals involving the misappropriation of public funds, and the collaboration of a top KMT official with a triad society to assassinate a Taiwanese author critical of President Chiang Ching Kuo, further undermined KMT legitimacy (Lo Shiu Hing 1990). Strikes and demonstrations broke out in 1986 and 1987. In 1987 the government bowed to popular pressures by deregulating the press, legalizing strikes and demonstrations, releasing political prisoners, and easing the restrictions on opposition political parties.

Since 1987 the DPP has struggled to build support for its independence proposals. Many Taiwanese believe China's threat that reunification will be enforced militarily if formal independence is sought, and the government could sentence two citizens to 11 and 10 years in jail in 1988 under National Security Law without fear of sparking revolts (Lo Shiu Hing 1990). The labour movement (explored in detail later), which was also instrumental in wringing democratic reforms from the government, has also failed so far to generate a united political voice. A Labour Party was established in December 1987, but by 1989 was already split when a breakaway group decided to establish a Workers' Party which preferred a more radical stance (*Far Eastern Economic Review*, 2 March 1989).

In the meantime, the ruling KMT was reworking itself, and in January 1988 appointed a Japanese educated non-mainlander – Lee Teng Hui – as President on the death of Chiang Ching Kuo (son of Chiang Kai Shek). The new President's stress on stability, discipline and Confucian moral values within a 'democratic' framework led Shim Jae Hoon (1989a) to liken him to Singapore's Lee Kuan Yew.

At the National Assembly elections in December 1991 the KMT claimed a stunning success, with 179 elected seats, compared with the DPP's 75. The DPP polled 24 per cent of the votes. One year later the national elections to the Legislative Yuan (Parliament) took place. The DPP had changed its emphasis on independence in favour of less controversial issues (including the US$ 303 billion spending plan). The KMT, on the other hand, campaigned on its leadership of a successful economy, and its responsibility in bringing in democratic reforms. (The KMT also had the advantage of controlling Taiwan's three television stations and the financial backing of big business.) The DPP improved its performance in getting 50 legislators elected with 31 per cent of the vote. The KMT gained 53 per cent of the vote. The result was a 161 member Parliament with 96 KMT, 50 DPP, and 15 Independent seats (*Far Eastern Economic Review*, 7 January 1993).

While the KMT still dominates in the early 1990s, significant changes have taken place. As well as granting relative freedom of speech and political organization, the government has taken notice of a growing environmentalist lobby. In October 1988 environmentalists invaded a petrochemical plant in Linyuan and forced its closure for four days. Protests also delayed construction of naphtha crackers and a fourth nuclear reactor (*Far Eastern Economic Review*, 16 March 1989). Significantly, the present *Six Year Development Plan* includes 'pollution control' in its list of 10 'high tech' priority industries, though the net effect may be an accelerated relocation of 'dirty industries' to the poorer South East Asian nations. Also promised within the plan is a US$ 29 billion spend on social security and welfare, US$ 29 billion on 'culture and education', and US$ 4 billion on health and medical care. If carried through Taiwan could emerge in the 1990s with the strongest welfare state among the ANICs, a change which would undermine the basis of protest of some elements of the opposition.

State-Labour Relations

Rather than simply repress organized labour (although strikes were banned until 1987) the state has traditionally attempted to exert a detailed control via KMT sympathetic (and KMT supported) unions. These are affiliated to, and overseen by, the Chinese Federation of Labour (CFL). Most unions are organized as enterprise unions, reporting through various craft and industrial and regional unions to the CFL. The government has encouraged employers to establish trade unions, and to give them a welfare role. Legislation also requires the establishment of factory councils in large organizations, and employers must contribute 15 per cent of profits to an Employee Welfare Fund. Hence Deyo (1989) refers to a 'state-mandated enterprise paternalism'. The state has typically played virtually no role in setting wages in the private sector.

The implications of trade union incorporation will be discussed later. Here, we will briefly mention changes in legislation and government policy, brought on by international and domestic pressures, in the 1980s. A Labour Standards Law (LSL) which improved compulsory pension and severance benefits and established a 48 hour working week and minimum monthly wages was introduced in August 1984. Then in 1989 the Arbitration Dispute Law was revised. The change meant workers were now allowed to strike if a first round of mediation failed, but required they return to work if arbitration was then called. The two other major changes in government policy which changed state-labour relations were the establishment of a Council of Labour Affairs (CLA, a Cabinet-level organization in 1988), and the relative freedom to organize politically which came with the lifting of martial law in 1987. The CLA gave off mixed signals, on the one hand wishing to emphasize its new role of up-grading labour conditions (including in the eyes of the US) and on the other, wishing to maintain the industrial relations order the KMT was still demanding in the absence of martial law (*Far Eastern Economic Review*, 8 September 1988). In 1992 it was announced that the CLA would be up-graded to a Ministry of Labour (*The Free China Journal*, 11 June 1992). Political freedoms meant the establishment of a Labour Party, and perhaps more importantly gave some trade unions the confidence to act more independently of the KMT. The trade unions had traditionally been led by KMT members, and they legitimated their roles on the grounds that a special relationship with government enabled them to negotiate the best deals for labour 'from the inside'. The KMT and the trade union leadership were clearly going to have to involve themselves in more propaganda if they were going to maintain credibility in the face of a rising awareness of trade union rights.

The industrial conflict which broke out in the late 1980s was a test of the new legislation and government policy, and was effectively, as in Korea, the beginning of a process of industrial relations readjustment. We will return to these events and the new industrial relations of Taiwan after a consideration of the characteristics of employers.

Employers

While one must not understate the importance of the small business sector in Korea, in Taiwan small and medium sized businesses have been more likely to play a leading role in the economy. Government employees apart, only 3.9 per cent of the workforce were employed in organizations with 500 or more workers in 1990. In the manufacturing sector alone the proportion was higher, at 9.5 per cent (table 4.11), but this still represents a relatively small number compared with Korea.

The striking contrast with Korea is suggested when comparing tables 4.11 and 3.13 (chapter three), though the data is not strictly comparable. However, a feel for the difference is gained when comparing 257,000 Taiwanese workers accounted for by *all* the manufacturing organizations employing 500 or more, with the employment of 160,000 workers by the giant Korean conglomerate, Hyundai, alone.

Table 4.11:   Employment by Size of Firm in Taiwan, 1990 ('000)*

	Govern-ment employees	Self-employed	2-9	10-29	30-49
All industries	987 (12.0)	1,032 (12.6)	3,198 (39.0)	1,114 (13.6)	452 (5.5)
Manufacturing	89 (3.3)	129 (4.8)	636 (23.5)	503 (18.6)	292 (10.8)

	50-59	100-499	500 persons or more	Total	
All industries	474 (5.8)	636 (7.6)	317 (3.9)	8,202	
Manufacturing	323 (11.9)	478 (17.7)	257 (9.5)	2,705	

* Figures in parentheses are proportion of total employees.

Source: Manpower Planning Department, Executive Yuan, Republic of China, *Monthly Bulletin of Manpower Statistics*, February 1990.

Public sector employers, as discussed above, are concentrated in the heavier, capital intensive areas such as petro-chemicals, steel and heavy machinery and equipment. As well as being linked to the military (Taiwan now has a significant capacity in the production of arms and military equipment) the public sector enterprises feed the smaller sized employers in the private sector with heavy capital equipment and raw materials for production. Significant numbers in the public sector are also employed to carry out R&D and technology projects, and to provide the link to the private sector in the diffusion of innovations. In the light of this public sector-private sector division of labour, the massive differential between average public enterprises wages and average private enterprises wages (table 4.12) is not so surprising: heavy industry public enterprises are more likely to employ skilled males, and the advanced role of public enterprises means they will have higher proportions of highly qualified employees.

Table 4.12 also demonstrates significant differentials *within* the private sector. Monthly earnings fall steadily by size of enterprise, down to 63.4 per cent of the 500-plus category for enterprises with less than 10 persons. Differentials related to sex are also striking. In 1989 females earned 52 to 80 per cent of males, and generally the bigger the employer the greater the differential.

Table 4.12:   Average Monthly Earnings per Worker by Size of Enterprise in Taiwan,
               1989 (NT$)

Employees per enterprise	Earnings	%*
9 or less persons	15,660	(63.4)
10 – 29	18,170	(73.6)
30 – 49	18,898	(76.6)
50 – 99	20,120	(81.5)
100 – 299	21,528	(87.2)
300 – 499	21,299	(86.3)
More than 500	24,687	
Private enterprise average	20,014	
Public enterprise employees	37,173	
Overall average	21,604	

* Percentages of earnings of employees in private sector firms employing 500 or more.

Source: Republic of China (1990).

Employer-State Relations

When the KMT took over Taiwan in the late 1940s there was no significant
local bourgeoisie. The government appropriated the industries left behind by
the Japanese colonialists, and could set up public enterprises in strategically
important areas without worrying about the interests of local employers. The
KMT's founder, Sun Yat Sen, in fact had an economic philosophy in which
key industries closely tied to national and public interests should be kept under
state control. In Taiwan, the state could implement the policy without opposition.
State-owned enterprises are typically profitable, and the surplus generated is a
major source of government income (Tang and Lin 1984). At the same, the state
encouraged private investments, whether local or foreign, in the export oriented
industries.

Unlike the Korean state, the government in Taiwan did not give special treatment to favoured private sector employers, although those employers willing to
develop along the lines desired by government have consistently been able to
take advantage of tax and other incentives, and the IDB keeps close contact with
businesses which ensures they are aware of developments. In Taiwan, private
sector employers never developed a close relationship with the state. This is not
altogether surprising given the divide between a government dominated by mainlanders and the rest of the population dominated by Taiwanese, speaking different
dialects and having had different historical experiences. The private sector, with
the exception of the textiles sector in the 1980s, has a weak national voice, and
gives little input into national industrial policy making (Wade 1990).

Hence while Taiwan has little in the way of a state-business elite, the state has been instrumental in persuading and assisting the private sector to develop in particular ways. The state has also been responsible for encouraging trade union recognition in the private sector, and legislation on factory councils and more recently labour standards have had a direct effect in shaping labour-management relations, issues to which we shall return.

Management and Management Styles

Taiwan's success in export markets in a range of sectors is typically attributed to the flexible industrial structure characterized by small and medium sized businesses which are capable of responding rapidly to shifting market conditions (Wu Rong I 1988). Enough has already been said to indicate a key role for the state as well, though this is not to undermine the importance of small and medium sized businesses, and here we will look briefly at the way they operate.

The characteristics of private Taiwanese-owned businesses have been related to a Chinese 'economic familism' (Lin Ho Lin 1991). The business is closely controlled by the owning family and trust is given only to family members and those persons with close obligational ties to the owner (Hamilton and Kao 1990). Employees, it is suggested, would prefer to be self-employed, and are willing to give only short term commitments. Employers jealously guard company secrets and prefer not to vest control in, or give discretion to, employees or 'professional' managers: delegation is too risky a business. This predominance of 'strong central, personal control and authority' (Whitley 1992) is related by *institutionalists* to the legacy of pre-industrial China, where authority was based on moral superiority and Confucian social rules rather than competence. China also lacked a codified legal system and there was a preference for personal, informal ways of managing conflicts over formal rules and procedures (Hamilton and Kao 1990). Hence, 'employment practices are not governed by standardized rules, but rather are highly personal and idiosyncratic to the particular relationship between the owner and the employees' (Whitley 1992, p.207). Whitley (p.207) goes further:

the combination of weak vertical integration of loyalties and identities, low rule formalization, weak village cohesion and loyalty beyond the family household, traditional conceptions of authority and equal inheritance practices in pre-industrial China has been an important – if not, indeed, determining – factor in limiting business owners' development of mutual dependence relations with their employees.

The practice of equal inheritance added a further characteristic – since each son would inherit a share of the family wealth on the death of the entrepreneur, when expanding the owner would be more likely to invest in non-related businesses than to vertically integrate. Non-entangled independent firms are more easily divided (Hamilton et al. 1990). Recent research seems to confirm that the larger as well

as the smaller Taiwanese business groups do indeed tend to be characterized by
unrelated diversification than their counterparts in other countries (Hamilton and
Kao 1990; Lin Ho Lin 1991).

Another characteristic is the extensive use of sub-contracting via *guanxi* networks inherited from imperial China. In the absence of large firms and vertical
integration, these enable the production of goods through 'satellite assembly systems'. Biggart and Hamilton (1990, p.15) give an example:

Taiwan is the world's largest producer of bicycles for export, yet has not a single large
bicycle factory. Instead, there are firms that manufacture parts and others that assemble
them to meet a retailer's specifications.

Further:

These "satellite assembly systems" dissolve when the orders stop. The individual firms
seek new product orders and form a new satellite assembly system with the next wave of
orders. Flexible, undercapitalized, and extremely sensitive to market demand, this type of
production system creates a sort of capitalism that rolls with market forces and does not
attempt to control them. Several people have called the Chinese industrial system "guerilla
capitalism".

In this way Taiwanese industrial and export success has been attributed to the
country's dynamic and highly flexible small Chinese family owned business
sector. Virtually the same arguments have been put forward for the equivalent
sector in Hong Kong, and we will explore some of the *institutionalists'* arguments
further there, and more theoretically in the concluding chapter. In Hong Kong
research has been conducted which demonstrates the negative aspects of Chinese
family business employment practices, and we might safely assume these negative
aspects apply at least to some degree in Taiwan too (see chapter five).

The final point in this section, however, is to point up the limitations of the
Chinese family business in Taiwan as a means of economic advance. Lin Ho Lin
(1991, p.28) summarizes:

in terms of the long run economic development, small scale seems more a liability than
an asset. Although flexible, most small firms operate at suboptimal scale and have higher
average costs. In addition, small firms cannot make technological innovations as well as
larger firms. Research and development are easier in larger than in smaller firms involved
in these activities. Larger firms, with longer time horizons of planning, are more willing to
take risks. With larger scale, they can, to a certain extent, internalize the externalities and
capture the benefits from innovation.

Employer-Labour Relations

A minimum wages law came into effect in 1956, and labour regulations have
limited overtime work, stipulated rest days and holidays, banned night work for
women and the under-16s, and established other minimum standards. However,

rapidly rising wages and full employment meant that such legal requirements were far below the average for the working population – for instance by 1976 the statutory minimum was only 10 per cent of average manufacturing wages (Rabushka 1987). Where labour unions existed these were KMT controlled and largely incorporated as enterprise unions, and served a role more of socializing and disciplining the workforce than of representing their interests. Hence Taiwanese employers traditionally have been able to operate with minimum legal interference, and with managerial prerogatives intact. Wages were set by the going labour market rates, and by most accounts the relationship between employer and worker has until recently been one of unquestioned authority on the part of the employer and obedience by the employee, but in the absence of trust between the two parties.

However, Deyo (1989) paints a slightly different picture. In the 1970s, the government increased pressure on employers to encourage the formation of enterprise unions, and to give the union a role in first, organizing workers' health and educational programmes, and second, rejuvenating the factory council system for the settlement of non-wage disputes. All this was intended to strengthen the company paternalism which was already enshrined in the legal requirement that employers contribute 15 per cent of all profits to an Employee Welfare Fund, administered jointly by employers, unions and workers. This attempted 'pre-emptive' strategy of labour control, of course, has its parallel in Singapore (see chapter two), and helps explain why the state, unlike in Korea and Hong Kong, has been able to avoid a significant direct role in the settling of grievances and disputes.

But while Singapore's pre-emptive strategy has, so far, worked, the measures taken in Taiwan were shown to be insufficient during the mid to late 1980s. The Labour Standards Law (LSL) which the government was forced to adopt in 1984 was rather more stringent and demanding of employers than previous legislation, and when martial law was lifted in 1987 many of the strikes which followed were justified on the grounds that the minimum standards of the law were not being met by employers. What this says about the Chinese preference for personal, informal ways of managing conflict is most interesting. Perhaps the workers' preference is less well informed by Confucian values! (We will return to this question in the final chapter.) The LSL guaranteed (in 1988) a minimum wage of NT$ 8,000 per month, a 48 hour working week, and various pension and other benefits. But although the official average wage in Taiwan was over NT$ 12,000 even for the smallest organizations (employing less than nine people) in the same year (and over NT$ 15,000 overall), many employers said they could not afford it. Undoubtedly, the rising wages which followed contributed to the outflow of capital, and even whole small Chinese family owned businesses, to mainland China where workers would be more willing to accept the pay and conditions they preferred to offer without question.

Labour

Between 1947 and 1949 leftist forces in Taiwan were liquidated. The KMT then encouraged union formation at plant, county and regional levels under the leadership of the party cadre, intended to pre-empt the possiblility of independent union acitivies at some point in the future (Koo et al. 1986). An unofficial labour movement emerged at the end of the 1980s during moves towards democratization, and there was an outburst of strike activity – not on the scale of that in Korea, but nonetheless highly significant, and contributing to a new climate of industrial relations in the 1990s.

Trade Union Organization

While strikes and collective bargaining were prohibited under martial law, unions were actively encouraged under strong KMT supervision (Johnson 1987). Detailed KMT controls over leader selection and all union activities meant that Taiwan's unions were 'no more than an arm of the government' (Koo 1987, p.174). As in Singapore, ruling party-union ties are close. In the early 1980s, Chen Hsi Chi, a KMT legislator *and* then President of the Chinese Federation of Labour (CFL), led a 'Factory as Home and School' movement, stressing labour-management cooperation and the 'positive participation' of workers in solving industrial problems (Deyo 1987b). The CFL functions at local, regional and national levels, and penetrates union leaderships right down to the enterprise level. It claims legitimacy on the grounds of its special relationship with government. KMT membership is a prerequisite for upward mobility within the CFL. There were no officer elections until 1975, and even in the late 1980s many seats on the CFL Board of Directors were still held by the original mainlanders (Kleingartner and Hsueh Yu 1991).

The success of KMT-controlled enterprise unions (success from the KMT's point of view, that is) is illustrated in union membership levels which were mostly on the rise from the 1950s through the 1980s. Membership rose every single year from 1955 (198,000 members) through 1986 (1.72 million members). 22.3 per cent of the total employed workforce were trade union members by 1986 (Deyo 1989). In 1989, the number had reached 2.42 million – 29.3 per cent of the employed population. The vast majority of these were industrial, manufacturing, transport and related workers: 'service workers' made up only around 12 per cent of total trade union membership (Council of Labour Affairs 1990).

Until 1987, labour affairs were dealt with by the Ministry of the Interior, but in 1987 the Council of Labour Affairs (CLA) was created, to function as a Cabinet level department within the executive branch of government, and signalling that workers concerns would no longer be an internal security matter. (In 1992 it was announced that the CLA was to become the Ministry of Labour.) However, the

CFL has remained the only legal national trade union centre (Kleingartner and Hsueh Yu 1991). The Taiwan Provincial Federation of Labour (TPFL) which is the CFL's largest affiliate with 63 per cent of total CFL membership in the late 1980s, refused to pay CFL affiliation fees for a period in 1989. This was a protest against the 11 out of 51 CFL Directors who were still in place as a result of their election in the mainland before 1949 (the TPFL was established in 1948 just prior to the establishment of the CFL in Taiwan in 1949). The TPFL would like the CFL to become more 'member centred', but while the CFL acknowledges change may be necessary to secure popular appeal in the new democracy, reform from within is slow (Kleingartner and Hsueh Yu 1991).

Attempts at reform of the labour movement from without have also occurred. Most recent strikes (described below) have been organized by unofficial enterprise centred organizations which have sprung up in response to specific grievances or incidents, and anti-government leaders in Taiwan have attempted to organize them. In December 1987 a Labour Party was launched, then in March 1989 a breakaway Workers' Party was formed, attempting to gain support from workers and orchestrate their discontent. And in 1988 some workers challenged the CFL by forming voluntary associations such as the Brotherhood of Unions and the Labour Union Alliance (Lo Shiu Hing 1990). A major coup for the alternative labour movement came in March 1988 when Kang Yi Yi, a member of the Labour Party, was elected Chairman of the China Petroleum Corporation's union, in the face of appeals from the company's President to keep the existing leadership in office. Kang was the first non-KMT member to head a major union (Moore 1988).

The alternative labour movement, however, faces two serious problems. First, the government has the ability to obstruct the formation of what Shim Jae Hoon (1989b) calls 'non-subvervient' unions – certain legal requirements must be met before a union can be officially established and the government can use technicalities to prevent or delay recognition. Secondly, and reflecting the youthfulness of radical labour, the movement has been characterized by factionalism: in particular, there is dispute as to whether the approach should be gradualist within existing laws, or more confrontational, including challenging the law (Shim Jae Hoon 1989b).

Industrial Conflict

While organized industrial action was simply banned until 1987, evidence of worker grievances and discontent comes from official industrial dispute figures. These show the number of recorded disputes rising steadily from 157 in 1971 to 700 in 1980, and involving between 2,000 and 27,000 workers in any one year (Deyo 1989). Trends in officially recorded labour disputes are shown in table 4.13.

As can be seen in table 4.13, the number of recorded disputes peaked at 1,943 involving 62,000 workers in 1989. Of the disputes recorded, most were

Table 4.13:   Labour Disputes in Taiwan, 1981-1991

	No. of disputes	No. of workers involved ('000)
1981	891	7
1982	1,153	10
1983	921	12
1984	907	9
1985	1,443	15
1986	1,485	11
1987	1,609	16
1988	1,314	24
1989	1,943	62
1990	1,860	34
1991	1,810	13

Sources: Republic of China (1990); *The Free China Journal*, 6 March 1992.

related to claims of unfair dismissal, wages arrears, health and safety issues, and welfare benefits. Almost invariably, disputes have been resolved through informal settlements and non-government arbitration.

What is not shown in table 4.13 is the number of strikes. In fact working days lost due to disputes were simply not recorded between 1973 and 1986 (prior to 1973 the most recorded in one year was 24,000 in 1970 – 2,000 to 3,000 was typical). However, the number of working days lost due to work stoppages were recorded at 2,000 in 1987, 9,000 in 1988, and a peak of 24,000 in 1989. Unrecorded stoppages may be much higher than the officially recorded figures – one dispute alone in 1988 accounted for the loss of 4,600 working days according to Shim Jae Hoon (1989b). Most stoppages were unofficial wild cat actions. Strike issues have focussed on wages, and on the failure of employers to adhere to the Labour Standards Law of 1984 (described earlier). Another issue, one which challenges a traditional management prerogative, has been the desire to make bonuses (which in Taiwan can be large) fixed and written into employment contracts, rather than being given at the whim of the employer according to their personal evaluations of individual workers (Shim Jae Hoon 1989b). Much of the outburst of labour unrest was concentrated in the large public utilities and government sanctioned monopolies such as the transport companies. (Examples of strikes are described by Shim Jae Hoon 1989b and Moore 1988.)

The CLA has given a slightly ambiguous response to workers' actions. On the one hand it has expressed the view that enforcement of the LSL could further the goal of industrial restructuring by adding to the pressure on labour intensive industries to either up-grade production or go overseas. On the other, it has implemented government policy on strike action which makes legal strikes difficult:

a majority of the union membership is required to endorse any strike action by secret ballot, and strikes are not possible when mediation or arbitration is in process. The result is a situation similar to that found in Singapore (see chapter two). The Arbitration Dispute Law, as revised in 1987, allows strikes after a first round of mediation, but requires a return to work if arbitration is called. The Miaoli bus drivers strike in August 1988 was the first legal strike in Taiwan's history, but became illegal after only three hours when the CLA called for arbitration on the grounds that the company provided a much needed service to commuters. Hence labour activists may have some justification in claiming that the government maintains a *de facto* ban on strikes (Moore 1988). Certainly, as is arguably the case in Singapore, a legal strike is effectively impossible without the tacit agreement of the government.

Despite these controls, the alternative labour movement probably can claim some responsibility for improvements in working conditions related to better enforcement of the LSL, and for improved wages in the late 1980s (see table 4.14), though the effects of trade union strength on the latter are impossible to separate out from labour market effects.

Table 4.14:   Manufacturing Wages in Taiwan, 1980-1989

	Monthly amount (NT$)	Increase on previous year (%)
1980	7,544	—
1981	8,730	15.7
1982	9,495	8.8
1983	10,129	7.3
1984	11,167	10.2
1985	11,456	2.6
1986	12,655	10.5
1987	13,940	10.2
1988	15,394	10.4
1989	17,585	14.2

Source: Republic of China (1990).

Since 1989 the number of strikes and labour disputes has reduced (*The Free China Journal*, 6 March 1992), and this is attributed by the CLA (and by at least one DPP leader) to the wider implementation of the LSL, and to a harmony in labour-management relations stemming from the adjustment of employers and unions to the new situation of greater participation and democracy. More detailed research would be necessary to throw further light on recent developments, but one might suspect that a major problem for the newly independent alternative trade union movement is the difficulty of challenging a still powerful and highly resourced – if discredited – incorporated trade union organization.

Kleingartner and Hsueh Yu (1991) are pessimistic of the possibilities for the KMT-controlled CFL to move beyond the status of labour controller and service provider – i.e. to bargain independently for workers. The future of the labour movement might depend more, then, on the ability of the unofficial unions to organize themselves into a competing Federation. To do so they would have to overcome serious obstacles: factionalism must be overcome; the hostility and the resources of state and employers will continue to stand in their way; and the small enterprise sector will always remain difficult to organize.

Conclusions and Prospects

The Taiwanese state has been subjected to serious challenges from alternative labour and democratic movements, but has so far managed to maintain a high degree of control by adapting to the new political context. Labour relations remain problematic, but the fragmentation of the labour movement has given the CLA breathing space to re-orientate itself to the new climate. Ambiguity is perhaps inevitable: on the one hand the government actively wants a more thorough enforcement of the Labour Standards Law which is now seen as a spur to up-grading and restructuring; on the other the maintenance of industrial relations stability remains one of the fundamental objectives of a state with an instinct to maintain order and control. The outcome has been the emergence of a set of state-labour relations with many features in common with those in Singapore. Managers and workers are encouraged to resolve their problems locally, but the state reserves the right to intervene through a legal machinery which means a more or less automatic government involvement where strikes (and lock-outs) are likely to occur. Effectively the state is in a position to selectively use the legal system (*against* or *for* organized labour) wherever it deems this desirable in its pursuit of national objectives.

State-employer relations are in many ways distant but relatively harmonious and unambiguous. Perhaps the most important area of potential disagreement is the flight of capital to mainland China which takes advantage of old village networks in Fujian province and elsewhere. While Chinese business capital is opportunistic and prefers to ignore political boundaries, the state would probably prefer that economic integration with China be held in check until the future of Taiwan-China relations become clearer. This may mean waiting to see what happens when Hong Kong is politically re-integrated with the mainland in 1997. Nonetheless the government has more often than not turned a blind eye to overseas investments in China.

While small businesses have served Taiwan well in their ability to adapt rapidly to changing world market conditions, key problems relate to the difficulties the small business sector has in moving into the highest value R&D intensive sectors, in investing in the most advanced capital equipment, and in weaning itself from dependence on Japanese technology. The government does acknowledge this problem, however, and the relatively low investment ratio which has been characteristic of the 1980s is, in the 1990s, being remedied with a massive state-led investment programme. This does not necessarily mean a reduced role for the private sector. Rather, small businesses will receive further support from government in their further development of a technological capability. This state-business relationship, the particulars of which are unique among the ANICs, arguably gives Taiwan a great advantage in its moves to restructure and advance in the 1990s: the flexibility of the small Chinese family business is maintained while the state ensures long term investment in the future is forthcoming.

Taiwan appears, then, set for relative political stability and continued economic growth through the 1990s. State-capital-labour relations remain problematic, though the problems are not on the scale of those found in Korea; economic growth, at least in the short term, is more or less guaranteed by Taiwan's huge reserves. In the longer term, much depends on the ability of the alternative labour and democratic movements to organize themselves and offer a coherent agenda for action, and on the outcome of the present round of economic and technological restructuring.

Chapter Five: Hong Kong

Hong Kong has existed as a British colony since 1843, but will be handed back to China in 1997. With China's gradual opening up to the external world since 1977, economic reintegration has been occurring in advance of political reintegration, and it is impossible today to understand the Hong Kong economy without reference to mainland activities and relationships. While these developments are discussed in some detail in this chapter, it is more difficult to predict the role of Hong Kong beyond 1997 when Britain and Beijing cannot even agree on the basic political structure which will apply after that date. Political uncertainty reached crisis proportions in the late 1980s and early 1990s, contributing to a brain drain which has added to other labour market problems, and causing a crisis of business confidence which arguably further shortens the already short term perspectives of much of the Hong Kongese business world. The entrepot trade which China's experiments in capitalism have increasingly generated for Hong Kong has contributed to the maintenance of full employment and a good living for business, but political uncertainties mean this chapter may, from 1997, have little more than a historical relevance.

Hong Kong is frequently held up as proof of the benefits of unfettered capitalism. Certainly among the ANICs it is the only country where the state has had a genuinely minimalist role in directing the economy: government policy has been one of 'positive non-interventionism'. In assuming increasing welfareist responsibilities since the 1960s, it would be wrong to characterize the state as simply overseeing a pure *laissez faire* capitalist system, but guidance in the form of positive discrimination for certain types of business or attempts to push the economy in certain directions through other means has been largely absent.

Hong Kong was the first of the ANICs to industrialize, and the colony has gradually shed its 'sweat-shop' image – in 1990 Hong Kong had the highest per capita GNP among the four ANICs. However, all is not well in the economy. There has been a serious failure to advance technologically and to up-grade manufacturing industries to higher value activities, and during the late 1980s and early 1990s there has been a decline in manufacturing sufficient for Hong Kong to be characterized as a case of *de*-industrialization. We explore the reasons for the crisis of manufacturing in this chapter.

The sweat-shop image, even in the 1990s, is not completely false. Relations between capital and labour are typically played out in small firms where the employment relationship is tentative and many employees lead a precarious existence. Small firms have certainly played a key role in Hong Kong's industrialization and economic growth, but the celebration of their success needs to be tempered with an acknowledgement of the problems associated with small firm employment, and also with acknowledgement of their economic limitations. In this chapter we examine the disadvantages, as well as the advantages, of the predominance of small businesses, and give attention to the peculiar forms of labour relations they generate in Hong Kong.

Economic Development and Economic Structure

Political changes in China and the nation's role in the Korean War led to a United Nations trade embargo in 1951 which curtailed, at least temporarily, Hong Kong's long standing role as entrepot. The rapid industrialization which followed, led largely by immigrants from Shanghai fleeing the mainland Communist regime, was in an important sense a process of the forced replacement of one role – entrepot, by another – export oriented manufacturer. By the end of the 1950s the remarkable transformation was already evident – *domestic* exports, led by textiles and clothing, had surpassed *re-exports*. In 1959 domestic exports accounted for 70 per cent of total exports. Unlike the other three ANICs, there was not even an attempt to use an import substitution strategy – as Haggard and Chen (1987, p.89) put it, Hong Kong was therefore 'the first of our four countries to enter the export game'.

Export Oriented Industrialization

Hong Kong did not benefit from the massive amounts of post-war aid which helped the development of the Korean and Taiwanese infrastructures and manufacturing capabilities, but the colony did find itself in the 1950s with a useful entrepot legacy. In particular, excellent port facilities and well developed commercial and financial services were both valuable for the attraction of foreign capital (to which the country was already open), for the financing of local manufacturing, and for the distribution and marketing of goods made for the Western world. Export-led economic growth was rapid – contributing to an overall growth rate of over eight per cent per year in the 1960s and 1970s (Sit and Wong 1989) – and significant, albeit erratic, growth during the 1980s gave Hong Kong the highest per capita income among the ANICs in 1990 (table 5.1).

The interruption in Hong Kong's growth in the early 1980s was due to uncertainties about the political future of the colony. As we shall document below, in the 1990s uncertainties are even greater, and the future of the Hong Kong economy beyond the 1990s is highly uncertain.

Manufacturing grew so rapidly that by 1961, when Korea for instance was only just beginning to embark on serious industrialization, a massive 43 per cent of the Hong Kong labour force was already employed in the manufacturing sector. This proportion peaked at nearly 50 per cent by the turn of the decade, then declined

Table 5.1:   GDP and Per Capita GDP in Hong Kong, 1980-1990

	GDP (US$ million)	Per capita GDP (US$)
1980	26,721	5,278
1981	29,038	5,608
1982	28,688	5,449
1983	26,679	4,991
1984	31,794	5,890
1985	33,439	6,129
1986	38,591	6,975
1987	47,587	8,477
1988	55,280	9,638
1989	64,036	11,286
1990	71,282	12,254

Source: Census and Statistics Department, Hong Kong, *Hong Kong Annual Digest of Statistics 1990.*

gradually to 40 per cent by the end of the 1970s. During the 1980s, the proportions engaged in manufacturing have declined due to various reasons, but principally, as we shall see, because of Hong Kong's renewed economic relationship with China as the mainland has gradually opened up again and embarked on its own experiments in capitalism. Table 5.2 summarizes the changing employment structure between 1980 and 1990.

As a proportion of the total labour force, manufacturing employment declined from almost 40 per cent in 1980 to only 26 per cent in 1990, and the fall is an absolute as well a relative one – the manufacturing work force shrunk by over 190,000 in the space of 11 years. Yet unemployment has shrunk to negligible levels over the same period – such has been the strength of the re-emergence of Hong Kong's role as entrepot to service trade between the mainland and the rest of the world. Services – especially in the distribution, trade, hotels and restaurants category – have expanded more than sufficiently to take up the slack. Interestingly, the decline of manufacturing employment and the rise of employment in import-export trading companies have occurred in similar proportions. Manufacturing employment fell by 190,302 between 1981 and 1990. Over the same period import-export company employment grew by 217,582. Manufacturing employment looks set to decline even further in the 1990s. By mid 1991 only 681,000 – around 25 per cent of the total workforce – was engaged in the manufacturing sector (*Far Eastern Economic Review*, 5 March 1992).

Clearly, the remarkable rise of export oriented manufacturing as the engine of growth in Hong Kong from the 1950s, and the equally remarkable decline of manufacturing as the most important source of employment in the 1980s and 1990s, is intimately bound up with the China connection. We will explore this

Table 5.2:   Changes in Employment Structure and Unemployment in Hong Kong, 1980-1990 ('000 persons)*

	1980	1985	1989	1990
Unemployed	87.3	83.6	29.7	36.6
	(3.8)	(3.2)	(1.1)	(1.3)
Public sector	136.2	174.9	187.9	189.9
	(5.9)	(6.6)	(6.8)	(6.9)
Manufacturing	907.5	847.6	791.5	715.6
	(39.1)	(32.3)	(28.5)	(26.0)
Construction	90.5	66.3	69.5	69.1
	(3.9)	(2.5)	(2.5)	(2.5)
Distribution, trade, hotels and restaurants	455.1	600.4	774.0	829.6
	(19.6)	(22.9)	(27.9)	(30.2)
Transport, storage and communications	77.3	95.4	126.0	132.8
	(3.3)	(3.6)	(4.5)	(4.8)
Private sector services	299.6	386.3	491.2	526.9
	(12.9)	(14.7)	(17.7)	(19.2)
Others	357.2	456.0	338.4	247.6
	(15.4)	(17.4)	(12.2)	(9.0)
Total labour force	2,323.4	2,626.9	2,778.5	2,748.1

* Figures in parentheses are proportions of the total labour force.

Source: Census and Statistics Department, Hong Kong, *Hong Kong Annual Digest of Statistics 1990.*

shortly. First, Hong Kong's export orientation is worth discussing in a little more detail.

Hong Kong's manufactured exports grew at an average rate of around 15 per cent a year through the 1960s and 1970s (Pang Eng Fong 1985). The growth of the manufacturing sector was financed primarily by domestic savings and foreign capital inflows rather than foreign loans, so that foreign debt dependence was never a serious problem. Domestic capital was responsible particularly for the growth of the traditional industries, especially textiles and clothing, while foreign capital was more likely to be invested in the newer electronics and related industries. This pattern of local and foreign ownership has continued into the 1990s. Foreign owned companies accounted for 22.2 per cent of total domestic exports in 1990: 78.1 per cent of their total overseas sales were in the electronics, electrical goods and watches and clocks categories, and accounted for 48.1 per cent of Hong Kong's domestic exports in these sectors. Locally owned companies accounted for the other four fifths of domestic exports: 49.4 per cent of their total overseas sales were in the textiles and clothing categories, and accounted for 91.6 per cent of Hong Kong's domestic exports in these sectors. Details of this striking pattern of ownership are provided in table 5.3.

Table 5.3:   Domestic Exports from Hong Kong by Ownership and Industry, 1990 (US$ million)

	Textiles and clothing	Electronics, electrical goods, watches and clocks	Others	Total
Locally-owned	10,455	4,924	7,732	23,111
Foreign-owned	965	4,569	313	5,847
Total	11,420	9,493	8,045	28,958

Sources: Calculated from data in Hong Kong Government Industry Department (1991a, 1991b).

The bulk of foreign manufacturing investments are by Japanese and US companies – accounting for around 30 per cent each of total cumulative investments, followed by China with around 10 per cent.

The structure of Hong Kong's exports is shown in more detail in table 5.4, which also documents recent trends.

Notable is the mixed performance of electronics and related sectors. In Hong Kong it is not wholly accurate to characterized these as 'modern' – the country was manufacturing TV sets for export even in the early 1960s. Telecommunications equipment and accessories (mainly telephones, fax machines, etc.) have significantly risen in importance during the 1980s, and electronics components and parts for computers have also risen in importance, but the largest electronics-related sector remains watches and clocks. Unlike the other ANICs, the 'electronics boom' of the 1980s has not had great effect.

On the other hand the 'traditional' industries are remarkable for their continued importance in domestic exports. Exports of plastic dolls and toys declined from 5.9 per cent of total exports in 1980 to a mere 1.7 per cent in 1989, but textiles and clothing combined still counted for 38.5 per cent of the total in 1990 (39.1 per cent in 1980).

Table 5.5 shows manufacturing employment trends in Hong Kong by sector, and these figures confirm the above comments.

Clothing and textile sectors combined accounted for 43.9 per cent of total manufacturing employment in 1990 (a proportion which held steady through the 1980s) whereas electronics and related sectors, if anything, declined slightly

Table 5.4: Domestic Exports by Principal Commodity from Hong Kong, 1980-1990 (US$ million)*

	Apparel and clothing	Watches and clocks	Textiles fabrics	Tele-communications equipment and accessories	Electronic components and parts for computers	Jewellery	Metal manufactures
1980	4,560.4 (34.1)	1,232.9 (9.2)	674.9 (5.0)	124.1 (0.9)	285.5 (2.1)	208.8 (1.6)	399.4 (3.0)
1985	5,757.9 (34.6)	1,165.1 (7.0)	794.2 (4.8)	595.0 (3.6)	868.0 (5.2)	369.0 (2.2)	376.4 (2.3)
1989	9,214.6 (32.1)	2,095.4 (7.3)	1,860.6 (6.5)	1,517.9 (5.3)	1,050.9 (3.7)	843.2 (2.9)	681.7 (2.4)
1990	9,251.9 (31.9)	2,348.6 (8.1)	1,901.5 (6.6)	1,626.0 (5.6)	1,234.9 (4.3)	882.2 (3.0)	579.9 (2.0)

	Plastic articles	Household equipment, electrical and non-electrical	Automatic data processing machines	Plastic dolls and toys	Others	Total
1980	154.1 (1.2)	386.7 (2.9)	0.6 (–)	789.8 (5.9)	4,549.7 (34.0)	13,366.9
1985	277.4 (1.7)	583.5 (3.5)	105.9 (0.6)	893.3 (5.4)	4,865.8 (29.2)	16,651.5
1989	614.0 (2.1)	545.1 (1.9)	506.3 (1.8)	486.0 (1.7)	9,315.6 (32.4)	28,731.3
1990	547.7 (1.9)	432.8 (1.5)	469.2 (1.6)	NA	9,683.9 (33.4)	28,958.3

* Figures in parentheses are percentages of total domestic exports.

Source: Census and Statistics Department, Hong Kong, *Hong Kong Annual Digest of Statistics*, various issues.

Table 5.5:   Manufacturing Employment in Hong Kong by Sector, 1980-1990*

	1980	1985	1989	1990
Wearing apparel	263,682 (29.1)	264,569 (31.2)	237,345 (30.0)	214,108 (29.9)
Textiles	127,609 (14.1)	110,606 (13.0)	113,487 (14.3)	100,150 (14.0)
Electrical and electronic machinery and apparatus	122,124 (13.5)	111,186 (13.1)	105,985 (13.4)	85,266 (11.9)
Plastic products	86,064 (9.5)	82,517 (9.7)	59,248 (7.5)	53,413 (7.5)
Fabricated metal products	84,240 (9.3)	61,773 (7.3)	54,670 (6.9)	50,942 (7.1)
Paper products, printing and publishing	39,075 (4.3)	44,297 (5.2)	51,878 (6.6)	53,024 (7.4)
Scientific and controlling equipment, photographic and optical goods	48,137 (5.3)	42,130 (5.0)	34,047 (4.3)	31,966 (4.5)
Non-electrical machinery	14,270 (1.6)	21,918 (2.6)	29,621 (3.7)	29,208 (4.1)
Furniture and wood products	18,753 (2.1)	12,721 (1.5)	10,245 (1.3)	8,646 (1.2)
Footwear	6,809 (0.8)	7,513 (0.9)	5,142 (0.6)	4,103 (0.6)
Others	96,700 (10.7)	88,385 (10.4)	89,851 (11.4)	84,771 (11.8)
Total manufacturing	907,463	847,615	791,519	715,597

* Figures in parentheses are percentages of the total manufacturing workforce.

Source: Census and Statistics Department, Hong Kong, *Hong Kong Annual Digest of Statistics*, various issues.

in importance. Perhaps more important in table 5.5 is the absolute decline of manufacturing as a source of employment, the reasons for which we shall return to.

Among other things, table 5.6 shows that by far the most important markets for goods manufactured in Hong Kong (the 'domestic exports' category) is the US, which took 29.4 per cent of the total in 1990. (This is only slightly down from 33.1 per cent in 1980.)

China is the next biggest market, taking 21.0 per cent of total domestic exports in 1990, up from only 2.4 per cent in 1980, and reflecting renewed economic relations with the mainland and the gradually increased importance of China as a market for manufactured goods. Also apparent in table 5.6 is the large positive balance with the US, and the trade deficit with Japan. This pattern was apparent in the other three ANICs, reflecting a dependence on Japan for capital imports: Hong Kong's deficit with Japan is by far the worst among the ANICs – Hong Kong imported from Japan 4.2 times more than it exported in 1990. The figures for Singapore, Taiwan and Korea were 2.7 times, 2.1 times and 1.5 times respectively. Table 5.7 confirms Hong Kong Kong's heavy dependence on capital imports (Hong Kong has negligible indigenous capacity in capital goods production and this is not changing) and shows an increasing proportion of imports falling into the capital goods category in the late 1980s – again a trend documented for the other ANICs. However, the increase of capital goods imports has been relatively slow, suggesting a failure to up-grade production facilities as is, arguably, necessary.

It is also worth pointing out the significance of consumer goods imports in Hong Kong compared with, say, Korea (compare table 5.7 with table 3.6 in chapter three). This is partly because Hong Kong makes fewer completed goods for local sale (the clothing sector is exceptional), being more likely to act as international sub-contractor (especially in electronics). It also relates to the relatively open market and relatively few restrictions on consumer goods consumption, whether imported or not, in Hong Kong.

Tables 5.6 and 5.7 also confirm the rapid emergence of the import-export trade for Hong Kong in the late 1980s. This parallels the decline of manufacturing employment, and we will return to discuss these phenomena shortly. First, there will be a brief caveat on the centrally important textiles and clothing, and electronics, sectors.

'Traditional' and 'Advanced' Sectors

It is worth dwelling on the traditional clothing and textiles industries because of their continued central importance both for Hong Kong's domestic export performance and as a source of employment. Yet this has been in the face of competition from the ASEAN countries (with cheaper factors of production, especially labour) for export markets in the West, and significant protectionist measures by Western countries attempting to defend their own textiles and clothing industries.

Li Kui Wai (1991) documents the protectionist trade measures imposed on Hong Kong's textiles and clothing exports in detail. The first – the 'Lancashire pact' – was imposed as early as 1959 by Britain. This pact imposed a restriction

Table 5.6:   Hong Kong's Exports and Imports by Country of Destination and Origin, 1980-1990 (US$ million)*

	Japan				US				China			
	Domestic exports	Re-exports	Imports	Balance	Domestic exports	Re-exports	Imports	Balance	Domestic exports	Re-exports	Imports	Balance
1980	456.7	431.6	5,028.2	-4,139.9	4,429.6	604.9	2,590.2	2,444.3	314.7	910.2	4,303.5	-3,078.6
1985	660.4	594.0	6,839.7	-5,585.3	7,395.8	1,885.3	2,807.2	6,473.9	1,947.3	5,900.4	7,559.4	288.3
1986	796.4	855.9	7,230.5	-5,578.2	8,233.2	2,866.9	2,974.1	8,126.0	2,310.5	5,242.8	10,465.8	-2,912.5
1987	1,216.5	1,252.8	9,218.6	-6,749.3	9,335.5	4,160.8	4,133.6	9,362.7	3,573.2	7,714.1	15,045.8	-3,758.5
1988	1,466.0	2,233.1	11,924.1	-8,225.0	9,344.1	6,344.0	5,300.9	10,387.2	4,877.3	12,166.0	19,953.1	-2,909.8
1989	1,670.3	2,854.9	11,949.0	-7,423.8	9,251.6	9,235.0	5,927.4	12,559.0	5,547.7	13,268.2	25,214.9	-6,399.0
1990	1,549.0	3,125.0	13,252.0	-8,578.0	8,509.0	11,250.0	6,640.0	13,119.0	6,086.0	14,219.0	30,274.0	-9,969.0

	Others				Total			
	Domestic exports	Re-exports	Imports	Balance	Domestic exports	Re-exports	Imports	Balance
1980	8,165.9	3,949.8	9,970.5	2,145.2	13,366.9	5,896.5	21,892.4	-2,629.0
1985	6,648.0	5,116.5	12,462.9	-698.4	16,651.5	13,496.2	29,669.2	478.5
1986	8,401.3	6,745.4	14,708.4	438.3	19,741.4	15,711.0	35,378.8	73.6
1987	10,907.4	10,305.6	20,056.9	1,156.1	25,032.6	23,433.3	48,454.9	11.0
1988	12,218.2	14,565.2	26,770.4	13.0	27,905.6	35,308.3	63,948.5	-734.0
1989	12,261.7	19,052.8	29,060.1	2,254.4	28,731.3	44,410.9	72,151.4	990.6
1990	12,814.0	24,483.0	32,210.0	5,087.0	28,958.0	53,077.0	82,376.0	-341.0

* Figures calculated on the basis of HK$ 5.1 to US$ 1 for 1980, and HK$ 7.8 to US$ 1 from 1985 to 1990.

Sources: Calculated from data in Census and Statistics Department, Hong Kong, *Hong Kong Annual Digest of Statistics 1990*; Hong Kong Government Industry Department (1991b).

Table 5.7: Structure of Hong Kong's Imports, 1980-1990 (US$ million)*

	Goods for re-export	Goods for domestic use			Total
		Food and consumer goods	Industrial materials and fuels	Capital goods	
1980	5,896.5	5,259.2 (32.9)	8,288.0 (51.8)	2,448.6 (15.3)	21,892.4
1985	13,496.2	5,632.6 (34.8)	8,260.5 (51.1)	2,280.0 (14.1)	29,669.2
1989	44,410.9	7,428.8 (26.7)	15,469.0 (55.6)	4,842.7 (17.4)	72,151.4
1990	53,076.8	6,919.4 (23.6)	17,117.4 (58.4)	5,262.2 (18.0)	82,375.6

* Figures in parentheses are percentages of domestic imports only.

Source: Census and Statistics Department, Hong Kong, *Hong Kong Annual Digest of Statistics*, various issues.

on exports of garments and piece goods to Britain to an annual total of 164 million yards. During the 1960s the pact was extended and refined, quotas being established for ever-finer categories of goods. Also in the 1960s, led by the US, arrangements were established through GATT to limit exports of cotton textiles from Hong Kong to various countries. In 1974, the first multi-fibre arrangement (MFA) allowed importing countries to impose restrictions on imports of a range of goods, including man-made fibres, unilaterally under certain conditions, and a Textile Surveillance Body was set up to police activities. Further protectionist measures were introduced during the 1980s, especially by the US, and in 1987 the first Hong Kong-EC textile agreement was signed. By 1988 60 per cent of Hong Kong's domestic exports of textiles and clothing products were subject to quota restraint (Poon 1992).

Li Kui Wai (1991) argues that the continued growth of the textiles and clothing sectors in Hong Kong defeated the 'zero-sum hypothesis' of protectionism. Instead of simply restricting output, Hong Kong manufacturers advanced technologically and shifted to the production of higher quality, higher value products, creating brand names as an instrument to create consumer loyalty. They have also continuously diversified production into categories of textiles and apparel for which quotas did not exist, or for which Hong Kong had space for expansion within the quota. Hence any loss or limitation within one specific export market would quickly be filled by another. Many Hong Kong manufacturers also established facilities or set up sub-contracting arrangements outside Hong Kong (in the

1980s and 1990s increasingly on the Chinese mainland, and most recently in Vietnam) in order to avoid quotas on goods shipped directly from the colony (Wong Yim Yu and Maher 1992). Li Kui Wai (1991, p.208) concludes that 'protectionism has acted indirectly as an engine of growth', and explains Hong Kong's ability to make the necessary changes described in terms of the large number of small Hong Kong firms which make up a flexible and responsive industrial structure.

Providing a more critical account, Lui Tai Lok and Chiu (1991) point out that while technological up-grading has occurred to a degree in some companies, the textiles and clothing industry has remained on the whole labour intensive – value added to output ratios hardly changed during the 1980s. Poon (1992) documents a textile industry more quick to up-grade technologically than clothing, but in spite of various government initiatives on the supply side (especially education and technical training) the overall extent of technological advance is limited. The high performance of these traditional sectors in fact appears to have been achieved, in the face of a tight labour market, *less* by technological advance than by the use of large numbers of legal and illegal immigrants from the Chinese mainland, and by the use of Hong Kong's significant informal sector, especially outworkers. In 1981 it was estimated that the textiles, clothing and footwear industries between them made use of around 42,000 outworkers, 35,000 of whom were women. The poor pay and conditions, and the insecurity, of these workers contributes to the low wage costs and flexibility of the industry, *and* reduces the urgency to apply more capital-intensive methods (Lui and Chiu 1991).

Perhaps more surprising is that to a significant extent the same chronic problem of weakness of technological level holds true of the 'advanced' electronics sector. Lui and Chiu (1991, p.18) quote the Hong Kong government's Industry Department as follows:

Hong Kong, while largely successful in competing in the international market as a subcontractor for many electronic consumer products, lacks well developed supporting industries and a substantial research and development capability. This makes it difficult for the industry to diversify into other areas of knowledge-intensive and potentially high value added production.

As Henderson (1989) points out, the electronics sector, like textiles and clothing, is characterized by the use of large numbers of small sub-contractors – in this case for the assembly of components and parts. Henderson does document a degree of technological up-grading, especially within US-owned semi-conductor plants, but like textiles and clothing there has been no sign of a step-change in value added to output ratios in the 1980s, and there is no sign of the development of any significant R&D capability or diversification into the highest value sectors. The contrast with Korea and Taiwan is striking.

Large numbers of small firms with little support or direction from the state, then, may have their advantages in terms of rapid response to market changes and protectionist measures, but their capability in moving to higher value production and up-grading technology is open to question. Sit and Wong (1989) explain that small firms have only short term relations with large firms, being used to absorb fluctuations in demand, and therefore (unlike small firms in Japan which have close and long term relations with big firms) they have little incentive to up-grade production facilities. Value added to output ratios are extremely crude indicators and can be misleading, but one might expect higher value activities, technological up-grading, and any deepening of an industry in terms of local content, to be reflected in higher ratios. As table 5.8 shows, while there may have been some improvement in textiles during the 1980s, both the clothing and electrical and electronics sectors show no improvement by this measure.

Table 5.8: Value Added and Gross Output in Selected Manufacturing Sectors in Hong Kong, 1979-1988 (HK$ million)

		Value added	Gross output	Value added - gross output ratio
Textiles	1979	3,957	16,604	23.8
	1984	7,294	29,076	25.1
	1988	12,925	47,445	27.2
Clothing	1979	6,553	21,742	30.1
	1984	13,171	41,309	31.9
	1988	17,858	59,771	29.9
Electrical and electronics products	1979	3,595	15,004	24.0
	1984	8,912	35,815	24.9
	1988	12,670	60,186	21.1
All manufacturing	1979	25,779	93,757	27.5
	1984	52,741	189,612	27.8
	1988	83,182	315,940	26.3

Source: Census and Statistics Department, Hong Kong, *Hong Kong Annual Digest of Statistics 1990.*

The rapid relative *and* absolute decline in the importance of manufacturing in Hong Kong at the end of the 1980s and early 1990s may be an indication of the limits to small business capabilities. However, causality is difficult to establish, for the *motivation* to up-grade for small companies (and indeed for large companies) has been absent in recent years for a *variety* of reasons: not only do small firms fear heavy capital investments because of their precarious existence, but at the same time as Hong Kong's entrepot role has emerged as important once again, soaking up employment in service sectors and reducing manufacturing labour force availability, the gradual opening up of China since 1977 has enabled Hong

Kong companies to increasingly locate production on the mainland where labour is abundant and cheap. The flow of Hong Kong FDI into China grew six-fold between 1983 and 1989 alone (Lui and Chiu 1991) and as we have documented in chapter one, has grown even faster since then. Further, within Hong Kong the growth of manufacturing wages has been held in check during the 1980s. As table 3.10 (chapter three) shows, despite Hong Kong having the highest ANIC per capita income by 1990, hourly compensation costs of production workers in manufacturing were significantly lower than the rest, including even Korea's where per capita income is less than half that in Hong Kong! These factors together explain why company survival has been possible without up-grading.

The wisdom of Hong Kong's government in more or less standing by and watching the decline of manufacturing is highly questionable. It makes Hong Kong's continued prosperity increasingly dependent on trade relations between China and the rest of the world. It could on the other hand be argued that the takeover of Hong Kong by China in 1997 means that even Hong Kong's medium term future is uncertain. Hence the best economic and industrial strategy is impossible to determine in a situation where Britain and China cannot come to agreement on what the precise role of (what will be) a small city in a huge country will be.

The China Connection

While the curtailment of international trade with China in 1951 led to Hong Kong's industrialization, it is the re-emergence of China-world trade in the 1980s which is now leading to Hong Kong's de-industrialization. Put simply, in the absence of government controls Hong Kong manufacturing capacity is transferred to the mainland in return for the re-export business which China generates. Table 5.6 showed that in 1980 re-exports constituted 30.6 per cent of total exports. But by 1987 re-exports were about to overtake domestic exports, and in 1990 re-exports were a huge 64.7 per cent of total exports. Table 5.9 confirms the importance of China in the re-export game – 58.1 per cent of the goods re-exported from Hong Kong in 1990 originated from China (up from 27.9 per cent in 1980).

The renewed entrepot role, together with the relocation of Hong Kongese manufacturing capacity on the mainland, means Hong Kong's economic integration with China is occurring in advance of its political integration. The Chinese government is well aware of this fact, and has been willing to threaten the use of its power which derives from Hong Kong's dependence on the mainland in negotiations with the British government over the terms and conditions of the colony's political transfer. In 1992 for instance the Chinese government threatened to cancel all commercial agreements signed between the Hong Kong government and the private sector before 1997, unless approved by Beijing (*The Guardian*, 2 December 1992). While China has agreed that Hong Kong's *laissez faire* capitalism

Table 5.9:   Country of Origin of Goods for Re-export from Hong Kong, 1980-1990
(US$ million)*

	Japan	US	China	Taiwan	Korea	Others	Total
1980	1,153.7	619.0	1,645.9	418.4	172.0	1,887.5	5,896.5
	(19.6)	(10.5)	(27.9)	(7.1)	(2.9)	(32.0)	
1985	2,381.9	1,225.8	4,439.5	1,112.9	470.1	3,901.4	13,531.6
	(17.6)	(9.1)	(32.8)	(8.2)	(3.5)	(28.8)	
1989	4,999.7	2,862.2	24,137.3	3,456.4	1,445.9	7,509.4	44,410.9
	(11.3)	(6.4)	(54.3)	(7.8)	(3.3)	(16.9)	
1990	5,420.5	3,139.7	30,821.8	3,882.4	1,488.5	8,323.9	53,076.8
	(10.2)	(5.9)	(58.1)	(7.3)	(2.8)	(15.7)	

* Figures in parantheses are percentage of total re-exports.

Source: Census and Statistics Department, Hong Kong, *Hong Kong Annual Digest of Statistics*, various issues.

can continue for 50 years after 1997, few people have complete faith that the Chinese government will not intervene.

Nonetheless, the most likely scenario for Hong Kong's future appears to be an increasing integration with the Chinese economy, and particularly with the neighbouring province of Guangdong which centres on the city of Canton. There has been talk of the development of a huge 'megalopolis' along the Pearl river delta in South East China which would take in a third of China's one billion population, and which would potentially give Hong Kong a key role in China's industrialization and trade expansion (Ma 1988). Already, Hong Kongese firms directly employ large numbers of workers directly in South East China – especially in Guangdong. One estimate put the number at three million in 1993 (*Financial Times*, 6 April 1993) which if correct is about the same as Hong Kong's own total work force, and these might be expected to increase even more in the future. Of course, this development is associated with the gradual liberalization of the labour market in China as part of the package of Chinese economic reforms (see Poon 1991 for details). Hong Kong could also be expected to take on increasing responsibilities for the import-export business and for a variety of commercial and financial services.

Presently, however, it is difficult to expand further on Hong Kong's future role: at the time of writing relations between Britain and Beijing are strained, to say the least, because of disagreements over Hong Kong's political future, and the outcome is likely to have an important impact on Hong Kong's economic future.

Labour Markets

As we have discussed, Hong Kong's labour market is characterized by an exceptionally high degree of flexibility which relates to the importance of small firms
and a large informal sector. Flexibility is reinforced by the weakness of organized labour in the colony, a point which will be discussed later in the chapter.
The influx of large numbers of immigrant workers from the mainland is a third
important characteristic of the labour market, and is one which helps explain the
continuation of relatively undeveloped industries in the face of rapid economic
growth. Net immigration peaked at a massive 180,000 in 1979. More stringent
controls brought the numbers down in the 1980s, but it was still estimated that
around 28,000 illegal immigrants entered Hong Kong in 1984 (Ng and Sit 1989).
However, an important aspect of the labour market which we have not yet discussed, and which in recent years has given Hong Kong its own unique 'labour
problem', is the abandonment of the colony by large numbers of professionals
and other highly qualified workers in the face of the impending takeover by China
in 1997.

In 1988 alone 44,211 Hong Kongese left for Canada, the US and Australia (the
most popular destinations), and most of these were highly skilled and professional
workers and their families (*The Observer*, 11 June 1989). (In the same year,
interestingly, Britain accepted only 776 Hong Kongese immigrants, and these had
to demonstrate close family connections or the ability to invest at least £ 150,000.
Not surprisingly, the Hong Kongese felt betrayed by their old colonial masters:
it could also be argued that Britain is missing out on an opportunity to take in a
highly educated, skilled and hard working population which would undoubtedly
contribute to Britain's economic well being.) Between 1987 and 1990 an estimated
180,000, most well educated and professionally skilled, left Hong Kong, adding
a 'brain drain' crisis to the more general problem of a serious labour shortage
which had been growing throughout the 1980s. For 1987 and 1988 alone it has
been estimated that Hong Kong lost 10 per cent of the stock of its engineers, 11 per
cent of its nurses and midwives, 13 per cent of its lawyers, doctors and dentists,
22 per cent of its accountants, and 35 per cent of its computer programmers and
systems analysts (Chiu and Levin 1993).

A whole variety of strategies developed by government and the private sector
have been developed in an attempt to stem the outflow of professional personnel, and to re-recruit those professionals who left the colony earlier in the 1980s
(C.F. Wong 1990). Inevitably, this has included the offer of higher salaries and
improved promotion prospects – the salaries of university academics in Hong
Kong in the early 1990s for instance were the highest in the world. And there
has been a real average salary increase of 65 per cent for managers and professionals between 1983 and 1991, compared with an average of only 10 per cent
for manufacturing employees over the same period (*Far Eastern Economic Review*, 5 March 1992). Despite such measures, the outflow has not been stemmed,

and at the same time the labour market more generally has become even tighter. Hence a series of measures in the late 1980s and early 1990s were introduced in an attempt to recruit foreign workers in a whole range of categories. Organized labour attempted – unsuccessfully – to resist labour import liberalization, claiming (undoubtedly correctly) that the wages of Hong Kongese workers would be undermined and that employers would be relieved of the pressures to up-grade technological capacity.

We have already documented several reasons why Hong Kongese firms have difficulty in up-grading technologically. This is now exacerbated by the fear among employers that any up-grading of *employees* will not produce returns in the long run – rather, employers may simply be equipping employees with the skills necessary to enable them to follow their predecessors overseas (Chiu and Levin 1993). The government has taken measures recently to greatly increase the proportions of school leavers entering higher education and to improve vocational training, and has recently opened a third Hong Kong University which is to be dedicated largely to management, science and technology. But such supply side measures may be too little too late to solve the labour market problems in the run up to 1997.

Summary

As the first export oriented manufacturer among the ANICs, Hong Kong made remarkable progress first in the traditional industries, especially textiles and clothing, and then the more advanced, especially electronics. The textiles and clothing sectors, led at first by the Shanghainese who fled the mainland during the Chinese revolution, have continued to play a central role in exports and in employment generation. This was made possible in the face of Western protectionism and competition from other Asian countries through, on the one hand, a highly flexible industrial structure related to the large numbers of small businesses and the informal sector, and, on the other, the use of waves of labour migrating from the mainland. It appears to be these factors, far more than any technological up-grading, which have enabled the traditional industries to remain world competitive. The electronics industry has been dominated by multinational corporations, especially from the US, though sub-contracting arrangements with small local companies have also been important.

Trade statistics show that Hong Kong suffers the same problem as the other ANICs with regard to technological dependence on Japan, and market dependence on the West, especially America. Western protectionism has not, however, led to significant overall balance of payments problems, even in the late 1980s and early 1990s. Recently, however, Hong Kong's dependence on domestically manufactured exports *per se* has declined markedly as the country has resumed its entrepot role and as manufacturing capacity has been relocated on the mainland via direct investments and sub-contracting. To the extent that these trends become predominant, it is difficult to compare the economy with other ANIC economies. Indeed, export oriented manufacturing may turn out to have been a brief interlude in Hong Kong's economic history – the first of the ANICs to industrialize could be set to become the first to *de*-industrialize.

The State

Economic Role

Compared with the three other ANICs, the government in Hong Kong has had relatively little direct role in the running of the economy. However, it would be wrong to suggest that the state has no economic role for two reasons. First, the state has played a role, albeit limited, in orchestrating the activities of business, including the myriad small, highly networked companies for which Hong Kong has been celebrated. Secondly, and far more importantly, on the supply side the government has played a significant role, particularly in the areas of infrastructure, education, social welfare, and the control of the supply of labour via immigration controls. Supply side measures have not *directed* Hong Kong's economy, but they could be characterized as *enabling* Hong Kong's unique form of capitalism.

With regard to the *orchestration* role of government, the Industry Department has taken a keen interest in the details of export quotas in the textiles and clothing industries, and has helped distribute allocations among different companies. The Hong Kong Productivity Centre provides training programmes and consulting services, and the Hong Kong Trade Development Council has offices around the world to promote Hong Kong exports and to feed back information on world market developments to Hong Kongese firms (Castells 1992). However, probably the closest Hong Kong has come to an attempt to direct the economy in specific directions was the establishment of an Industry Development Board in 1980, which was charged with the task of planning, monitoring and advising on programmes for the provision of support and technical back-up facilities for industry. The Industry Development Board was the outcome of the recommendations of a government appointed Advisory Comittee on Diversification (set up in 1977) which found that measures were necessary to overcome the problems of increasing restrictions on exporters imposed by importing countries. Another outcome of the committee's deliberations was the Industry Department's attempt to attract multinational investments in new industries in order to diversify the export base, and to persuade existing industries to up-grade technology and shift to higher value added (Poon 1992). However, government intervention was limited to persuading and cajoling (note the contrast with Taiwan) and the impact of such measures has been restricted by Hong Kong's industrial structure. As Poon (1992) points out, surveys among Hong Kong's manufacturers suggest an increased *awareness* of the availability and nature of modern technology, but not an increased rate of adoption. Even in the 'advanced' electronics sector:

investment in technology is made when the market need exists and when the equipment payback period is short ... with few exceptions, the bulk of the industry comprises small and medium sized operations manufacturing consumer products typically assembled from imported components. Little is spent on technology development work such as product design and process improvement. The industry is becoming more and more specialized in the production of fad products such as TV games, electronic watches and telephones. ... With these characteristics, it is not surprising that the electronics industry in Hong Kong is not capital and technology intensive (Poon 1992, p.217-8).

Clearly persuasion is inadequate to the task of industrial restructuring in Hong Kong, but the state has been unwilling to shift its 'positive non-interventionist' stance – firms might or might not desire, but certainly have learned not to expect, government protection or assistance (Lin and Chyaun Tuan 1988). And in recent years the state has observed not just the failure of industry to make great technological strides, but also the absolute decline of manufacturing, with rather less alarm than would certainly be apparent among other ANIC governments. Indeed, whereas the response of the Taiwanese government to serious problems related to industrial structure at the turn of the decade has been a massive boost in government investments in the economy (see table 4.10 in chapter four), the public share of gross domestic fixed capital formation in Hong Kong has actually *declined* from 14.7 per cent in 1981 to 12.7 per cent in 1990.

The government has, then, deliberately avoided attempting to direct the economy through, for instance, the use of state owned companies in strategic areas, or giving protection or preferential treatment to favoured sectors, or even setting targets for output and exports, etc. However, supply side measures have provided an institutional context within which capital and labour operates, and which must be understood in order to explain the economy.

Private companies are encouraged to engage in as many activities as possible, including utilites; hence the public sector employs only around seven per cent of the working population (table 5.2). However, the government has used its ownership of land (most land is Crown land which the government leases but does not sell) to manipulate the land market to generate revenues which have been used for infrastructural development and, most importantly, to develop industrial estates, flatted factories, and state subsidized housing for workers. Castells (1992) points out that while GDP grew by a factor of 13 between 1949 and 1980, government expenditure grew 26-fold over the same period. Infrastructure provision helps create the framework for the activities of small businesses which would otherwise be less likely to able to afford to build or rent their own factories.

As described earlier, education is also given significant and increasing state support. In 1987 the Hong Kong government's per capita expenditure on education was US$ 224. This was a long way short of Singapore's US$ 422 per capita spend, but well above Korea's and Taiwan's at US$ 92 and US$ 142 respectively (Deyo 1992).

The massive public housing programme in Hong Kong provides subsidized appartments for about 45 per cent of the population, and since the late 1960s, partly in response to growing public concern about poverty, there has been a great expansion in state provision of health facilities, educational institutions, and other social services. Deyo (1992) estimates Hong Kong's social expenditures at 53.1 per cent of total government expenditure in 1987 – the highest among the ANICs. Housing and community services took up 35.9 per cent of this expenditure, and education 34.4 per cent, a pattern similar to that found in Singapore (in Taiwan and Korea government expenditures on housing and community services amounted to around six per cent of their social expenditures budget, and total levels of social expenditure were much lower). Castells (1992) argues that Hong Kong's 'colonial welfare state', by shifting responsibility for the worker's well being onto government's shoulders, has allowed employers to concentrate on pure business matters and made it easier for them to shrink and expand the labour force according to variations in demand in the knowledge that the state provides a safety net. At the same time, the safety net means would-be entrepreneurs, relying on small personal savings and family support, are more likely to be willing to take gambles on risky business ventures.

If the emergence of a welfare state in Hong Kong helps explain the continuation of small and medium sized companies, waves of immigration from mainland China have underpinned the maintenance of relatively low wages and therefore the ability of companies to continue in their pursuit of labour intensive manufacturing. Immigration was particularly high in the mid to late 1970s – hundreds of thousands of immigrants, mostly young unskilled males, entered Hong Kong during the 1960s and 1970s, being welcomed by employers hungry for cheap labour (Lui and Chiu 1991). The labour shortages of the 1980s were dealt with by employers more through locating manufacturing facilities on the mainland than through labour imports, though the acute labour shortage at the turn of the decade led to the government giving permission for the recruitment of large numbers of immigrant workers – and not just the professionally skilled – once again.

To sum up, the government of Hong Kong did not, as in the case of each of the other three ANICs, play any decisive role in the country's industrialization. Export oriented manufacturers received few special favours and were offered no protection, and even in the 1980s when the state perhaps began to acknowledge the inadequacies of dogmatic 'positive non-interventionism', little was done beyond attempts to persuade. But Hong Kong is not the Friedmanite *laissez faire* paradise some people still imagine. In Britain, the state reluctantly began to take on welfare responsibilities from employers at the turn of the last century; in Hong Kong the colonial administration held out until the 1960s but finally had to give in to popular pressure. The government's increasing welfareist role since the 1960s has contributed, albeit indirectly, to Hong Kong's unique economic characteristics.

Legitimacy

Political extremists of the British Monarchist persuasion apart (of which there are still surprisingly large numbers), few would doubt that the fact that Britain was not forced out of Hong Kong soon after World War II was a simple function of the Chinese Communist revolution in 1949. China ceded Hong Kong island to Britain in 1842 following the Opium War under the Treaty of Nanking, and later in the nineteenth century Britain acquired the Kowloon peninsula after China's defeat in the Anglo-Chinese War (1860), then the New Territories on a 99 year lease in 1898. For the most part, China-world trade via Hong Kong was sufficient for the locals to make a good living. But Hong Kong's role as entrepot suddenly came to an end following the Chinese revolution, and the colony continued to exist in most important respects independently of China until the late 1970s, when the mainland began to gradually open itself to political and economic relations with the capitalist West.

For the period between the Chinese revolution and China's re-opening – roughly the 1950s through the 1970s – the colonial administration might not have been seen as *legitimate*, but the alternative of rule from Beijing was sufficient to make it, for the majority, *acceptable*. And for many, the success of export oriented industrialization might have made the word *palatable* more appropriate. The 1984 Sino-British agreement which hands sovereignty over the whole of Hong Kong from 1997 to Beijing, unsurprisingly, stirs the emotions of the Hong Kongese, who generally see themselves as very definitely Chinese but equally certainly not Communist. The Tiananmen Square massacre of pro-democracy protestors by government-instructed troops in China in 1989 dashed any faith the Hong Kongese might have had in Beijing's promises, and an air of uncertainty and trepidation (and occasionally panic) has hung over the colony since then.

Hong Kong is ruled from Britain via an appointed Governor of Hong Kong, who oversees an Executive Council (which operates like the Cabinet in Britain) and a Legislative Council (Legco). Legco is made up largely of civic and business leaders appointed by the government, and local leaders are also co-opted onto various consultative and statutory bodies. Electoral participation is limited to Urban Council (Urbco) and District Board elections. Urbco and District Boards are local advisory councils with some elected members who are invited to give opinions on government policy through District Officials. Not surprisingly given their 'public parks and libraries' role, voter turnouts have been very low (Lo Shiu Hing 1990). Hence while the colonial government's attempts to incorporate the Hong Kong elite and its willingness to consult the local populations on some issues may have had some importance, it hardly explains the fact that its power has not been seriously challenged (apart from a limited confrontation by local Communists in the late 1960s) until the 1980s.

Further, unlike the other three ANICs, the government of Hong Kong cannot derive legitimacy from the country's economic performance. The government did grudgingly take on responsibilities for housing, education and social welfare provision, but played no serious role in the strategic direction of the economy.

Yet it would be wrong to say that the Hong Kong government has enjoyed *no* legitimacy, and this relates to several factors. First, if we take a definition of democracy broader than 'one man one vote' so that electoral participation becomes only one element, then Hong Kong does not fair so badly. Unlike other authoritarian states, including Korea, Singapore and Taiwan, Hong Kong has showed a relatively high degree of tolerance towards dissent. Hong Kongese citizens are largely free to organize and to express their opinions without fear of political imprisonment, and there is a free press – there is in fact even a free circulation of pro-Peoples' Republic of China and pro-Kuomintang newspapers (So and Kwitko 1990). Secondly, the government's acceptance of a welfareist role has limited some of the extremes of poverty which might otherwise have given grounds for radical protest. Thirdly, small businesses have not been discriminated against (as, arguably, they have been in Singapore and Korea), giving a large segment of the population the possibility of upward mobility: as Chu Yin Wah (1992a) puts it, the Chinese business culture of entrepreneurialism has been allowed to flourish. Finally, and most obviously, the British could be seen as effectively freeing Hong Kong's population from a forced participation in (or subjugation to) mainland politics.

Nonetheless, anti-colonial sentiment was occasionally expressed through the 1960s and 1970s, and again in the 1980s when the future of Hong Kong was at stake and the issue of democratization in advance of 1997 became a central political issue for an overt political movement. This 1980s movement was led primarily by Hong Kong's 'new middle class' (So and Kwitko 1990). This is made up of young professional university and college educated graduates whose political inclinations were formed in the 1970s by participation in pressure groups which protested against the government's 'bureaucratic arrogance', the lack of local control, and the problems of urban life. Encouraged by the successes of democratic movements elsewhere in Asia, especially those in Korea and Taiwan, and by China's apparently softening stance towards Hong Kong's political and economic future, the democratic movement called for direct elections to Legco, and for the future election of the Hong Kong Chief Executive by one person one vote. The 1984 Joint Declaration had in fact stipulated 24 elected members to be included in Legco, with these numbers to build up to a more significant percentage by 1997. While the democratic movement demanded that this become reality, Britain was slow to move, and at the time of writing there were still no elected Legco members. This was in part due to opposition to early Legco elections by Beijing *and* by local capitalists in Hong Kong, who feared the new middle class, if their candidates were elected, would seek higher taxes, more regulations, and more welfare for the poor, which would all damage their own interests (So and Kwitko 1990).

Transition to China

It is naive to think that Britain has Hong Kong people's interest at heart; they enjoy the notion of doling out democracy. If we have to suffer, it is preferable to be ruled by the hypocritical British. (Ms Chow, office administrator, cited in *Financial Times*, 4 December 1992).

Britain continued to stonewall on demands for democracy even during the 1980s and as late as 1990. Following the Tiananmen incident, a delegation of Executive Council and Legco members led by Baroness Dunn asked Mrs Thatcher, then British Prime Minister, to ensure that a full half of Legco members would be directly elected at the scheduled 1995 Legco elections. Immediately after Tiananmen in 1989 the Baroness had also asked Mrs Thatcher for up to three million visas for residents of Hong Kong who might want to seek assylum in Britain. The British government turned down both requests (*The Observer* 13 December 1992).

In late 1992, however, the 'hypocritical' British did an about-face, when the new Governor of Hong Kong Chris Patten (who was appointed when he lost his seat at the British parliamentary elections) announced he would institute almost exactly what Baroness Dunn had requested in 1990. Mrs Thatcher gave her full support to Patten's announcements and congratulated him on a 'marvellously constructed speech'. Democracy was not the first concern of the Hong Kongese people, she said patronisingly, but recently they had come to want to play a greater role in their own affairs (*The Observer* 13 December 1992). Beijing's anger at Britain's impudence – the announcement was made prior to any agreement with the Chinese government – led to threats about Hong Kong's economic future which caused the stock market to plummet, and the Chinese Peoples' Liberation Army conducted military exercises close to the colony with the scenario of 'the capture of Hong Kong in six hours without a shot being fired' (*Sunday Times*, 6 December 1992). Even some of the most outspoken pro-democracy Hong Kongese were alarmed at British hypocrisy and apparent diplomatic failure – Ms Chow was expressing a widely shared sentiment.

However, if few have faith in the British and the colonial government, *no one* trusts Beijing. The Chinese government has, throughout the 1980s and into the 1990s, gone to great lengths to assure the population of Hong Kong that their immediate economic future is secure, and China's renewed economic relations with the First World has given Hong Kong huge amounts of highly profitable import-export business which is material proof of Hong Kong's potential continued prosperity. But China is politically volatile, and Tiananmen sent shock waves through Hong Kong which will continue to reverberate for some time to come. One measure of the lack of faith in Beijing is of course the flight of the middle classes, many of whom are trading material well being in Hong Kong for safe havens in the West. Even if China does not welch on its promises, it will take a long time for confidence to return.

State-Labour Relations

As with other interest groups, Hong Kongese labour has been largely free to organize and express its demands. Unlike the other three ANICs, there has been no systematic attempt by the state either to incorporate the labour movement or to suppress its more militant elements. Even a strike by 2,000 of Cathay Pacific's cabin crew in January 1993 – a strike which caused serious disruption to the national air carrier and which could easily have been seen as threatening the national interest – failed to draw any direct action from the government (*Far Eastern Economic Review*, 4 February 1993). Nor has there been any significant attempt to influence wage levels (though immigration control has an obvious and very important indirect effect): such a move would contradict the government's 'positive non-interventionist' ideology. Legco is of course dominated by business interests, and organized labour is not taken very seriously. Draft bills relating to employment matters are typically circulated among Hong Kong's major employers for comment, but not to Hong Kong's trade unions (Ng Fung Sau 1988). A tripartite Labour Advisory Board, chaired by the Commissioner for Labour, has existed since the 1930s for consultation on labour law and policy formulation. However, the board has limited prerogatives, and is largely concerned only with the discussion of specific questions put to them.

Where the role of government *has* been important is with regard to legislation detailing minimum standards and conditions of employment, which has been increased since the 1960s (though the issues of wages and working hours remain basically unregulated). Similarly, legislation relating to Labour Tribunals introduced in the early 1970s means government can adjudicate over disputes of rights, though it can only offer advice on disputes of interest: the jurisdiction of the Labour Tribunal is restricted to claims arising from breaches of the terms of a contract of employment. However, the Labour Relations Service of the Labour Department, which is charged with the responsibiity of attempting conciliation, may claim some contribution to the industrial peace which has characterized Hong Kong since the early 1980s. The 1975 Labour Ordinance gave the Commissioner for Labour the legal power to conduct enquiries where trade disputes occurred or were suspected to be likely to occur, and to provide a conciliation and non-binding arbitration service. Since the Ordinance was introduced, the Labour Relations Service has claimed responsibility for the resolution of over 80 per cent of Hong Kong's recorded trade disputes (Ng and Sit 1989).

As in Britain itself, then, the state's direct role in industrial relations has been minimal, but unlike Britain trade unions have always been relatively weak and employees poorly organized. Employer prerogatives in Hong Kong firms are exceptionally strong. What the future holds is another matter. Labour unions have sent delegates to China to express concerns over the future rights of workers, but what the future relationship between the state and labour will be when China resumes control is as uncertain as any other aspect of Hong Kong's political future.

Employers

One of the most remarkable features of employment in Hong Kong is the typically small size of employment establishments, which gives Hong Kong far lower employment concentration ratios than in Korea or Singapore. According to Deyo (1989), in the 1980s the mean size of factories in Hong Kong was less than half that even in Taiwan, and around a third that in Korea and Singapore. Industrialization was in fact associated rather peculiarly with a significant *decline* in average firm sizes. In 1950 the mean size of manufacturing establishments was 55.2, declining to 45.1 in 1960, 27.8 in 1970, and 19.6 in 1980 (Tam 1990). During the 1980s the mean size reduced less rapidly, but still fell to 14.9 per in 1990 (table 5.10). In Singapore in 1990 the mean size of manufacturing establishments was a relatively massive 92.5.

As can be seen in table 5.10, in 1990 only 4.1 per cent of the manufacturing labour force worked in organizations employing 1,000 and over (down from 6.5 per cent in 1980), while 48.5 per cent worked in organizations employing less than 50 (up from 41.3 per cent in 1980). The importance of small establishments is similar to the case in Taiwan (compare table 4.11 in chapter four).

Another interesting feature is the relatively small differentials in wages in Hong Kong (table 5.11). Apart from the smallest organizations employing less than nine people, differences in wages by establishment size in Hong Kong are rather less than in Korea or even Taiwan (compare table 5.11 with tables 3.14 and 4.12). Indeed the highest wages are paid in medium rather large sized companies. This might be explained in relation to a context where there is minimal government interference in the workings of the labour market, and where trade unions are weak in large as well as small companies.

Overview of Employer Characteristics

England and Rear (1981) provide a typology of employing organizations in Hong Kong according to size, form and capital origin. They distinguish between small and large privately owned Cantonese, large privately owned Shanghainese, joint stock American, joint stock British, and government. To this list it would now be worth adding Japanese multinationals. In examining employer characteristics we will focus on the predominant small Chinese family run enterprise, but it is worth very briefly commenting on the other types of enterprise.

Table 5.10:   Manufacturing Employment by Firm Size in Hong Kong, 1980-1990

Number of persons engaged		1980	1985	1989	1990
1 – 9	Establishments	29,747	32,827	34,802	35,915
	Persons engaged	117,124	121,291	129,666	130,957
10 – 19	Establishments	6,970	6,760	7,270	6,366
	Persons engaged	93,898	90,156	97,739	87,038
20 – 49	Establishments	5,119	5,040	4,735	4,219
	Persons engaged	157,222	154,161	145,104	136,092
50 – 99	Establishments	2,111	2,016	1,919	1,520
	Persons engaged	144,974	137,110	131,443	113,673
100 – 199	Establishments	895	904	741	668
	Persons engaged	122,680	122,734	100,345	91,280
200 – 499	Establishments	410	393	346	302
	Persons engaged	120,353	117,266	103,178	91,307
500 – 999	Establishments	117	99	88	77
	Persons engaged	77,567	67,257	58,611	50,173
1000 – 1999	Establishments	36	23	24	18
	Persons engaged	46,752	29,143	29,510	22,565
2000 and over	Establishments	4	3	2	2
	Persons engaged	11,570	9,782	7,386	7,132
Total	Establishments	45,409	48,065	49,926	49,087
	Persons engaged	892,140	848,900	802,983	730,217

Source: Census and Statistics Department, Hong Kong, *Annual Digest of Statistics*, various issues.

The large family owned Shanghainese companies brought their business skills and technical knowledge to Hong Kong in the late 1940s. They concentrated their activities in cotton spinning and weaving: England and Rear (1981) estimate that in the 1970s 75 per cent of Hong Kong's cotton spinning industry was Shanghainese owned and managed. As employers they have an authoritarian reputation, being intolerant of trade unions, but with a paternalistic bent. In the 1950s and 1960s, various welfare benefits were provided to workers including free meals, dormitory accomodation for single workers, and subsidized flats for some married workers who displayed 'good conduct'. Shanghainese paternalism declined during the 1970s as the state increasingly took on welfare responsibilities: this, combined with the tight labour market, led to significant labour turnover problems which previously had not troubled the Shanghainese.

Table 5.11: Average Annual Earnings per Worker by Size of Establishment in Hong Kong Manufacturing, 1988 (HK$ '000)

Persons engaged	'000 HK$	%*
≤ 9	36.0	60.8
10 – 19	52.5	88.7
20 – 49	57.1	96.5
50 – 99	59.2	100.0
100 – 199	61.0	103.0
200 – 499	61.6	104.1
500 – 999	62.4	105.4
> 1,000	59.2	100.0
Overall average	55.4	

* Earnings compared to earnings of employees in establishments employing 1,000 or more persons.

Source: Census and Statistics Department, Hong Kong, *Hong Kong Annual Digest of Statistics 1990.*

American multinationals, concentrated in electronics, arrived in Hong Kong relatively late, and according to England and Rear (1981) they established their own style with individualistic relations with workers and generally a refusal to recognize trade unions. Japanese multinational manufacturers are also concentrated in electronics, but their style differs somewhat from the American. Although not offerring life time employment, seniority based promotion and the like, evidence suggests they do practice on-the-job training, intensive appraisals, and some aspects of total quality control (Tsang Chiu Hok 1992; Song Hui Szc 1992). Further, it has been suggested that job security is higher than in American companies, and that there are attempts to persuade employees to remain with the company through compensation schemes which include length of service and internal training elements (Nikei et al. 1983).

Locally based British firms have of course been engaged in a wide variety of sectors and are among the largest employers in Hong Kong. England and Rear comment that they have substantial political influence, their directors being well represented on the Executive and Legislative Councils and on government advisory committees. Like the large Shanghainese employers, paternalistic provision was commonplace up to the 1970s, but unlike the Shanghainese they have been relatively tolerant of trade unions. Following serious trade disputes in the late 1960s, the response of British companies (and public sector employers) was to set up joint consultative committees – a form of workforce consultation which has been widely practiced in Britain.

We will discuss the predominant small Chinese business organization following a brief caveat on employer-state relations.

Employer-State Relations

As mentioned, Hong Kong's business leaders, particularly the British but also large and increasing numbers of Chinese, are co-opted onto government committees and the like, and there is little doubt that Hong Kong's government has acted in a way which largely suits the business elite. In recent decades this means the state has come to shoulder the burden of welfare provision and has established a legal framework for employment relations, but has for the most part left capital free to work in the way it pleases, and indeed to come and go as it pleases, without interference. Employers Associations are relatively loosely organized and weak in Hong Kong (Ng Fung Sau 1988), but then the political environment has more or less obviated the need for employers to have a collective voice. The contrast with Singapore and Korea, both of whose governments have directed capital, albeit in different ways, could not be more striking. Hence, apart from the issue of the transfer of power back to China in 1997 (in which some Hong Kongese business leaders have taken a keen political interest) there has been little conflict between business and government.

As Hamilton (1992) argues, while Japanese and Korean capitalisms are creations of political economy, overseas Chinese capitalism in Hong Kong is a case of successful capitalism with little in the way of a state structure. Hamilton goes further, arguing that Chinese capitalism fills 'an economic space, not a political space', that boundaries cannot be put on economic endeavour, and that Chinese economic institutions, not just in Hong Kong but *wherever* overseas Chinese capitalists ply their trades, are 'extensions of relational networks'. Hence an understanding of (predominant) Chinese small business enterprise in Hong Kong is dependent less on locating the form of capitalism to 'a time in history or a place in the world' (the political economy approach) than on coming to terms with the logic of Chinese business organization which is basically the same at different times and in different places. Without necessarily accepting the whole sweep of Hamilton's argument, he does have a point – compare the discussion below with that of Chinese small businesses in Taiwan in chapter four.

Management in the Small Chinese Business

The characteristics of Chinese family businesses have been related to their origins in pre-Communist mainland China, where the environment was one of patrimonial authority, aloof government, a freedom for entrepreneurs, and traditions of equal inheritance (Redding and Whitley 1990). The Chinese Confucian-informed culture is said to impart a respect for authority and a natural acceptance of hierarchy (Tricker 1990). These translate, it is suggested, into peculiar features of business management and specific kinds of relations with employees.

Chinese family businesses are highly centralized with a heavy reliance on one dominant executive (Redding and Whitley 1990). There is little in the way of a divorce of ownership and control. Of course, this would very likely be characeristic of *any* small business anywhere in the world, but Tricker (1990) finds that even in larger Chinese enterprises the same centralization of decision making holds true. Tricker (1990, p.204) comments that:

Responsibility for day to day activities of production and operations may be delegated to managers, but even then with frequent re-arrangements and what would be considered, by Western executives, interference in delegated responsibilities. Responsibility for financial and personal matters typically remains with the owner.

In a study which compared Hong Kong and UK firms, Reid and Lee (1989) found that planning was far more centralized in the Hong Kong firm, confirming the above point. At the same time they documented a lesser degree of formality and institutionalization of the planning process, and this appears to be repeated in other aspects of business management.

Some of the potential dysfunctions of the typically small size of Chinese businesses are overcome by the use of relational networks between different businesses called *guanxi* networks (Hamilton 1992). Horizontal relations between businesses, often based on kinship and sub-ethnic ties, enable small businesses to carry on activities which would be virtually impossible for a small business in other circumstances. Hence in Hong Kong small businesses can manage, among themselves, to export to the rest of the world: most exports are handled by local import-export firms, which are themselves often small (the mean size of Hong Kong's import-export firms was 5.6 persons in 1989 according to a government survey), and which network with 'related' small manufacturing organizations. In order to meet specific orders, the manufacturing firms will then if necessary network among themselves, for instance to meet a particularly large order (Castells 1992).

Within the Chinese business organization relations are typically described as 'paternalistic' or 'benevolent autocratic', and these are held to derive from the Chinese acceptance of the hierarchical principles of Confucian social order. However, perhaps even more important to the Chinese than a generalized respect for authority, is a concern with the family. For the business owner, as for the employee:

the firm is just an instrument for the service of the family. The locus of primary loyalty lies outside the firm. It is the persistence and aggrandizement of the family tradition, not the firm, which commands loyalty and commitment (Tam 1990, p.176).

Further:

Firms as seen as family property in the Chinese universe, and this proves to be an insurmountable barrier for integrating the employer and the employees. The nurtured route is reserved for those who are related in one way or another to the owning family whereas the self-made route is trodden by those who are not. Those who are related will be on a fast track, ending up eventually in the ownership echelon. Those who are not related are given limited career movement, and they face an upper ceiling barring them from the top (Tam 1990, p.173).

Hence Tam characterizes the relationship between employer and employee as one of *distrust*, and documents a job insecurity problem for the employee, and a high labour turnover problem for the employer. In such a circumstance, 'owners are forced to centralize, delegation is a risky affair, and direct supervision becomes necessary' (p.177). The lack of loyalty and trust is also reflected in extensive subcontracting – the market is considered more reliable than employees – and this in turn helps explain the drive towards the further proliferation of small businesses. Employees, on the other hand, finding their career aspirations blocked by the familial monopoly over ownership and control, are likely to use the organization as a short term means of developing sufficient capital and skills to set up their own small business. This is confirmed by surveys of entrepreneurs in Hong Kong.

Another feature of Chinese family businesses which contributes to the persistence of small firms is inheritance patterns. According to Chinese customs, wealth is inherited not by the eldest son; rather wealth is distributed among *all* the sons. As Redding and Whitley (1990, p.100) point out:

Even if in practice unequal inheritance is practiced in many expatriate Chinese communities, the strong cultural preferences for equal division of family property acts as a constraint on the reproduction of large, stable economic enterprises controlling substantial resources. As long as they are viewed as part of the family asetts and governed by family obligations, such enterprises, by being continually broken up, are unlikely to continue as major economic actors.

In fact few firms survive beyond two or three generations.

Combining these various features of Chinese family businesses – family centredness, equal inheritance, employer-employee distrust, and extensive *guanxi* networking – together with limited state intervention, produces an 'ideal type' which Tam calls a *centrifugal* pattern of development in Hong Kong, which contrasts with a *centripetal* pattern in Japan. Such a pattern has its advantages – flexibility and market responsiveness as we have documented, and Tam adds rapid innovation diffusion to the list. It also has its limitations, primarily those related to technological advance and R&D capability which typically depend on large organizations with long term objectives and large amounts of available capital. The Taiwanese state supports its Chinese family businesses in an attempt to overcome their weaknesses; the Hong Kong state does not.

Employer-Labour Relations

Turner et al. (1980; 1991), England and Rear (1981) and Ng and Sit (1989), have provided the most detailed accounts of workplace industrial relations in Hong Kong, and this section draws on these works. Employee relations within small Chinese enterprises, where the owner may also be a worker, hardly call for formalized communication and bargaining mechanisms. The owner has virtually complete managerial prerogatives, and communication and bargaining are direct. Typically there will be a core of family labour and skilled permanent employees, and labour sub-contracting, piecework and outwork will be used to meet demand fluctuations. Showing little loyalty, non-family employees will be mobile between firms in response to even minor variations in pay, and some of them will use the firm instrumentally to develop skills which can form the basis of their own small businesses (Ng and Sit 1989).

Large numbers of highly mobile casual labourers are sometimes organized into 'gangs', whose leader will offer their collective services to small companies for short periods of time. This is known as the 'ambulatory' system. But even though they will sometimes work under the roof of the contractor for significant periods, the Principal is exempt from the normal employer liabilities of provision of sickness benefit, holidays, redundancy pay and the like. Ng and Sit (1989, p.170) comment that:

The lack of unequivocal employment bonds defining relationships with and within the 'ambulatory' work group hence reduces these workers to a marginal legal position, generally held to fall outside the protective ambit of the Employment Ordinance.

Gang mobility does enable workers to take advantage in tight labour market conditions in order to improve their remuneration. But this is short run – long term income is unstable and job securtiy fragile. The benefits to employers of such a system, on the other hand, are clear: informal workers give a production flexibility such that production capacity can be cut or multiplied literally overnight. They are also relatively cheap, giving savings which off-set the fact that average labour costs in Hong Kong are around five times those on the mainland in the Shenzhen Special Economic Zone (Chu Yin Wah 1992b).

Hence the relationship between employer and employee for large but not calculable numbers of the population is unstable, distant, and lacking in responsibility and commitment. Indeed, ambulatory and outworkers, who are often paid only piece rates, do not have an 'employer' in the full sense of the term.

Larger organizations, as we mentioned earlier, tend to be more paternalistic, though welfare provision has become less important since the 1970s. On the whole managerial prerogatives are strong and unchallenged. Collective bargaining does still occur in the traditional trades between craft unions and employers' associations or individual firms, but this tradition derives from pre-industrial craft and trade guilds, and has lost much of its efficacy. Rates vary widely from the standards established in union-employer association bargaining, and the rates established are not in any case legally binding.

In the manufacturing sector, collective bargaining is almost non-existent, especially in the labour intensive clothing and electronics industries, and the same is true of the private sector services. However, trade disputes have occasionally broken out over specific issues, and these will be discussed below. Perhaps surprisingly, the restaurant trade is exceptional in having well organized unions which have established collective agreements with some larger employers, and which serve as a benchmark for the rest of the trade.

Ng and Sit (1989, p.63) describe 'the closest approximation to modern collective bargaining in the Western sense' as occurring in the public sector, and in one utility company (Cable and Wireless which specializes in telecommunications and recognizes a house union). In these cases collective agreements cover substantive issues such as wages and holidays, and they also have procedural rules relating to grievances, strikes, etc. It is also in the public sector that British style joint consultative committees (JCCs) have been adopted. (JCCs were encouraged by the government since the late 1960s as a means of improving communications between employer and employee, and are similar in intent to Labour Management Relations Committees in Korea.) JCCs are not a legal requirement and have largely been ignored elsewhere.

Many legislative items were passed during the 1960s and 1970s which prescribe minimum standards on health and safety, maternity leave, redundancy pay, holidays, etc., and as we shall see below increasing numbers of employees have taken advantage of the more favourable legal climate. But apart from this, and except in a handful of exceptional cases, employees rely on market forces and the benevolence of the employer for their quality of working life.

Labour

Since the late 1950s legislation has been increasingly favourable not just to the rights of individual labourers, but to organized labour. The right to strike (which, interestingly, is not specified in British law) was granted in the 1961 Trades Union Ordinance, and successive legislation via the 1968 Employment Ordinance, the 1975 Labour Relations Ordinance, and a 1977 ammendment to the 1961 Trades Union Ordinance, all strengthened the legal framework for the existence and development of independent trade unions (Turner et al. 1980). Yet trade unions remain weak, poorly organized and ineffective except in the public sector, and official industrial action is uncommon. In this section we will examine the incidence of disputes and their resolution, then the characteristics of Hong Kongese labour organizations, before offering some explanations for the weakness of organized labour.

Industrial Conflict

For the whole of the post-war period labour disputes in Hong Kong which have led to work stoppages have been quite rare, and during the 1980s have declined to negligible proportions. Table 5.12 shows the incidence of work stoppages and the number of worker days lost from 1951 to 1990.

Table 5.12:   Work Stoppages in Hong Kong, 1980-1990

	Work stoppages	Worker days lost
1951-60*	7.8	37,689
1961-70*	18.3	38,968
1971-75*	35.6	30,487
1976-79*	37.5	21,559
1980	37	21,069
1981	49	15,319
1982	34	17,960
1983	11	2,530
1984	11	3,121
1985	3	1,160
1986	9	4,907
1987	14	2,773
1988	8	2,345
1989	7	3,270
1990	15	3,495

* Annual average.

Source: Census and Statistics Department, Hong Kong, *Hong Kong Annual Digest of Statistics*, various issues; Ng Sek Hong and Sit Fung Shuen (1989).

During 1967 there were an unknown number of strikes connected with the Hong Kong riots and disturbances, which in turn were related to the cultural revolution in China. These were deemed illegal and ommitted from public records (Turner et al. 1991), and public order legislation was used effectively in their curtailment (Deyo 1989). Up to that point the Communist led Federation of Trade Unions (FTU) had overtly led strike actions, but from then increasingly took a 'background' role, giving help or guidance to strike committees but assuming a more conciliatory role. In 1982 Deng Xiao Ping announced China's intention to resume control over Hong Kong in 1997, and from that point the FTU leadership, in sympathy with China's concern to avoid capital flight, discouraged strikes 'in the interest of Hong Kong's prosperity and stability' (Turner et al. 1991, p.70). While the incidence of work stoppages were declining steadily during the 1970s, these events help explain the abrupt decline from 1982.

However, officially classified 'trade diputes', which usually imply a breakdown of negotiations or a refusal by the employer to negotiate in the first place, and which frequently involve non-strike direct action such as a sit-in, have increased in incidence from an average of 113 per year during 1968-1974, to over 150 per year in the 1980s. 18 per cent of all trade diputes from 1968 to 1986 were due to wages issues, but the majority were caused by issues of employment security. Trade disputes are typically initiated by small groups of workers, often in unorganized industries and without trade union support. Also on the rise have been the number of 'grievances' referred to Hong Kong labour officers. The numbers recorded have increased from an average of around 5,000 per year in the 1970s to around 20,000 per year in the 1980s. 'Grievances' are much more likely to concern matters of 'right' as opposed to the substantive demands characteristic of work stoppages and trade disputes. Turner et al. (1991, p.77) conclude that:

the combined evidence of the increased number of spontaneous trade diputes, of the extraordinary and continuing rise in officially handled grievance claims, and of our own survey on grievances at work, suggests a considerable body of workplace discontent which finds only limited satisfaction in public or employer policies – and a negligible expression through trade unionism.

It would be wrong, therefore, to characterize Hong Kong employees as being either 'happy with their lot' or acquiescent. Rather, the failure of trade unions to effectively organize and lead workers in the pursuit of their interests and the parallel rise in the ability of employees to seek legal redress, has meant workers have been more likely to attempt to settle their grievances and disputes with employers through the services of the state and through the law rather than through the trade union and organized collective action.

Trade Union Organization

In the post-war period trade union membership reached its height in 1977 and has consistently declined since then. Table 5.13 shows trends in membership and union density since 1967.

As well as the decline in union density since its peak in 1977, table 5.13 also shows a fragmented, and increasingly fragmenting, trade union movement, with increasing numbers of small trade unions. The two competing national organizations of trade unions are the Hong Kong Federation of Trade Unions (FTU) which is pro-Beijing, and the Hong Kong and Kowloon Trades Union Council (TUC) which is pro-KMT. There are also independent trade unions. Their fortunes since since 1968 are documented in table 5.14.

The percentage of trade union members belonging to unions affiliated to the FTU and TUC has declined since the 1970s, though their total membership has not collapsed. More significant has been the failure of national organizations to

Table 5.13: Trade Union Membership and Trade Union Density in Hong Kong, 1967-1986

	Working population ('000)	No. of trade unions	Trade union membership ('000)	Trade union density (%)
1967		224	165.6	
1970		272	196.3	
1973		283	295.7	
1977	1,926.0	313	404.3	21.0
1980	2,370.0	357	384.3	16.2
1983	2,540.0	382	352.3	13.9
1986	2,701.5	403	367.3	13.6

Source: Hong Kong Registrar of Trade Unions, *Annual Reports*, cited in Ng Fung Sau (1988).

Table 5.14: Trade Unions Affiliation in Hong Kong, 1973-1986

	Membership					
	FTU	%*	TUC	%*	Independent trade union	%*
1973	170,047	(57.0)	35,391	(12.0)	45,340	(15.0)
1978	214,047	(54.0)	33,471	(8.0)	76,727	(19.0)
1983	167,993	(47.7)	34,564	(9.8)	112,327	(35.9)
1986	169,802	(46.2)	31,477	(8.6)	166,066	(45.2)

* Percentage of total membership.

Source: Hong Kong Registrar of Trade Unions *Annual Reports*, cited in Ng Fung Sau (1988).

recruit while the working population has been rapidly growing. On the other hand independent trade unions, while not growing sufficiently to prevent an overall decline in union density, have assumed a greatly enhanced importance in Hong Kong. These unions are mostly public sector white collar unions which organize groups such as teachers, nurses, social workers and even office clerks in the civil bureaucracy (Ng and Sit 1989).

Perhaps even more remarkable than the figures in tables 5.13 and 5.14 are those found in table 5.15, which show a decline in unionization in all sectors except public services.

As Turner et al. (1991) point out, while public sector white collar unionization has advanced, it has receded almost everywhere else. 'Islands' of unionization are still important in some sectors, e.g. transport workers and public utility workers,

Table 5.15:   Sectoral Distribution of Union Membership in Hong Kong, 1976 and 1986

	% of workforce unionized in 1976	% of workforce unionized in 1986
Manufacturing	11	6
Construction	15	8
Transport and communications	63	38
Public utilities	50	24
Financial services	18*	11
Trade and catering		7
Other private sector services	19	18
Public services	38	50

* % for Financial services and Trade and catering.

Source: Turner *et al.* (1991).

but even here union strength is on the decline. Most remarkable from table 5.15 is the exceptionally low unionization rate in manufacturing industries, the area in which one would normally expect one of the highest levels of union activity. By 1986 the percentage of the manufacturing work force which was organized had fallen to a mere six. Deyo (1989) contrasts the difference between the light industries employing relatively unskilled persons characteristic of Hong Kong, and the heavy industries employing relatively skilled persons in larger companies in Korea, to explain Hong Kong's lesser potential for proletarian consciousness and therefore trade union organization, but a *six per cent* density can surely not be explained by these structural factors alone.

Trade Union Weakness

Why then, are are Hong Kong's unions weak in a legal and economic context in many respects highly favourable to trade union organization? The *laissez faire* economists might argue that the market, being allowed to do its allocative work without interference, gives Hong Kongese workers the best deal they could expect without the need for trade union representation. From this point of view the public sector would be the only exception where non-market mechanisms for wage determination might be necessary. Further, to the extent that the market has 'worked', Hong Kongese employees enjoy job opportunities and opportunities for self development in a context of rapid growth. That is, Hong Kong's employees enjoy a degree of real self-determination. But the experiences of other countries would tell us that in itself such an argument is inadequate.

Another popular but problematic argument is that the Hong Kongese are family centred and that in work they are individualistic and materialistic, which works against solidaristic collective organization. Again in itself this is unconvincing, and is based on a stereotypical view of Hong Kong's work force. However, in relation to the small business sector, there may be a point here. As we described, small businesses provide a precarious existence for the bulk of the work force, the employment relationship is tentative, and labour turnover is high. In such circumstances unionization would be difficult regardless of the orientations of the workers, but of course the circumstances are likely to create an individualistic mentality which might in turn reinforce a difficulty in union organization. Further, in the 'good times' when unions would normally be most likely to be able to recruit, these workers *are* able to take advantage of market forces and demand higher wages without a trade union.

A general problem for the trade union movement has been the traditional split between the pro-Communist and pro-KMT factions. Significant parts of Hong Kong's population may understandably be wary of aligning themselves to a political ideology. And further, the pro-Communist FTU, which was traditionally the most active and militant, has increasingly taken a 'soft' line in the light of Beijing's desire to prevent capital flight in advance of 1997. Political in-fighting among national trade union leaders has continued through the 1980s and into the 1990s, trade unions have continued to be fragmented, and the independent trade unions which have grown in importance have parochial interests restricted to a few sectors (Turner et al. 1991).

Three more general factors may help account for trade union weakness in Hong Kong, although again none of them in themselves are sufficient explanations. First, both employers and employees have accepted a role for the state in the settlement of trade disputes, and to a lesser extent employer grievances. To the extent that the state has been successful in resolving disputes to the satisfaction of the parties concerned the need for direct employer-employee bargaining is obviated. Secondly, the ideology of employers in Hong Kong is generally one of antagonism towards trade unions, which are seen as unnecessary fetters on management prerogatives. Union organizers and sympathizers are not unlikely, if found out, to be faced with dismissal (Deyo 1989). Thirdly, and perhaps most importantly, the successive waves of legal and illegal immigrant labour from mainland China, which have accounted for a large amount of Hong Kong's expanding working population, in the 1960s and 1970s in particular, and especially in manufacturing industries, are extremely difficult to organize, and may be used by employers to undermine the organization of other workers.

Conclusions and Prospects

Over a century of British colonial rule has left Hong Kong an emphatically Chinese city. This is something of an irony when we compare Hong Kong to Singapore, where 'Western' and 'Japanese' values and institutional forms have had a much more pervasive influence since independence under a Chinese dominated ruling party. Hong Kong's 'Chinese-ness' finds wide cultural and social expression, but most important here is its expression in business. 'Positive non-interventionism' has allowed Chinese entrepreneurs and Chinese business organization to dominate large and important sectors of the economy with relatively little direct interference from the state. But while this has had its advantages, there have been disadvantages, for labour obviously but also for economic development.

For large segments of the labour force, the absence of state discrimination against small business organizations has provided wide opportunities for economic advance and personal and family development. Hong Kong has countless examples of 'poor man made rich'. However, with small business dynamism comes, for many others, a precarious existence and an absence of the rights normally afforded 'employees'. The extent of mistreatment, discrimination and the like, is impossible to calculate but is undoubtedly big. The poor state of collective representation is reinforced by a failure of nationally organized trade unions to take a more commanding role in advancing the interests of workers, and by the waves of immigration which have been in part responsible for dampening the effects on workers' wage increases a tight labour market might otherwise have had. However, and contrary to popular perceptions, the state has had a significant role in limiting the negative aspects of Hong Kong's 'free labour market', first by providing channels and mechanisms for the airing of grievances and the settlement of trade disputes in the absence of mechanisms internal to firms, and secondly in its provision of welfare benefits, and particularly housing, which has reduced the extent of the worst poverty.

For economic development, positive non-interventionism has allowed Hong Kong's highly flexible industrial structure, and in particular the export oriented sectors, to do its work in 'naturally' adjusting to market variations and changes in protectionist policies in the advanced nations. But on the negative side Hong Kong's industry has failed to up-grade technologically, to diversify into the highest value sectors, and to develop anything remotely resembling a technological and R&D capability of its own. Hong Kong has remained highly dependent on traditional clothing and textiles industries, and on its role as international subcontractor in electronics. The country has serious structural problems.

All this has been over-shadowed in recent years by, on the one hand, the absolute decline of manufacturing, and on the other, the re-emergence of Hong Kong as entrepot. Hong Kong has increasingly relocated its manufacturing capacity on the mainland, and employment has shifted to the services, especially those associated with the import-export business. Both these developments are occurring due to

China's trade liberalization since 1977, and indicate an economic integration in advance of the political integration scheduled for 1997.

Extrapolating from recent developments, Hong Kong's future role would appear to be likely to continue to focus on export-import trade, and on the provision of financial and commercial services, perhaps increasingly to the vast and rapidly developing area of South East China. The government's allowing the manufacturing sector to decline, however, is highly questionable. The resulting increased economic integration with and dependence on China will arguably leave Hong Kong more vulnerable to Beijing's control even if Beijing does not welch on its promise to allow a significant political independence after 1997. However, given the extreme political uncertainties which exist at the time of writing, and which seem unlikely to go away in the run up to 1997, it is impossible to take a commentary on the future of industry and labour in Hong Kong any further.

Chapter Six: Labour and Industry in East Asia

In the light of the failure of conventional economics to account for the rapidity and evident success of East Asian industrialization, sociological accounts, particularly those of the Weberian persuasion, have become fashionable. There are two popular schools of thought. One attributes the characteristics of East Asian entrepreneurialism, business organization and work ethics to pre-modern belief systems – usually neo-Confucianism – which have continued into the modern period, and which we term here the *new culturist* perspective. The second calls itself *institutionalism*. It also attributes modern East Asian organizational forms to pre-modern cultures, but defines culture more broadly as a set of social arrangements and patterns of behaviour. Both these perspectives, it is argued, have added to our understanding of East Asian patterns of modernization, but equally they can be guilty of post-hoc rationalization and carry the danger of determinism.

Following a discussion of these different explanations of East Asian economic success, a discussion of contemporary change in East Asia is provided which lays emphasis on the (sometimes differing) interests, values and motives of the actors in the East Asian economy. The intention is to provide a summary account focussed on recent and present developments which shows how the inter-relations, and sometimes conflict, between the actors fashion the modern industrial orders of East Asia.

Explanations of East Asian Business Success

Political Economy

There can be little doubt that foreign aid (in the cases of Korea and Taiwan) and the inheritance of infrastructural facilities (in the cases of Singapore and Hong Kong) gave the ANICs a useful basis upon which their programmes of industrialization were built. They were also fortunate in embarking on export oriented growth strategies just as world trade and international capital mobility were taking off. But as Clegg et al. (1986) have demonstrated, economists have failed to provide convincing arguments for the superior performance of the ANICs *vis à vis* competitor regions, in Africa and Latin America for instance, which in some respects were in a better position in the 1950s.

In the 1980s and into the 1990s, it is in the face of *adverse* world trade conditions that the ANICs, and the Asia-Pacific region as a whole, have continued to defy conventional economic logic. Foreign aid has long since gone, Western markets have been far less 'soft' since the end of the 1970s, and there have been increasing measures taken by the West to make East Asian goods less competitive in American and European markets. Yet it is in exactly this period that Japan has emerged as undisputed world leader in many of the higher value product areas, and the ANICs have restructured rapidly to become more capital and knowledge intensive. Such has been the advance that Kaplinsky (1991) could describe the US, with detailed justification, as being in danger of 'shooting itself in the foot' by insisting on pursuing issues of intellectual property rights in East Asia.

The ASEAN4 as well are doing better than might be expected. Although embarking on export oriented strategies at a less opportune time than the ANICs (Nolan 1990), success in attracting multinational direct manufacturing investments (recently especially from the ANICs themselves) to become well established *export platforms* in labour intensive sectors has led on to the more ambitious goal (for Malaysia and Thailand at least) of achieving NIC status.

If conventional economics has failed to explain relative economic success, the political economists of the world dependencies school – the *dependendistas* - have not fared any better, as explained in detail by Limqueco et al. (1989). Faced with overwhelming evidence of East Asian economic success, the original dependency theorists who argued that a *de-development* of Asia was occurring had to admit the existence of development, but characterized this as *dependent development*. In the latter characterization, technology and the international division of labour are still under the control of the 'international bourgeoisie', and there remains a hierarchy of core-periphery relations. The difference is that the international division of labour occurs *within* industrial (and tertiary) activities. But while a hierarchy of core-periphery relations clearly *does* exist – and most strikingly so in the Asia-Pacific region – the experience of the ANICs, and more recently the ASEAN4, would nonetheless suggest that there is, as Limqueco et al. (1989, p.176) put it, 'substantial domestic room for maneouvre ... even with a strong presence of MNCs'.

None of this is to deny the importance of world market economics, or the inter-dependencies which exist between national economies, and one of the main purposes of this book is to explain the dependency relations within which states, capital and labour operate. It is, indeed, exactly such politico-economic understandings which have enabled governments to formulate strategies for successful economic growth. What it does suggest is that the fate of the Asia-Pacific nations was not and is not pre-determined and that in order to understand industrialization and contemporary economic change we need to examine the ways in which the economic actors have interacted to fashion dynamic economies. This has been the intention throughout this book. But before going on to draw some comparisons and conclusions, we will turn attention to two theoretical perspectives which have emerged in the last decade or so which claim a superiority to economics in their explanatory power.

The New Culturists

The *new culturists* find a more or less direct link between an East Asian 'culture', usually defined as a set of values, and a set of business practices which lead to economic success. For Kolm (1985) it is *Buddhism* which provides the values. For instance the Buddhist idea of linear progress with no limit to possible improvement results in:

the pursuit of unlimited improvement which characterizes these countries. A Western factory normally sets itself a quality goal – for example 95 per cent of the items produced free of defects – and is satisfied if it arrives at that goal. This never happens for a Japanese company: the objective is always 100 per cent perfection, one can therefore practically always achieve an improvement over the actual situation, one can always make progress, and they attempt to do so. ... The idea of perfection, the notion of the perfect thing, is far more present in this way of thinking than in the West (Kolm 1985, p.236-7).

For the majority of *new culturists* however, it is not Buddhism, but Confucianism, which underpins business organization, methods, and ultimately economic growth, and it is on the latter which we shall focus.

In a book published in 1979 Herman Kahn hypothesized that the common cultural roots of the East Asian countries, under the world market conditions of the post-war period, gave a comparative advantage for successful business activity. The common cultural roots lay in *neo-Confucianism*, and during the past decade or so many scholars, journalists, politicians and other pundits have implicitly accepted, or explicitly argued for, a *neo-Confucian* explanation of economic growth in Japan and the ANICs.

Classical Confucianism derives from Confucius's teachings in China around 500 B.C. Confucius (Kong Fu Ze) was a high civil servant known for his wisdom who came to be surrounded by disciples who recorded his teachings. He preached worldly, practical ethics for day-to-day behaviour derived from his understanding of Chinese history (Hofstede and Bond 1988). *Neo-Confucianism*, associated with the teachings of Chu Hsi around 250 B.C., accepted a 'supernatural order' or 'divine law', but placed emphasis on the same practical guide to behaviour. Chu Hsi said that observance of the moral codes for action laid down by Confucius was the Mandate of Heaven (Kim Byung Whan 1992). Neo-Confucianism identifies 'five human relationships' and mandates 'ten righteousnesses' as guides for behaviour within those relationships as follows: the father should have a deep love of the son, who should display filial piety; the ruler should act benevolently towards the minister, who should be loyal; the husband should act righteously towards the wife, who in return should be submissive; elders should display kindness towards juniors, who should behave deferentially; and friends should act with fidelity towards each other. The only equal relationship specified is the friend-friend relation, but even here hierarchy is likely to enter the relation, for instance if one friend is older than the other. Kim Byung Whan (1992) hence suggests that the common theme is superior and subordinate: the superior is responsible for justice; the subordinate must behave with obedience. The behaviours of the superior should be guided by the 'five essential virtues' of benevolence, righteousness, wisdom, propriety, and trustworthiness.

Neo-Confucianism spread later from China to Korea and Japan to become important ideologies in pre-modern times, and was carried by Chinese migrants to Singapore and the Malacca Straits (and elsewhere in South East Asia) in the nineteenth and twentieth centuries. The classic texts of Confucianism have been far less widely read among Asians than, say, the Bible among Europeans and Americans (or indeed among Asians!), and at those periods in history when the texts were studied, this was usually only among the literate elites. Only a tiny minority of East Asians today could even recite the 'ten righteousnesses' or 'five essential relationships' (though Lee Kuan Yew is trying to change this for the ethnic Chinese Singaporean population). Nonetheless, it is claimed that the neo-Confucian ethical codes of conduct within relationships are rigidly adhered to in day-to-day behaviour among the majority of Japanese, Koreans and Chinese.

Whilst the most naive of the *new culturists* have simply stated that since conventional economic explanations of East Asian business success have failed, the explanation must lie in 'culture', more serious scholars have attempted to demonstrate how *neo-Confucianism* provides the ideological or spiritual underpinnings for capitalistic development. As intimated earlier in the book, these scholars accept Max Weber's (1930) thesis of a cultural basis for economic activity, but reject any notion that Western Protestantism is the only, or the best, philosophic foundation for capitalism (which, rightly or wrongly, is how Weber has often been interpreted as arguing). Shepard et al. (1989) have put the more serious version forcefully. For Weber (1930), central to Protestantism (to be accurate, specifically Calvinism) is the doctrine of *vocation*: man is naturally idle or sinful, so work, which implies delayed gratification, is the highest form of moral activity, and this leads to an accumulation of capital rather than consumption. Thrift, savings and investment become fundamental values. The equivalent in neo-Confucian belief, say Shepard et al. (1989), is the search for harmony (*chung yung*) which is achieved by behaviour which benefits the whole of society, and also leads to the self-denial and ascetism necessary for capital accumulation.

Also central to Calvinist belief is the doctrine of *predestination*. Since man cannot know whether he is elected or damned, he behaves as if he is elected and looks for a sign of his salvation – i.e. material well-being. Predestination is an individual affair, so this gives rise to a rugged individualism which translates into entrepreneurial behaviour. Neo-Confucianism, on the other hand, advocates the ceaseless pursuit of perfection (*jen*) which translates into the behaviours associated with the 'ten righteousnesses' within the 'five human relationships'. This underpins what Shepard et al. (1989) call a 'humanistic bureaucracy' and a 'humanistic approach to management', and this is a key area where they take issue with Weber. Weber, they say, saw filial piety and familism as barriers to the *impersonal rationality* which characterizes capitalism. But for the *new culturists*, neo-Confucian human relations can *underpin* capitalist endeavour. That is, employees are treated like family members, who reciprocate with hard work as if they *were* family members. And, 'seeking employee welfare can be as strong a motivating mechanism for capitalistic activities as the profit motive' (Shepard et al. 1989, p.319).

Kim Byung Whan (1992, p.77) similarly describes the five human relationships as 'an almost perfect set of ethical codes for industrial society': loyalty to the ruler translates into company loyalty; the benevolence of parents translates into a benevolent management style; senior-junior relationships translate into an acceptance of hierarchy; and trustworthiness among friends becomes cooperation between co-workers. The 'humanist' line of argument is also pursued by Riddle and Sours (1984) who claim that Confucianism gives rise to competitiveness in services as well as manufacturing, because of the collectivist as opposed to the individualist orientation. In their words, 'an innate cultural valuing of human interaction provides a crucial competitive edge in the effective functioning of service provision' (p.196).

The humanist argument, of course, assumes that the neo-Confucian ethical code of conduct applies in work organizations as much as it does in other, including family, institutions. For Pascale and Athos (1981, p.192), herein lies another key difference between the East and the West:

By an accident of history, we in the West have evolved a culture that separates man's spiritual life from his institutional life. This turn of events has had a far-reaching impact on modern Western organizations. Our companies freely lay claim to mind and muscle, but they are culturally discouraged from intruding upon our personal lives and deeper beliefs.

By implication a great advantage of Eastern forms of capitalism, and one which Pascale and Athos, among others, believe the West should copy, is the blurring of distinctions between work and non-work life which in the West are associated with an instrumental, calculative orientation on the part of both employer and employee.

But while the *new culturist* perspective on the success of East Asian capitalism has proved seductive to so many scholars from Eastern *and* Western countries, there are so many problems with the perspective that it would prove tedious to list them all here. Instead, we focus on four key problems: of post-hoc rationalization; of gross assumptions about causal links; of racism; and of an absence of historical understanding. These problems bedevil all the *new culturist* accounts of East Asian economic success to greater or lesser degrees.

The *post-hoc* nature of *new culturist* accounts was discussed briefly in chapter one. The problem is that sociologists and psychologists have decided *after* success has become evident to seek the explanation *in the very culture* which culturists previously held, if anything, to stand in the way of success. The re-interpretation of classic texts is for this reason suspicious, and unconvincing (Lubeck 1992). Further, there is a tendency simply to attribute the residual, unexplained phenomena – e.g. that portion of economic growth which cannot be accounted for by conventional economics, or those aspects of organization structure which do not fit the logic of conventional organization theory – to 'culture'. Kim Byung Whan (1992, p.87), for instance, in an attempt to explain relatively high age-wage profiles in Korea and Japan, proceeds with the following methodology:

In order to identify the socio-cultural effect on earnings, all other possible factors affecting age/pay relationships will be taken into account at first. ... As there is no other plausible model so far to which one can attribute the remaining effect, it will be attributed to the socio-cultural factor, namely neo-Confucianism in Korea and Japan.

Whether such an approach is scientific is not a debate we will enter into here. What it does not do is further our understanding.

The second problem, or perhaps set of problems, of the *new culturist* account relates to the nature of causal links between culture and economic success which are posited. These problems stem from different interpretations of what is important in the 'root culture', and through what mechanisms these translate into economic success. The accounts of Shepard *et al.* (1989) and Riddle and Sours (1984) refer to the 'humanism' of neo-Confucian ethics. Others, however, have stressed the importance attached to education or, as Hofstede and Bond (1988), a Confucian work ethic. The latter authors identify a 'cluster of values' which they refer to collectively as 'Confucian dynamism': these are perseverance, thrift, a sense of shame, and the hierarchical ordering of relationships by status. The problem is, the more one reads, the longer becomes the list of values identified by various authors as representing the essence of neo-Confucianism. If there is confusion about the 'root values', then establishing causal links is clearly going to be difficult. But the confusion becomes magnified when we find that the things to which culture are linked can also vary. While Shepard et al. emphasize the link between a 'humanistic culture' and a 'humanistic bureaucracy' and 'humanistic management' (with life-time employment, consensus decision making, etc.) which in turn accounts for business success, they also link a neo-Confucian 'perseverance' to successful manufacturing methods:

The focus on the ceaseless pursuit of renovation finds its expression in modern East Asian management practices, especially in quality control (QC) and zero defects (ZD) programmes. The process of improving quality or pursuing zero defects has such deep cultural roots that people in other cultures may sometimes find it difficult to understand, learn or adopt (Shepard et al. 1989, p.314).

(Readers will note the similarity between this 'neo-Confucian' account and Kolm's 'Buddhist' account of Eastern quality management.)

The stress on education in some accounts of neo-Confucian root values has the most obvious link to economic success. A literate and numerate population is obviously going to have an advantage over an uneducated one. Bond and Hofstede's (1988) 'cluster of values' which make up 'Confucian work dynamism', on the other hand, are held to underpin the sorts of entrepreneurship associated with

East Asia. And a final *new culturist* argument worth mentioning is that which links the predilection on the part of workers to behave deferentially or obediently towards their bosses to business success. In this case neo-Confucian *human relations* are again the root values, but the emphasis here is on employee acceptance of managerial prerogatives rather than employer paternalism. This perspective would perhaps find support in the fascinating (and highly controversial) work of Japanese pycho-analyst Takeo Doi (1973) who argues that the Japanese carry a child-like craving for dependence (*amae*) into their adult lives.

The confusion arising from all these different interpretations of what is important in the 'root culture' (and indeed what *is* the root culture), and how the root values link through to particular practical behaviours which account for economic success, are considerable, though I have tried to summarize some of the causal links popularly identified in figure 6.1.

Are we to take it that the important values are hierarchical human relations, or a reverence for education, or persistence, or thrift or shame, or some combination of these and/or others? And is it company paternalism, authoritarian management, worker obedience, employee literacy, management techniques, or simply a strong work ethic which provides the link through from culture to business success? Further, why are the causal links between culture, values, and action only one way? Surely there can be no doubt, for instance, that mass education has given the ability to challenge the expectation of worker obedience; and surely economic success, to the extent that material well-being arises, can itself undermine the very work ethics held to have led to that success. As Clegg et al. (1990, p.40) put it:

if the post-Confucian hypothesis is to be accepted, then the highly differentiated consumption characteristic of (Japan's) success would appear to undermine the productive basis of this post-Confucian economic culture's core values of familism, deferred consumption and disciplined order.

The third problem is the danger of racism. One reason why the *new culturist* argument is important is that it serves as a powerful corrective to (often racist) notions of Western cultural superiority. The problem is that the characteristic stereotyping and blanket generalizations can lead to an implicit, if unintended, racism on the part of the *new culturist* perspective as well. Neo-Confucianism was originally a specifically Chinese ideology, and its spread has been limited largely to the Mongoloid races of East Asia (unlike Buddhism which spans many races). Hence when Lee Kuan Yew justified an immigration policy which would favour 'culturally assimilable' workers from Hong Kong, Korea and Taiwan over 'jolly' Thais and Filipinos who might 'unsettle the local population', he was justifying a policy which effectively discriminated against the non-Mongoloid Asian races. While probably the majority of the *new culturists* are not racists – indeed are sometimes vehemently anti-racist – the general thrust of their argument can be interpreted as claiming a cultural superiority which translates rather too easily into a racial superiority. The *new culturists*, then, need to be extremely careful in

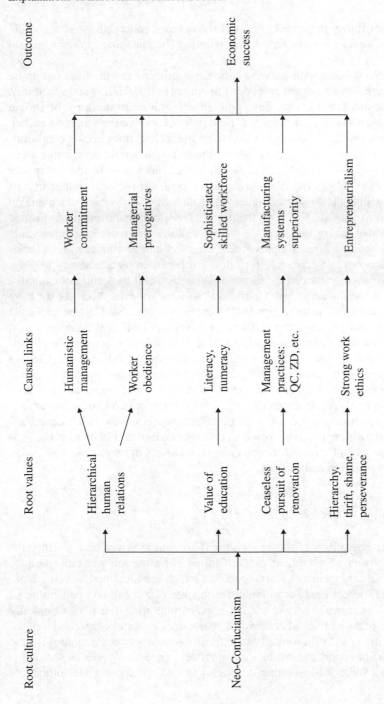

Figure 6.1: New Culturist Interpretations of East Asian Business and Economic Success

their analyses if they prefer not to bolster the not inconsiderable racist sentiment which already exists in some East Asian nations. (That the same applies to sexism is obvious.)

The fourth problem with the *new culturist* approach, and the final one to be discussed here, is the frequent absence of historical understanding and specificity. As Hofstede and Bond (1988) have pointed out, culture in the form of certain dominant values may be a necessary condition for economic growth, but a culture in itself is not a sufficient condition. Also important are certain market conditions and a supportive political context. Most *new culturists* would accept this argument and point, as do Hofstede and Bond, to the coincidence of the emergence of a global market from the 1950s with radical post-war political change in East Asia, as providing the conditions under which an East Asian version of capitalism was allowed to flourish. However, the discussion of political economy is limited to its role in *releasing the potential* of the culture, and there is a remarkable lack of discussion of the complex inter-play of culture, political system, business organization, and economic fortunes. Further, there is a tendency to gloss over the differences between the forms of capitalism and the nature of capitalist endeavour in the different 'neo-Confucian' societies of East Asia. As we have seen in the previous chapters, Japanese, Korean, and overseas Chinese capitalist organizations have emerged in different political and historical contexts which have given rise to different management styles and different forms of employer-employee relations. The Japanese *kaisha*, the Korean *chaebol*, and the Chinese family business represent quite different routes to capital accumulation, and if there is any causal relation between neo-Confucianism and organizational form, then, *ipso facto*, there must either be three very different neo-Confucianisms, or neo-Confucianism must provide a range of alternative values which have been selectively drawn upon and endorsed in different countries. Either way, the neo-Confucian argument, *in itself*, becomes next to useless in explaining East Asian business organization and success.

The Institutional Perspective

Some of the limitations of the *new culturist* account are overcome by an *institutional* approach which relates modern forms of business organization to pre-modern social arrangements – arrangements which are identified as being quite different in different East Asian countries in spite of a common neo-Confucian ideology. From this perspective culture remains important, but is more broadly defined as a pattern of social behaviours rather than a set of beliefs, and this enables a sensitivity to the historically specific differences between nations. Like the *new culturist* approach, the institutional approach appeals to Weberian sociology, but interprets Weber's ideas rather differently (for a discussion see Hamilton and Kao 1987).

As we described in the chapters on Korea, Taiwan and Hong Kong, and in the brief discussion of Japan in chapter one, these countries have rather different forms of characteristic business organization. To re-cap briefly, Japanese industry is dominated by giant corporations which have close horizontal links with financial institutions and trading houses, and which vertically organize smaller companies into *keiretsu* groups of (often dedicated) suppliers. Relations between big and small companies are characterized by 'obligational contracting'. The core work forces of the big companies enjoy life-time employment and a range of welfare benefits, and in return are expected to display loyalty and commitment. Peripheral workers – those employed on a temporary basis in the larger companies or those employed in the smaller organizations – enjoy relatively poor terms and conditions. Korean conglomerates – the *chaebol* - are less likely to sub-contract work, and less likely to cooperate with each other than are the Japanese corporations. They are family controlled and their relations with employees are characterized by authoritarianism and by some accounts nepotism. The Chinese family businesses which are so important in Taiwan and Hong Kong are mostly small and owner-controlled. There is a preference for sub-contracting through *guanxi* networks over business expansion and delegation to employees because of the extreme distrust of non-family members.

In the case of Japan, the characteristics of the giant corporations have been related to the collective traditions and inter-family collaboration of the Tokugawa village, which had considerable political autonomy. The *Shogun* (then in the Meiji period the Emperor) played a coordinating role, but there was a separation of reigning from ruling which largely left the villages to their own devices to control themselves. This was achieved by the village headman who sought a consensus from the leading families on policies and actions. The village identity, inter-family trust and consensus decision making characteristic of the Tokugawa period are reflected, it is suggested, in modern business organizations through company loyalty, high levels of trust and mutual obligation between business partners and managers (hence the separation of ownership and control), and the delegation of authority to managers and work groups (Whitley 1992).

In Korea, the *chaebol* are held to practice the sort of patrimonialism characteristic of the pre-modern regionally based *yangban* elites. Inter-*chaebol* competition reflects the competition of the *yangban* elites for the favour of the royal Patriarch, and within the conglomerate the head (*haejang*) exercises centralized control through a personal staff (Biggart 1990). The low level of trust in, and commitment to, employees, is held to reflect the mistrust between clans and weak inter-family cooperation within the pre-modern villages compared with Japan (Whitley 1992).

In Hong Kong and Taiwan, the Chinese family business is related to the 'economic familism' which derives from Imperial China, where village cohesion was even weaker than in Korea, and where the state was even more aloof. Authority was based on moral superiority more than competence or law, and conflicts of interest were dealt with in personal, idiosyncratic ways (Hamilton and Kao 1990).

From this perspective it was natural that trust would not be extended beyond the family and the closest of friends, so that Chinese businesses came to prefer to rely on extensive short term sub-contracting rather than (non-family) employees. Further, the practice of equal inheritance among sons (in contrast to Japan and Korea) restricts the size to which businesses can grow, and helps explain the fact that few business organizations last more than two or three generations (Tam 1990).

Institutionalism, then, overcomes some of the limitations of the *new culturist* accounts of East Asian forms of capitalism. By sensitizing us to historically and geographically specific social formations, this approach points up key differences within that group of societies which have been strongly influenced by neo-Confucian ethical codes. Hence, for instance, the 'humanistic management' identified by the *new culturists* may be specifically a *Japanese* form of management, and the 'entrepreneurialism' identified by Hofstede and Bond (1988) may be most particularly Chinese. Chinese economic familism may, indeed, explain the alleged instrumentality of the Chinese Singaporean work force: working for large anonymous organizations simply cannot have the same meaning as running one's own business or working for one's own family. In this circumstance, neo-Confucianism promotes a *non-work* ethic!

Institutionalism can also have its drawbacks, prime among which is the danger of explaining the modern predominantly or solely in terms of the pre-modern, and being guilty of the same determinism and processes of post-hoc rationalization as characterizes the *new culturists*. The opposite perspective, which sees all modern organizations and societies as converging towards pluralistic forms because of the demands of industrialization and technology (originally put forward by Kerr et al. 1960) may now be discredited, and primarily by the East Asian example, but the rapid rise of Christianity and popular demands for political democracy in modern East Asia, to give just two examples, surely cannot be accounted for by reference to pre-modern social formations. Institutionalism is a broad school, and includes works, such as Kinzley's (1991) account of business ideology in interwar Japan, which points up the importance of the pursuit of particular ideologies and forms of organization by individuals and groups with specific interests in their dominance. In Japan the ideology of 'industrial harmony', which made appeals to pre-modern values and social formations, won the day (for the time being) but only by beating off the challenges of counter-ideologies and alternative visions of the future of industry and industrial relations. In this sense industrial harmony in Japan was a *modern* creation. The best *institutionalist* accounts are alive to ideology *and* counter-ideology, to conflict *as well as* 'harmony'. The danger of the institutional approach is the tendency to neglect the alternative ideologies which are occasionally pressed forward and the interests which dominant ideologies serve.

This leads us to a second potential problem with the institutional approach. The tendency (which again is not universal in this broad school) is to focus on elites, particularly business elites, and to lose sight of the differences of interest and the conflicts inherent in societies. Specific forms of organization or social arrangements, be they pre-modern or modern, serve the interests of some better than others, and appeals to 'cultural roots' on the part of elites are often no more than attempts to legitimate inequalities, exploitation, or particular courses of action.

To use the example of Japan again, the 'high trust' relations held to characterize employer-employee relations in modern organizations are at least part myth. Some Japanese scholars have recently had works translated into English which would suggest the opposite of high trust relations, even for that minority of core workers who enjoy life-time employment and other privileges (Ogasawara 1992; Tabata 1989; Yamamoto 1990). Rather than being trusted, workers are closely monitored on their performance and behaviour, and retribution (sometimes in the form of public humiliation) for any misdemeanour is swift. Similarly, total quality management, far more fundamentally than being an avenue of worker participation, as is popularly assumed, is a means of exerting tight employer control over employee performance through an efficient system of surveillance (Sewell and Wilkinson 1992).

Another example of the way social arrangements serve specific interests comes from Hong Kong. For the institutionalists, conflicts within Chinese businesses are managed in personalistic ways which relect preferences derived from Imperial China. As Whitley (1992, p.206-7) argues:

positional authority based on formal relationships has not developed to nearly the same extent as in Japanese, or even Korean, companies. ... Formal rules and procedures which would constrain this authority reflect upon the personal merits of the owner in much the same way as criticism of particular decisions implied the personal unworthiness of those in authority in pre-industrial China. As a result, employment practices are not governed by standardized rules but rather are highly personal and idiosyncratic to the particular relationship between the owner and individual employees.

Yet as we discussed in chapter five, when Hong Kongese employees were given the opportunity of seeking legal redress against the worst exploitations through the introduction of employment legislation in the 1960s and 1970s, and in the absence of strong trade unions, they flocked to the courts. Personal means of conflict resolution, it seems, is a preference restricted to a particular interest group – i.e. employers. And to confirm that Turner et al. (1991) were not wholly misguided in their analysis of industrial relations in Hong Kong, and to demonstrate that the Hong Kong case is not an anomoly, we can compare recent events in Hong Kong with those in Taiwan. Here, it was mostly *violations of the Labour Standards Law* (introduced in the mid 1980s in response to popular local demand and international pressures) which were the basis of the wave of strike activity in the late 1980s. Again, the Taiwanese case raises serious questions about the assumed Chinese preference for personalistic means of conflict resolution beyond those who would benefit from an absence of a legal basis for authority.

Institutionalism, then, is a powerful rejoinder to convergence theory. It reminds us of the importance of history, and it points to alternative means of capital accumulation. But it carries the dangers of historical determinism, of losing sight of differing interests and values within populations, and therefore of losing sight of choice in alternative visions of the future.

Industry and Labour in East Asia

Conventional economics, dependency theory, and Frobel et al.'s (1980) theory of a new international division of labour have all failed to explain economic development in East Asia. Weberian sociological accounts, and some implicitly Durkheimian accounts such as that by Pascale and Athos (1982), have emerged to contend with those of political economists. But while still fashionable, and while in their own ways they do make important contributions to our understanding, they carry their own problems and are equally subject to counter-factual examples as are previous theories. As Clegg et al. (1990) point out, it is unlikely that any univariate explanation can come to grips with such a complex phenomenon as East Asian economic development, and certainly no grand theory is proposed here. However, the author would argue that an understanding of the East Asian economies is dependent not simply on arm chair theorizing, valuable though that sometimes might be, but from empirical investigations into the characteristics of, and the relationships between, the actors in the economies under question. This book has attempted to draw on such investigations to provide insights into the workings of the economies of East Asia. By stressing the roles of *actors*, it is intended to provide an account which is not deterministic, which does not suggest cast-iron laws, but which acknowledges what Limqueco et al. (1989) call 'room for maneouvre'. It is to acknowledge that the future of industry and labour in East Asia will be the outcome of *choices* to be made *in the light of*, never wholly determined by, either world economic developments or local cultural affinities; and that these choices will be the outcome of indeterminate and complex political processes. We conclude, then, with a summary and commentary on the players in the East Asian economies, their inter-relationships, and the choices now facing them.

States, Development and Democratic Transitions

Any serious analysis of economic growth in the Asia-Pacific has to include consideration of the role of strong states, both for their strategic guidance of capital and for their key role in developing and controlling labour forces through, for instance, educational and welfare provision, immigration policy, and employment legislation. (See Appelbaum and Henderson 1992 for an edited collection of articles which provides an extensive discussion of states and development in East Asia.)

But in the 1980s many East Asian governments found their authority as well as legitimacy under threat and were forced to embark on democratic transitions, most dramatically in the Philippines, and then in other countries as well. In Taiwan, international pressures and broad based 'islander' opposition built up sufficiently to force the 'mainlander' KMT government to lift martial law in 1987, and a democratic government (with an 'islander' President) was installed by the early 1990s. The KMT remained in power, but only after making wide ranging concessions to opposition groups, which now have a significant number of representatives in seats of political power. The situation in Korea is similar: in this case, the opposition labour movement played a more central role in bringing down the notorious Chun regime, though again the democratic movement was broad based. Again like Taiwan, many concessions were made and restrictions lifted, and the ruling DLP managed to hold on to power under a changing leadership at the 1992 national elections, but now facing a more confident and powerful group of democrats. In both Korea and Taiwan, the opposition groups are understandably fragmented and still in the process of making their own transitions from merely *opposing* government policies to formulating their own alternative policies into sufficiently sophisticated and coherent agendas to provide more positive alternatives to the ruling political elites. The ruling elites on the other hand still occasionally lapse into repressive measures while publicly avowing their commitment to democracy and widespread political participation. But while these fledgeling democracies may take some time to mature, it seems unlikely that there will be a reversion to purely authoritarian rule.

Assuming purely repressive authoritarianism does not re-emerge, the important question is whether the Taiwanese and Korean states will come to behave similar those in Western democracies or, as in Singapore (Deyo 1989) the ruling elites will attempt to pre-empt opposition through a more effective penetration of grass roots organizations and incorporation of independent trade union, and perhaps other, leaders. Taiwan appears to be struggling to do this through, for instance, attempting to revive the flagging fortunes of the Chinese Federation of Labour (CFL), whereas the Korean political elite has little in the way of a sympathetic base to start from, and faces continued antagonism in its relationships with employers as well as trade unions and other groups such as environmentalists. Korea's short term economic difficulties could also present problems for the state. Unlike Taiwan, the nation does not have massive foreign reserves which can be drawn on to ensure short term economic growth, and with growth a degree of legitimacy. Korea seems the most likely candidate, then, to emerge with a form of political pluralism familiar to the West.

Singapore's political elite has not been seriously challenged, even in the late 1980s, and active pre-emptive measures and the refusal of the state to be complacent undoubtedly explain this in large part. The promise in the 1980s of a 'softer' style of leadership by the 'new guard' PAP politicians has been slow in forthcoming, and the question of whether a certain softness will emerge when Lee Kuan Yew eventually leaves the political scene must remain an open question. Certainly the style of government in Singapore owes a great deal to the style of its charismatic leader, but the 'new guard' is now well trained and well versed in the language of 'Asian values', 'orderliness' and 'nation building'. Change might be more likely to come, then, not from within the PAP, but from without from would-be dissidents who might fear Goh less than the authoritative Lee. In the meantime, it is business as usual in Singapore.

Hong Kong's political future is anyone's guess. The colonial administration finally gave way to demands for democracy (though many, with good reason, suspect the announcement of democratic reforms is more some sort of snub at Beijing than a genuine concern for the rights of the Hong Kongese), but the first elections to Legco, scheduled for 1995, come only two years before political re-integration with China. This hardly gives time to even *practice* running a democracy and acting independently before takeover, which will undoubtedly make Beijing's task of establishing control much easier than it otherwise might have been. In the meantime, many of those fortunate enough to be blessed with large amounts of capital or professional skills are voting with their feet and leaving the colony in advance of 1997.

Let us now turn to the relations of states with capital and labour, and assess the implications of recent political developments for those relations.

State-Capital Relations

Although Singapore has formally been a democracy since the 1960s, *all* the ANICs in the early years of development were characterized by ruling political elites with extraordinary power, and industrialization took place without serious opposition, including from underdeveloped local bourgeoisies. However, relations between state and capital are fundamentally different in each country, with important consequences.

In Hong Kong, capital has been left to its own devices under the policy of non-interventionism, and appears to have failed in developing world manufacturing competitiveness. The country's rapid de-industrialization in the late 1980s and early 1990s may be related to richer pickings in the import-export trade associated with China's market liberalization, but it is doubtful whether, in the absence of state support or guidance, the small Chinese family business would have been capable of leading the economy beyond the role of international sub-contractor or into higher value areas, or even of heavily automating production (Poon 1992).

The Taiwanese government, on the other hand, has consistently played a leading role in industrial development through direct ownership of heavy industry sectors and through support and guidance of the relatively small Chinese family businesses which have dominated the export oriented sectors. Taiwan has hence effectively combined the advantages of its highly flexible and responsive small businesses operating within *guanxi* networks with those of state plans which have served to guide the economy along strategic paths through a range of incentives and trade measures (Wade 1990). During the 1990s the state has extended its role as capitalist itself with a massive public spending programme under the *Six Year Development Plan*, reflected in the growth of the government's share of fixed capital formation from 17 per cent to 30 per cent between 1987 and 1992. The plan probably reflects the state's lack of trust in private capital alone to lead Taiwan's restructuring beyond a certain level (investment ratios had dropped alarmingly in the 1980s) and certainly it relects a willingness on the part of the government to use whatever means it can to achieve national economic objectives.

The Korean government has also consistently provided support and guidance to industry, including underwriting foreign loans to local capitalists as well as the usual mix of incentives and protection against foreign competition in areas considered strategically important. However, Korea was exceptional in that by the 1970s the *chaebol* had grown so large and powerful that they could pose a threat to the established political elite. At the same time as the state and employers relied heavily on each other, a degree of antagonism, which occasionally broke out as open conflict, developed over national economic policies and the freedom of big business to engage in the activities it chose without state interference (Biggart 1990).

Singapore is the exceptional country in its heavy reliance on foreign rather than domestic capital, and especially in the export oriented manufacturing sectors. While on the one hand this has meant a relief from the need to monitor and control a local bourgeoisie, the Singaporean government, from the beginning, identified the imperative to create a climate which would be entirely conducive to internationally mobile capital. Singapore's big foreign employers have not challenged the state politically, nor have they shown any desire to do so, but it is employers' needs, probably more than in the case of the other ANICs, which have been paramount. State-capital relations in Singapore, then, are characterized by a massive dependence of the state on foreign employers which probably gives those employers a greater degree of power than they realize. Although the political elite has rarely said so, it must be exasperated by the complaceny – if not hostility – of foreign employers towards the PAP's attempts to engage them in the creation of an industrial community in Singapore. Nor is there any sign that this will change in the immediate future – the economic success which foreign capital has brought means that despite the problems it brings it would be a brave step to change course now. Although there are recent attempts to diversify and to become a 'brain centre', the dependence on foreign capital is as great as ever, and the dramatic switch in policy which would be necessary for the creation of a stronger local bourgeoisie appears unlikely.

In Taiwan and Korea state-capital relations *have* changed in recent years, partly because of changed international and domestic political pressures as well as changing economic environments. The most dramatic manifestation of change in both countries is the massive outflow of foreign capital since the late 1980s which was enabled by economic liberalization measures, but motivated by the search for cheaper labour in the face of tight labour markets and dramatically rising wages domestically. Capital flight has been most dramatic from Taiwan, including to mainland China where Chinese businesses take advantage of old networks in Fujian and other provinces. The state appears ambiguous about economic relations with China, officially disapproving but in practice turning a blind eye – clearly Taiwan could benefit enormously from capital involvement in China, but the political implications are another matter. But while capital has more freedom to move across political boundaries, both the Korean and Taiwanese states have so far kept their hands firmly on the tiller at home. In Taiwan the state has increased its direct involvement in the economy through its massive spending programme, and in Korea there is currently an attempt to break the power of the *chaebol* through a forced gradual economic de-concentration. Whether Hyundai's Chung Ju Yung's failed efforts to weaken the ruling party at the national elections in 1992 was the last gasp attempt of the *chaebol* to maintain and extend their influence remains to be seen. In the meantime the state is in a position (arguably has a mandate) to attempt to change fundamentally the characteristics of big business, but must recognize its continued dependence on big business to lead the desired economic restructuring. The future of state-capital relations in Korea, then, are highly uncertain.

Hong Kong, finally, is characterized by arms-length state-capital relations, and there has been no sign that this will change in the run up to 1997. In the eyes of a colonial administration which has little apparent concern for things like economic structure, and which actually advocates letting the economy shift wherever 'the market' desires, the economy is probably 'doing well'. But this will soon be history: economic re-integration with China is going ahead, and the Hong Kongese capitalists on the mainland already appear to be pursuing the same sorts of business practices they have become accustomed to in Hong Kong (though this is an area in need of serious research). Whether this will continue after 1997 is another matter: the future of state-capital relations beyond 1997 are in the hands of a Beijing government which is going through its own shifts in economic policy directions.

State-Labour Relations

The image of repressive authoritarian political regimes controlling labour on behalf of capitalists left free to engage in the worst exploitations was never a wholly accurate representation, but like all myths contained a grain of truth. As the ANICs have matured, however, so the worst exploitations have become less common, and indeed the divides between rich and poor have not, as might have been expected, widened significantly as measured by concentrations of income. This has been due in part to increasingly tight labour labour markets over the period of industrialization, but also the fact that, Hong Kong apart, the states in question have pursued (albeit their own versions of) *national* social and economic objectives *through* capital, rather than allowing them to be dictated by capital. Indeed, one would not be wholly wrong in suspecting a large measure of socialist ideology in each of the ANICs except Hong Kong, and even here the state has reluctantly accepted a responsibility for the provision of housing and educational facilities.

Generally, however, labour has not been trusted to organize and bargain for itself (again Hong Kong is the exception) but rather has been subject to guidance and control from above. In Singapore, Korea and Taiwan there were systematic attempts to incorporate labour within the state apparatus through the creation of affiliations between ruling party and peak union organization. Singapore, where PAP and NTUC elites became so closely inter-related as to be virtually indistinguishable, and where trade unions accepted productionist and socializing roles, was manifestly the most successful in its drive to incorporate. Korea was the least successful, the leadership of the official union movement having little credibility in spite of state-mandated Labour-Management Councils within enterprises. Repression has been the method preferred over more subtle means of controlling labour in this country.

More generally, it has been the state in Singapore which has been the most vociferous in its attempts to influence the values and attitudes of the work force, though it has been less successful in winning the hearts and minds of the workers than of their official representatives. Taiwan's 'factory as home' campaign expressed similar sentiments to those expressed by Singapore's PAP-NTUC elite, but appears to have been equally unsuccessful. In both countries, the *familist* orientation of the populations would be likely to contradict the notion of *company* loyalty: equally importantly, both Singapore's foreign employers and Taiwan's Chinese family businesses have been reluctant to adopt long term relationships with their workers. In Taiwan's case the company welfareism which does exist is mostly state-mandated. In Singapore where the state is limited to persuading rather than forcing the hand of (foreign) employers, company welfareism and employee participation have simply been given the thumbs down.

Singapore again stands out in the state's ability to control wages. This was demonstrated vividly in the early 1980s when the 'tripartite' recommendations of the NWC to substantially raise wages as part of the economic restructuring programme were accepted by employers across the board, and again in the mid 1980s when what were effectively wage cuts were endorsed by the NTUC, and again implemented across the board, in the light of the recession. Neither has the substantial labour immigration into Singapore been allowed to affect wages in adverse ways. The government carefully manipulates the number of foreign workers in specific sectors of the economy, and imposes variable levies on their employment to prevent downward wages pressures, in the process maintaining the balance between the need to supply labour to employers and the push for economic restructuring. In Taiwan, wages in the private sector were deliberately left to the market, and in Korea the state has simply not had the authority to enforce wage controls on the giant *chaebol* (though it has been willing to step in on behalf of the *chaebol* to quell labour demands when the need has arisen).

Legislation has, of course, favoured managerial prerogatives in Singapore, Korea and Taiwan, most strikingly again in Singapore where extensive employer rights are mandated in detail. All three countries have also introduced tough trade union legislation which has limited unions' representation, bargaining and political rights, and a close surveillance has been exercised over would-be independent trade union movements. In Singapore legal strikes are all but impossible without the tacit consent of the government, whereas in Taiwan and Korea (until democratization) strikes were simply banned.

Hong Kong has so far been ommitted from discussion because in virtually every respect the country stands out as exceptional in the relations between state and labour. There has been little attempt at incorporation, the state has made only weak attempts to affect management-labour relations at company level, and there is a deliberate avoidance of wages control. Hong Kong has also been exceptional (until recently) on the legislation front, where trade union and employment law guarantees trade union rights and stipulates minimum terms and conditions. More generally, the state has also deliberately avoided involvement in industrial disputes, except where employers or employees have actively called on the services of the Labour Department. For various reasons related to Hong Kong's economic structure and the unions' inability to organize however, trade unions in the private sector, and expecially manufacturing, have been ineffectual. This does not reflect, as the authorites would prefer to believe, a contented work force. Nor does it reflect, as one possible version of the *new culturist* thesis would have it, an 'obedient' work force. Rather, the work force finds itself limited to non-union avenues of grievance expression (Turner et al. 1991).

Neither, of course, should the work forces be simply characterized as 'docile' in the other three ANICs, and this was brought home most forcefully in the outbursts of strike activity in Taiwan and Korea during their democratic transitions. The Taiwanese and Korean independent labour movements can claim as many heros and martyrs as can the labour movements of Western countries. Labour gains in the form of better wages, terms, conditions, hours of work, etc., are most clear cut (and best documented) in the case of Korea. But in both countries the rights and freedoms of trade unions have been extended, and legislation also now provides some safeguards against the worst exploitation for non-unionized workers. Although it is early days, more pluralistic forms of industrial relations seem likely in both countries. The governments of Korea and Taiwan would clearly like to revive the fortunes of their peak union organization allies – the FKTU and the CFL – but the only way these 'puppet' organizations are likely to gain credibility and legitimacy within new democracies is through establishing some distance from government and behaving at least a little more independently.

Capital-Labour Relations

Although there are always exceptional companies, as Samsung is reputed to be in Korea, one thing all the ANICs have in common with regard to characteristic capital-labour relations is that they are different from those in Japan. Enterprise based trade unions are predominant in Korea and Taiwan, and there has been an attempt to pursue the Japanese model of industrial relations in Singapore, but in none of these countries do employers appear to have put in the effort necessary to create an identification between company and union.

Taiwan has probably come closest, but it is the KMT which has driven local union organization, and KMT party cadres which have provided the leadership. It is also Taiwan which, in the 1980s, has had the highest union density among the ANICs; again, however, this reflects the KMT's influence rather than either employer choice or employees' ability to independently organize. The mandatory Factory Councils and the forced contribution of 15 per cent of profits to an Employee Welfare Fund also appear to have had little impact on industrial relations. Management-labour relations are reported to be characterized by an authoritarian management style and an absence of trust between the parties which reflects Chinese cultural preferences. The lack of Japanese style controls over labour was confirmed when martial law was lifted in 1987. Immediately there was an outbreak of wild cat strikes, with strike organizers justifying their actions mainly by pointing to gross violations of the Labour Standards Law by employers. In the late 1980s and early 1990s the Taiwanese alternative labour movement has been characterized by factionalism. But even if factional disputes can be overcome, the problem of organizing workers in Chinese family businesses – perhaps because of their 'Chinese-ness' and certainly because of their small size and geographic dispersal – will remain.

The predominance of small, and increasingly small, Chinese family businesses in Hong Kong helps explain the weakness of the labour movement there in spite of liberal trade union laws. Trade union weakness also relates to the split between Beijing oriented and KMT loyal peak organizations, the former having changed its stance from militant to conservative in the light of China's concern not to cause capital flight before 1997. As in Taiwan, employer-labour relations more generally are by all accounts characterized by instrumentalism and distrust.

In Singapore too, employer-labour relations tend to be distant. Here more than anywhere employer prerogatives are enshrined in legislation which is strictly enforced where necessary, and while the state would prefer employers to take on welfareist roles and involve NTUC affiliates in Japanese style employee involvement programmes, employers remain indifferent. The decline of trade union density in the 1980s and into the 1990s clearly reflects the inability of the NTUC to find a legitimizing role for itself, but while its future may appear bleak, it is not beyond the PAP-NTUC elite to find some means or other of reviving its fortunes.

Since democratiztion in 1987 it is Korean trade unions which have emerged as the strongest and best able to mobilize workers in industrial action in spite of the youthfulness of the leadership of independent trade unions. Deyo (1989) relates this strength to the economic structural conditions of Korea (especially the relatively large numbers of skilled male workers in heavy industry and the goegraphical concentration of workers in urban areas) and to the failure of the state to develop pre-emptive strategies for labour control. It is also presumably related to the antagonisms of labour towards employers which built up over nearly three decades of autocratic rule by managements. Korea, then, is characterized by state-capital, state-labour *and* capital-labour conflict.

Conclusions

In the light of the fact that theories of East Asian development have consistently been proved wrong by East Asian experience and East Asian counter-factuals, it is probably correct to say that we do not yet have the detailed understanding of this complex region to provide a convincing account. But perhaps nor should we expect to. The real world has always defied social scientific logic in one way or another, and change in East Asia continues to occur at a faster pace than is realistically possible to keep track of. It is also imperative, in the author's view, that we acknowledge 'room for maneouvre', and recognize that economic outcomes are dependent on the inter-play of ultimately *indeterminate* relationships between actors. What we can do by way of a conclusion, however, is attempt an assessment of how well equipped the ANICs appear to be, in the light of the above discussion to cope with the new economic realities discussed in chapter one.

To summarize the economic situation, the ANICs make up the second of three tiers in a fairly clear cut division of labour and technology within the AP9, with Japan sitting on top and the ASEAN4 at the bottom. Import-export data suggests unambiguously that the ANICs' technological dependence on Japan (and the ASEAN4's technological dependence on both Japan and the ANICs) has deepened over the past decade. At the same time the ANICs' dependence for export markets on the advanced West has also deepened. This could change if a market for finished goods can emerge in the Far East sufficient to make up for any cut-backs in trade with the West. There are some signs of consumer goods market growth, and China's liberalization, if it continues, could lead to the establishment of the biggest market in the world. But so far the figures suggest the dependency on exports to the West will continue for some time. In the meantime, the increased difficulties of exporting standardized mass produced goods to the West has added to the imperative to further restructure into higher value areas. The question then becomes one of whether the ANICs can escape, or somehow live with, their dual dependencies, in a way which still ensures economic growth.

A small city state with a working population of a little over a million is always likely to have limited economic diversity and to be a provider of niche services. For this reason, and because of Singapore's extraordinary dependence on foreign direct investment and on domestic exports, the country remains even more vulnerable to exogenous economic and political developments than the other ANICs. Singapore is also so tightly integrated with ASEAN that its future is dependent on the future of that region. The ability of the state to meet the needs of multinational capital is dependent in part on state vigilance and the PAP-NTUC 'symbiosis', which guarantees a compliant, if instrumental, work force, and a stability of industrial relations and wages. Any major shift in state policy which might arise if the PAP lost its grip or was reformed from within could have serious consequences for the pattern of economic development, though in the short term this seems unlikely. Meeting the needs of multinational capital, which has demonstrated its ability and willingness to pull out at short notice, has meant tough social and political measures which have alienated large segments of the population, an alienation which may in some respects stand in the way of ambitions to make Singapore a 'creative' brain centre. But Singapore's economic future through the 1990s appears relatively secure in the context of ASEAN growth and continued foreign confidence in the country.

Having the only political administration with a clear ideological commitment to an economic philosophy – 'positive non-interventionism' – Hong Kong has also been the slowest to up-grade its manufacturing base, which has remained primitive compared with the other ANICs. But any debate over the merits of *laissez faire* ideology in hong Kong have been over-shadowed by a rapid de-industrialization associated with the transfer of manufacturing capacity to the mainland and the re-emergence of the colony as entrepot. Hong Kong is already partly integrated economically with the mainland. Political re-integration means massive uncertainty about the future of state-capital-labour relations after 1997.

The trade imbalance crisis suggests that Korea has probably been the most severely affected by its technological dependence on Japan and its market de-pendence on the West. Labour militancy since 1987 exacerbated the problems by greatly increasing labour costs and reducing exploitation, which has damaged the competitiveness of Korean exports, and the state has been hampered in its ability to take rapid short term remedial measures by the power of the *chaebol* as well as the power of organized labour. The state was given a new legitimacy in 1992 at the national elections, and has vowed to finally curtail the ability of the *chaebol* to thwart national economic objectives. But the political pluralism which now char-acterizes state-capital-labour relations could hamper the speedy implementation of economic policy and blunt its decisiveness. The important question appears to be whether sufficient national consensus can be forged to ensure the pursuit of common national economic goals in the new democracy.

Taiwan also now appears to be a test bed for the hyposthesis that East Asian industrial and economic advance was dependent on all-powerful states. While employers have not been capable of challenging the state in the past because of their small size, the dilution of control over 'islanders' by the KMT 'mainlanders' associated with the democratic transition could conceivably allow the development of a collective private sector employer voice. The collective voice of an independent labour movement could also conceivably strengthen despite present problems of organization and factionalism. In Taiwan as well then, a certain political pluralism has begun to emerge, and is unlikely to go away. An advantage over Korea, however, is the breathing space afforded Taiwan to readjust by massive foreign reserves which guarantee the short term future.

There are many reasons to be pessimistic for the economic futures of the ANICs. In particular these relate to dependencies which stand as obstacles to further growth, and democratic transitions (in Korea and Taiwan) which erode the ability of strong states to direct the economies unilaterally. But we could identify equally difficult obstacles ten years ago. Perhaps in another ten years time we will be documenting another 'miracle'.

References

Abdullah, R.S. (1991) "Management Strategies and Employee Response in Malaysia", Unpublished PhD thesis, Cardiff Business School, University of Wales, College of Cardiff, Cardiff.

Amnesty International (1980) *Report on an Amnesty International Mission to Singapore*, London, Amnesty International Publications.

Amsden, A. (1989) *Asia's Next Giant: South Korea and Late Industrialization*, Oxford, Oxford University Press.

Appelbaum, R. and Henderson, J. (eds.) (1992) *States and Development in the Asian Pacific Rim*, London, Sage.

Arotcarena, G., Tan, T.W. and Fong Hoe Fang (1986) *The Maid Tangle: A Guide to Better Employer-Employee Relationship*, Singapore, Katong Catholic Book Centre.

Aryee, S. and Wyatt, T. (1989) "Central Life Interests of Singaporean Workers", *Asia-Pacific Journal of Management*, 6 (2), pp.281-291.

Azumi, K. (1969) *Higher Education and Business Recruitment in Japan*, New York, Columbia University Press.

Bai Moo Ki (1990) "Recent Developments in Korean Labour Conditions", Paper presented to the CAER Seminar on The Korean Economy, University of New South Wales, November.

Bank of Korea (various years) *Monthly Balance of Payments*, Seoul, Bank of Korea.

Bank of Korea (various years) *Monthly Statistical Bulletin*, Seoul, Bank of Korea.

Berger, P. (1987) *The Capitalist Revolution: Fifty Propositions About Prosperity, Equity and Liberty*, London, Wildwood.

Biggart, N. (1990) "Institutionalized Patrimonialism in Korean Business", *Comparative Social Resarch*, 12, pp.113-133.

Biggart, N. and Hamilton, G. (1990) "Explaining East Asian Business Success: Theory Number Four", *University of Wales Business and Economics Review*, 5, pp. 11-16.

Bureau of Labour Statistics, US Department of Labour (1991) *International Comparisons of Hourly Compensation Costs for Production Workers in Manufacturing*, Report 817, November, Bureau of Labour Statistics, US Department of Labour, Washington DC.

Caiden, G. and Jung Yong Duck (1985) "The Political Economy of Korean Development Under the Park Regime". In Kim Bun Woong, Bell, D. and Lee Chong Bum (eds.), *Administrative Dynamics and Development: The Korean Experience*, Seoul, Kyobo, pp.20-31.

Castells, M. (1992) "Four Asian Tigers with a Dragon Head: A Comparative Analysis of the State, Economy and Society in the Asian Pacific Rim". In Appelbaum, R. and Henderson, J. (eds.), *States and Development in the Asian Pacific Rim*, London, Sage, pp.33-70.

Census and Statistics Department, Hong Kong (various years) *Hong Kong Annual Digest of Statistics*, Hong Kong, Census and Statistics Department.

Cha Dong Se (1988) "Korea Approaching a Developed Economy Regime". In Dutta, M. (ed.), *Asian Industrialization: Changing Economic Structures*, Volume I, Part A, Greenwich, Connecticut, JAI Press, pp.83-108.

Chan Heng Chee (1976) *The Dynamics of One Party Dominance: The PAP at the Grass Roots*, Singapore, Singapore University Press.

Chan Heng Chee and Evers, H. (1978) "National Identity and Nation Building in Singapore". In Chen, P. and Evers, H. (eds.), *Studies in ASEAN Sociology*, Singapore, Chopmen, pp.117-129.

Cheah Hock Beng (1988) "Labour in Transition: The Case of Singapore", *Labour and Industry*, 1 (2), pp.258-286.

Cheng Soo May (1986) "Worker Participation as a Strategy in Labour-Management Relations in Singapore", Paper presented to the Sociological Association of Australia and New Zealand Annual Conference, University of Queensland, 30 August-2 September.

Chew Soon Beng and Chew, R. (1984) "The Limitations and Implications of GDP Growth for Singapore", *Singapore Management Review*, 6 (1), pp.77-83.

Chew Soon Beng, Chew, R. and Chan, F. (1992) "Technology Transfer from Japan to ASEAN: Trends and Prospects". In Tokunaga, S. (ed.), *Japan's Foreign Direct Investment and Asian Economic Interdependence*, Tokyo, University of Tokyo Press, pp.111-134.

Chiu, S. and Levin, D. (1993) "From a Labour Surplus to a Labour Scarce Economy: Challenges to Human Resources Management in Hong Kong", *International Journal of Human Resource Management*, 4 (1), pp.159-189.

Chng Meng Kng, Low, L. and Toh Mun Heng (1988) *Industrial Restructuring in Singapore: For ASEAN-Japan Investment and Trade Expansion*, Singapore, Chopmen.

Cho Woo Hyun (1990) *Korea's Industrial Relations System: Its Past, Present and Future*, Central Officials Training Institute, Seoul.

Choi Jeong Pyo, Kang, Cheol-Kyo and Chang, Jee-Sang (1991) *Chaebol*, Seoul, Bee Bong.

Chu Yin Wah (1992a) *State History, Development Strategies, and the Democratic Movements in South Korea, Taiwan and Hong Kong*, Working Paper no. 43, Institute of Governmental Affairs, Research Program in East Asian Business and Development, University of California, Davis.

Chu Yin Wah (1992b) *Informal Work in Hong Kong*, Working Paper no. 36, Institute of Governmental Affairs, Research Program in East Asian Business and Development, University of California, Davis.

Chua Beng Huat (1985) "Pragmatism of the Peoples' Action Party Government in Singapore: A Critical Assessment", *South East Asian Journal of Social Science*, 13 (2), pp.29-46.

Clegg, S., Dunphy, D. and Redding, G. (1986) "Organization and Management in East Asia". In Clegg, S., Dunphy, D. and Redding, G. (eds.), *The Enterprise and Management in East Asia*, Hong Kong, University of Hong Kong, Centre of Asian Studies, pp.1-34.

Clegg, S., Higgins, W. and Spybey, T. (1990) "'Post-Confucianism', Social Democracy and Economic Culture". In Clegg, S. and Redding, G. (eds.), *Capitalism in Contrasting Cultures*, Berlin, de Gruyter, pp.31-78.

Clifford, M. (1988) "Appearances are Deceptive", *Far Eastern Economic Review*, 11 February, pp.56-62.

Clifford, M. and Moore, J. (1989) "Squeezed by Success", *Far Eastern Economic Review*, 16 March, pp.84-89.

Clutterbuck, R. (1984) *Conflict and Violence in Singapore and Malaysia: 1945-1983*, Singapore, Graham Brash.

Council for Economic Planning and Development, Republic of China (various years) *Taiwan Statistical Data Book*, Taipei, Council for Economic Planning and Development, Republic of China.

Council for Economic Planning and Development, Republic of China (1992) *The Six Year National Development Plan of the Republic of China*, Taipei, Council for Economic Planning and Development, Republic of China.

Council of Labour Affairs, Republic of China (1990) *Yearbook of Labour Statistics 1989*, Taipei, Council for Labour Affairs, Republic of China.

De Bettignies, H. (1982) "Can Europe Survive the Pacific Century?", *Euro-Asia Business Review*, 1 (1), pp.10-15.

Dhanabalan, S. (1983) "Censorship to Prevent Erosion of Values", *Speeches: A Selection of Ministerial Speeches*, 7 (1), pp.60-66.

Deyo, F. (1981) *Dependent Development and Industrial Order: An Asian Case Study*, New York, Praeger.

Deyo, F. (1987a) "Coalitions, Institutions and Linkage Sequencing – Toward a Strategic Capacity Model of East Asian Development". In Deyo, F. (ed.), *The Political Economy of the New Asian Industrialism*, Ithaca, Cornell University Press, pp.227-248.

Deyo, F. (1987b) "State and Labor: Modes of Political Exclusion in East Asian Development". In Deyo, F. (ed.), *The Political Economy of the New Asian Industrialism*, Ithaca, Cornell University Press, pp.182-202.

Deyo, F. (1989) *Beneath the Miracle: Labor Subordination in the New Asian Industrialization*, Berkeley, University of California Press.

Deyo, F. (1992) "The Political Economy of Social Policy Formation: East Asia's Newly Industrialized Countries". In Appelbaum, R. and Henderson, J. (eds.), *States and Development in the Asian Pacific Rim*, London, Sage, pp.289-306.

Doi, T. (1973) *The Anatomy of Dependence*, Tokyo, Kodansha International.

Domingo, R. (1985) "'Kanban': Crisis Management Japanese Style", *Euro-Asia Business Review*, 4 (3), pp.22-24.

Dore, R. (1973) *Origins of the Japanese Employment System*, London, Allen and Unwin.

Douglass, M. and DiGregorio, M. (1991) "Industrial Transformations and the Division of Labour", Paper presented to the Workshop on Industrial Restructuring and Regional Adjustment in Asian NIEs, East-West Centre, Hawaii, 18-20 September.

Eckert, C. (1990), "The South Korean Bourgeoisie: A Class in Search of Hegemony", *Journal of Korean Studies*, 7, pp.115-148.

Economic Committee Report to the Ministry of Trade and Industry, Republic of Singapore (1986) *The Singapore Economy: New Directions*, Singapore, Ministry of Trade and Industry.

Economic Planning Board, Republic of Korea (various years) *Annual Report on the Economically Active Population Survey*, Seoul, Economic Planning Board, Kaohsiung.

Endo, K. (1991) "Satei (Personal Assessment) and Inter-worker Competition in Japanese Firms", Unpublished paper, Department of Economics, Yamagata University, Yamagata.

England, J. and Rear, J. (1981) *Industrial Relations and Law in Hong Kong*, Hong Kong, Oxford University Press.

Enright, D. (1969) *Memoirs of a Mendicant Professor*, London, Chatto and Windus.

Export Processing Zone Administration (various years) *Export Processing Zone Concentrates*, Kaoshiung, Export Processing Zone Administration.

Fallows, J. (1988) "Japan is Not Korea", *Atlantic*, October, pp.22-33.

Frobel, F., Heinrichs, J. and Kreye, O. (1980) *The New International Division of Labour: Structural Unemployment in Industrialized Countries and Industrialization in Developing Countries*, Cambridge, Cambridge University Press.

George, T. (1973) *Lee Kuan Yew's Singapore*, Kuala Lumpur, Eastern Universities Press.

Gereffi, G. (1992) "New Realities of Industrial Development in East Asia and Latin America: Global, Regional and National Trends". In Applebaum, R. and Henderson, J. (eds.), *States and Development in the Asian Pacific Rim*, London, Sage, pp.85-112.

Goh, S. (1984) "Soft-selling the Productivity Movement", *Productivity Digest* [Singapore], 3 (1), pp.28-35.

Gordon, A. (1985) *The Evolution of Labor Relations in Japan: Heavy Industry, 1853-1945*, Cambridge, Massachusetts, Harvard University Press.

Gow, I. (1989) "Japanese Technological Advance: Problems of Evaluation", *European Management Journal*, 16 (2), pp.127-133.

Haggard, S. and Cheng Tun Jen (1987) "State and Foreign Capital in the East Asian NICs". In Deyo, F. (ed.), *The Political Economy of the New Asian Industrialism*, Ithaca, Cornell University Press, pp.84-135.

Hakam, A. (1983) *Deliberate Restructuring of the Newly Industrialized Countries of Asia – the Case of Singapore.* Occasional Paper no. 36, School of Management, National University of Singapore, Singapore.

Hamilton, G. (1992) *Overseas Chinese Capitalism*, Working Paper no. 42, Institute of Governmental Affairs, Research Program in East Asian Business and Development, University of California, Davis.

Hamilton, G. and Kao Cheng Shu (1987) "Max Weber and the Analysis of the East Asian Industrialization", *International Sociology*, 2 (3), pp.289-300.

Hamilton, G. and Kao Cheng Shu (1990) "The Institutional Foundations of Chinese Business: The Family Firm in Taiwan", *Comparative Social Research*, 12, pp.95-112.

Hamilton, G., Orru, M. and Biggart, N. (1987) "Enterprise Groups in East Asia: An Organizational Analysis", *Shoken Keizai*, 161, pp.78-106.

Hamilton, G., Zeile, W. and Kim Wan Jin (1990) "The Network Structures of East Asian Economies". In Clegg, S. and Redding, G. (eds.), *Capitalism in Contrasting Cultures*, Berlin, de Gruyter, pp.105-130.

Hanazaki, M. (1992) "Industrial and Trade Structures of Asian Newly Industrialized Economies". In Tokunaga, S. (ed.), *Japan's Foreign Direct Investment and Asian Economic Interdependence*, Tokyo, University of Tokyo Press, pp.49-72.

Henderson, J. (1989) *The Globalization of High Technology Production: Society, Space, and Semiconductors in the Restructuring of the Modern World*, London, Routledge.

Higashi, C. and Lauter, G. (1990) *The Internationalization of the Japanese Economy*, Second edition, Boston, Klewer.

Hirata, A. (1992) "Economic Interdependence in Asia and the Pacific", *Journal of Japanese Trade and Industry*, 11 (2), pp.35-38.

Ho, K.C. (1991) "Industrial Restructuring and the Dynamics of City State Adjustments", Paper presented to the Workshop on Industrial Restructuring and Regional Adjustment in Asian NIEs, East-West Centre, Hawaii, 18-20 September.

Hofstede, G. and Bond, M. (1988) "The Confucius Connection: From Cultural Roots to Economic Growth", *Organizational Dynamics*, 17, pp.5-21.

Hong Kong and Shanghai Bank (1988) *Taiwan*, Hong Kong, Hong Kong and Shanghai Bank.

Hong Kong Government Industry Department (1991a) *1991 Survey of Overseas Investment in Hong Kong Manufacturing Industries*, Hong Kong, Hong Kong Government Industry Department.

Hong Kong Government Industry Department (1991b) *Industrial Investment in Hong Kong: Statistical Tables 1991*, Hong Kong, Hong Kong Government Industry Department.

Hooley, R. (1988) "A Comparative Study of Manufacturing Productivity Among ASEAN Countries". In Dutta, M. (ed.), *Asian Industrialization: Changing Economic Structures*, Volume I, Part A, Greenwich, Connecticut, JAI Press, pp.349-359.

Irwan, A. (1989) "Business Patronage, Class Struggle, and the Manufacturing Sector in South Korea, Indonesia and Thailand", *Journal of Contemporary Asia*, 19 (4), pp.398-434.

Ishizuna, Y. (1990) "The Transformation of Nissan – the Reform of Corporate Culture", *Long Range Planning*, 23 (3), pp.9-15.

Jansen, K. (1991)"Thailand: The Next NIC?", *Journal of Contemporary Asia*, 21 (1), pp.13-30.

JETRO (Japan External Trade Organization) (1992) *White Paper on Overseas Investment*, Tokyo, JETRO.

Johnson, C. (1987) "Political Institutions and Economic Performance: The Government-Business Relationship in Japan, South Korea and Taiwan". In Deyo, F. (ed.), *The Political Economy of the New Asian Industrialism*, Ithaca, Cornell University Press, pp.136-164.

Josey, A. (1980) *Singapore: Its Past, Present and Future*, Singapore, André Deutsch.

Jun Jong Sup (1985) "The Paradoxes of Development: Problems of South Korea's Transformation". In Kim Bun Woong, Bell, D. and Lee Chong Bum (eds.), *Administrative Dynamics and Development: The Korean Experience*, Seoul, Kyobo, pp.56-75.

Kamata, S. (1983) *Japan in the Passing Lane: An Insider's Account of Life in a Japanese Auto Factory*, London, Allen and Unwin.

Kaplinsky, R. (1991) "Industrial and Intellectual Property Rights in the Uruguay Round and Beyond", *Journal of Development Studies*, 25 (3), pp.373-400.

Kenney, M. and Florida, R. (1988) "Beyond Mass Production: Production and the Labour Process in Japan", *Politics and Society*, 16 (1), pp.121-158.

Kerr, C., Dunlop, J., Harbison, F. and Myers, C. (1960) *Industrialism and Industrial Man*, Cambridge, Massachusetts, Harvard University Press.

Kim Byung Whan (1992) *Seniority Wage System in the Far East*, Aldershot, Avebury.

Kim Choong Soo (1991) *Wage Policy and Labour Market Development of Korea*, Seoul, National Institute for Economic System and Information.

Kim Hwang Joe (1990) "The Labour Movement in Korea". In Kim, Dalchoong and Healey, G. (eds.), *Korea and the United Kingdom: Political and Economic Trends and Issues*, Seoul, Institute of East and West Studies, pp.153-196.

Kim Taigi (1990) *The Political Economy of Industrial Relations in Korea*, Seoul, Korea Labour Institute.

Kim W. Chan and Terpstra V. (1984) "Intraregional Foreign Direct Investment in the Asian Pacific Region", *Asia-Pacific Journal of Management*, 2 (1), pp.1-9.

Kim Won Bae (1991) "Industrial Restructuring and Employment in Asian NIEs", Paper presented to the Workshop on Industrial Restructuring and Regional Adjustment in Asian NIEs, East-West Centre, Hawaii, 18-20 September.

Kim Young Rae (1991) "Defining the Role of Labour in the Democratic Political Process", Paper presented to the International Conference on the Role of Labour in the 21st Century Korea, Soongsil University, Seoul, 31 October-1 November.

Kinzley, W. (1991) *Industrial Harmony in Modern Japan: The Invention of a Tradition*, London, Routledge.

Kleingartner, A. and Hsueh Yu, S. (1991) "Taiwan: An Exploration of Industrial Relations in Transition", *British Journal of Industrial Relations*, 29 (3), pp.427-445.

Kolm, S. (1985) "Must One be Buddhist to Grow? An Analysis of the Cultural Basis of Japanese Productivity". In Koslowski, P. (ed.), *Economics and Philosophy*, Tübingen, J.C.B.Mohr (Paul Siebeck), pp.221-242.

Koo, H. (1987) "The Interplay of State, Society, Class, and World System in East Asian Development: The Cases of Korea and Taiwan". In Deyo, F. (ed.), *The Political Economy of the New Asian Industrialism*, Ithaca, Cornell University Press, pp.165-181.

Koo, H., Haggard, S. and Deyo, F. (1986) "Labor and Development Strategy in the East Asian NICs", *Items*, 40 (3), pp.64-68.

Korea Development Institute (various years) *Quarterly Economic Outlook*, Seoul, Korea Development Institute.

Korea Employers' Federation (various years) *Quarterly Review*, Seoul, Korea Employers' Federation.

Korea Employers' Federation (1990) *Industrial Relations in Korea 1990*, Seoul, Korea Employers' Federation.

Korea Employers' Federation (1991) *Brief on Economy and Industrial Relations*, September, Seoul, Korea Employers' Federation.

Korea Labour Institute (1992) *International Statistical Review 1992*, Seoul, Korea Labour Institute.

Korea Labour Institute (various years) *Quarterly Review*, Seoul, Korea Labour Institute.

Krislov, J. and Leggett, C. (1984) "Singapore's Industrial Arbitration Court: Changing Roles and Current Prospects", *The Arbitration Journal*, 40 (1), pp.18-23.

Kuah Khun Eng (1990) "Confucian Ideology and Social Engineering in Singapore", *Journal of Contemporary Asia*, 20 (3), pp.371-383.

Kumazawa, M. (1994) *The Light and the Dark Side of Japanese Management*, Boulder, Westview Press.

Lee Dae Chang (1990) "Demand and Supply of Science-Technology Manpower and their Projections in Korea", Paper presented to the International Conference on Technological Manpower, Korea Institute for Economics and Technology, Chung Ang University, Seoul, 20 February.

Lee Kam Hon (1989) "The Emerging Pacific Century". In Kaynak, E. and Lee Kam Hon (eds.), *Global Business: Asia-Pacific Dimensions*, London, Routledge, pp.425-434.

Lee Sheng Yi (1978) "Business Elites in Singapore". In Chan Heng Chee and Evers, H. (eds.), *Studies in ASEAN Sociology*, Singapore, Singapore University Press, pp.38-60.

Lee Won Duck (1989) *Economic Growth and Earnings Distribution in Korea*, Seoul, Korea Labour Institute.

Leggett, C. (1984) "Airline Pilots and Public Industrial Relations: The Case of Singapore Airlines", *Indian Journal of Industrial Relations*, 20 (1), pp.27-43.

Leggett, C. (1988) "Industrial Relations and Enterprise Unionism in Singapore", *Labour and Industry*, 1 (2), pp.242-257.

Leggett, C., Wong, E. and Ariff, M. (1983) "Technological Change and Industrial Relations in Singapore", *Bulletin of Comparative Labour Relations*, 12, pp.55-75.

Li Kui Wai (1991) "Positive Adjustment Against Protectionism: The Case of Textile and Clothing Industry in Hong Kong", *The Developing Economies*, 29 (3), pp.197-209.

Lim Chong Yah (1984) *Economic Restructuring in Singapore*, Singapore, Federal Publications.

Lim, L. and Pang Eng Fong (1984) "Labour Strategies and the High-tech Challenge", *Euro-Asia Business Review*, 3 (2), pp.27-31.

Limqueco, P., McFarlane, B. and Odhnoff, J. (1989) *Labour and Industry in ASEAN*, Manilla, Journal of Contemporary Asia Publishers.

Lin Chin Yuang (1988) "Taiwan's Declining Investment Ratio and its Persistent Trade Surplus in the United States". In Dutta, M. (ed.), *Asian Industrialization: Changing Economic Structures*, Volume I, Part A, Greenwich, Connecticut, JAI Press, pp.139-158.

Lin Ho Lin (1991) *Chinese Economic Familism and the Diversification of Economic Organizations: A Study of Taiwanese Business Groups*, Working Paper no. 40, Institute of Governmental Affairs, Research Program in East Asian Business and Development, University of California, Davis.

Lin, T.B. and Chyuan Tuan (1988) "Industrial Evolution and Changes in Trade Environment: A Case Study of Consumer Electronics and Textile/Garment Industries in Hong Kong". In Dutta, M. (ed.), *Asian Industrialization: Changing Economic Structures*, Volume I, Part A, Greenwich, Connecticut, JAI Press, pp.159-186.

Linder, S. (1986) *The Pacific Century: Economic and Political Consequences of Asian-Pacific Dynamism*, Stanford, Stanford University Press.

Littler, C. (1982) *The Development of the Labour Process in Capitalist Societies*, London, Heinemann.

Liu, M. (1990) "Kinder and Gentler?", *Newsweek*, 10 December, pp.32-36.

Lo Shiu Hing (1990) "Political Participation in Hong Kong, Korea and Taiwan", *Journal of Contemporary Asia*, 20 (2), pp.239-253.

Low, P. (1984) "Singapore-Based Subsidiaries of US Multinationals and Singaporean Firms: A Comparative Management Study", *Asia-Pacific Journal of Management*, 2 (1), pp.29-39.

Lubeck, P. (1992) "Malaysian Industrialization, Ethnic Divisions, and the NIC Model: The Limits to Replication". In Applebaum, R. and Henderson, J. (eds.), *States and Development in the Asian Pacific Rim*, London, Sage, pp.176-198.

Lui Tai Lok and Chiu, S. (1991) "Industrial Restructuring and Labour Market Adjustment under Positive Non-interventionism: The Case of Hong Kong", Paper presented to the Workshop on Industrial Restructuring and Regional Adjustment in Asian NIEs, East-West Centre, Hawaii, 18-20 September.

Ma, T. (1988) "The Canton Connection", *Far Eastern Economic Review*, 28 July, pp.48-49.

Manpower Planning Department, Executive Yuan, Republic of China (1990) *Monthly Bulletin of Manpower Statistics*, Taipei.

McDermott, M. (1992) "The Internationalization of the South Korean and Taiwanese Electronics Industries: The European Dimension". In Young, S. and Hamill, J. (eds.), *Europe and the Multinationals: Issues and Responses for the 1990s*, Aldershot, Elgar, pp.206-231.

Milton-Smith, J. (1986) "Japanese Management Overseas: International Business Strategy and the Case of Singapore". In Clegg, S., Dunphy, C. and Redding, G. (eds.), *The Enterprise and Management in East Asia*, Hong Kong, Centre for Asian Studies, University of Hong Kong, pp.395-412.

Ministry of Labour, Republic of Korea (various years) *Yearbook of Labour Statistics*, Seoul, Ministry of Labour, Republic of Korea.

Ministry of Labour, Republic of Singapore (various years) *Singapore Yearbook of Labour Statistics*, Seoul, Ministry of Labour, Republic of Singapore.

Ministry of Trade and Industry, Republic of Singapore (1990) *Economic Survey of Singapore 1990*, Singapore, National Printer.

Mok, K. (1980) "Feasibility Study for Promoting Industrial Democracy in Asia: The Singapore Case". In International Labour Office (ed.), *Industrial Democracy in Asia*, Bangkok, Friedrich Ebert Stiftung, pp.293-319.

Moore, J. (1987) "Japanese Industrial Relations", *Labour and Industry*, 1 (1), pp.140-155.

Moore, J. (1988) "Summer of Discontent", *Far Eastern Economic Review*, 8 September 1988, pp.116-117.

Morishima, M. (1982) *Why Has Japan Succeeded? Western Technology and the Japanese Ethos*, Cambridge, Cambridge University Press.

Morris-Suzuki, T. (1992a) "Re-shaping the International Division of Labour: Japanese Manufacturing Investment in South East Asia". In Morris, J. (ed.), *Japan and the Global Economy*, London, Routledge, pp.135-153.

Morris-Suzuki, T. (1992b) "Japanese Technology and the New International Division of Knowledge in Asia. In Tokunaga, S. (ed.), *Japan's Foreign Direct Investment and Asian Economic Interdependence*, Tokyo, University of Tokyo Press, pp.135-152.

Munday, M., Morris, J. and Wilkinson, B. (1992) *Factories or Warehouses? A Regional Perspective on Japanese Transplant Manufacturing in the UK*, Working Paper no. 18, Japanese Management Research Unit, Cardiff Business School, Cardiff.

Muraoka, T. (1986) *ASEAN: The Regional Economic Collaboration in Perspective*, Occasional Paper no. 3, Institute of Social Studies, Centre for Contemporary Asian Studies, Chinese University of Hong Kong, Hong Kong.

National Defense Counsel for Victims of Karoshi (1990) *Karoshi: When the Corporate Warrior Dies*, Tokyo, Mado-Sha.

National Trades Union Congress (1970) *Why Labour Must Go Modern!*, Singapore, NTUC.

Negandhi, A., Yuen, E. and Eshghi, G. (1987) "Localization of Japanese Subsidiaries in South East Asia", *Asia-Pacific Journal of Management*, 5 (1), pp.67-79.

Ng Kiat Chong (1983) "Labour-Management Cooperation System: National Productivity Board's Perspective". In National Productivity Board (ed.), *Proceedings of the Tripartite Convention on Work Excellence through Joint Consultation*, Singapore, National Productivity Board, pp.22-27.

Ng Fung Sau (1988) "Industrial Relations in Hong Kong", Unpublished MBA dissertation, Cardiff Business School, Cardiff.

Ng, N. (1984) "The Implementation of Work Improvement Teams in the Singapore Civil Service", *Productivity Digest*, pp.82-108.

Ng Sek Hong and Sit Fung Shuen (1989) *Labour Relations and Labour Conditions in Hong Kong*, London, MacMillan.

Nikei, Y., Ohtsui, M. and Levin, D. (1983) "A Comparative Study of Management Practices and Workers in an American and a Japanese Firm in Hong Kong". In Ng Sek Hong and Levin, D. (eds.), *Contemporary Issues in Hong Kong Industrial Relations*, Hong Kong, University of Hong Kong, Centre for Asian Studies.

Nolan, P. (1990) "Assessing Economic Growth in the Asian NICs", *Journal of Contemporary Asia*, 20 (1), pp.41-63.

Oehlers, A. (1991) "The National Wages Council of Singapore: Issues for Consideration", *Journal of Contemporary Asia*, 21 (3), pp.285-300.

Ogasawara, K. (1992) "Japanese Personal Appraisal: Individualized Race for Power and Imposed Involvement", Paper presented to the Conference on Japanese Management Styles: An International Comparative Perspective, Cardiff Business School, Cardiff, 28-29 September.

Okumura, H. (1991) "Enterprise Groups in Japan", *JCR Financial Digest*, April, pp.1-4.

Oliver, N., Morris, J. and Wilkinson, B. (1992) "The Impact of Japanese Manufacturing Investment on European Industry". In Young, S. and Hamill, J. (eds.), *Europe and the Multinationals: Issues and Responses for the 1990s*, Aldershot, Elgar, pp.185-231.

Oliver, N. and Wilkinson, B. (1992) *The Japanization of British Industry: Developments in the 1990s*, Oxford, Blackwell.

Orru, M. (1991) *Institutional Cooperation in Japanese and German Capitalism*, Working Paper no. 35, Institute of Governmental Affairs, Research Program in East Asian Business and Development, University of California, Davis.

Ouchi, W. (1981) *Theory Z: How American Business Can Meet the Japanese Challenge*, Boston, Addison Wesley.

Pang Eng Fong (1981) "Singapore". In Blum, A. (ed.), *International Handbook of Industrial Relations: Contemporary Developments and Research*, US, Connecticut, Greenwood Press, pp.481-497.

Pang Eng Fong (1982) *Education, Manpower and Development in Singapore*, Singapore, Singapore University Press.

Pang Eng Fong (1985) "Distinctive Features of Two City States' Development", Paper presented to a Symposium on In Search of an East Asian Development Model, Asia and World Institute (Taipei) and Council on Religion and International Affairs (New York).

Pang Eng Fong and Lim, L. (1982) "Foreign Labour and Economic Development in Singapore", *International Migration Review*, 16 (3), pp.548-575.

Park Duk Je (1992) "Industrial Relations in Korea", *International Journal of Human Resource Management*, 3 (1), pp.105-124.

Park Se Il (1988) "Republic of Korea: Bank A", "Republic of Korea: Bank B", "Republic of Korea: Engineering Company A", "Republic of Korea: Electrical Appliance Company A". In International Labour Office (ed.), *Technological Change, Work Organization and Pay: Lessons from Asia*, Geneva, ILO, pp.57-64, 65-70, 99-106, 125-134.

Park Young Ki (1990) *Labour Relations and Labour Regulation*, Unpublished paper, Institute for Labour and Management, Sogang University, Seoul.

Park Young Ki (1992) 'Korea'. In Deery, S. (ed.), *Labour Law and Labour Relations in the Pacific*, Melbourne, University of Melbourne Press.

Pascale, R. and Athos, A. (1982) *The Art of Japanese Management*, Harmondsworth, Penguin.

Patarapanich, S., Leggett, C. and Wilkinson, B. (1987) "Labour Management in Singapore: The Management of Thai Workers in the Construction Industry", Paper presented to the International Industrial Relations Association Second European Regional Congress, Herzlia, 13-17 December.

Poon, T. (1991) "Labour Contract System in China", Paper presented to the APROS Conference on New Trends in Organizations, Technologies and Information Systems, University of Marketing and Distribution Sciences, Kobe, 25-28 June.

Poon, T. (1992) "Western Technology in a Chinese Context: The New Technologies and the Organization of Work in Hong Kong". In Marceau, J. (ed.), *Re-working the World: Organizations, Technologies and Cultures in Comparative Perspective*, Berlin, de Gruyter, pp.205-235.

Presidential Commission on Economic Restructuring (1988) *Realigning Korea's Priorities for Economic Advance*, Seoul, Presidential Commission on Economic Restructuring.

Pucetti, R. (1972) "Authoritarian Government and Academic Subservience: The University of Singapore", *Minerva*, 10 (2), pp.223-241.

Pucik, V. (1985) "Managing Japan's White Collar Workers", *Euro-Asia Business Review*, 4 (3), pp.16-21.

Rabushka, A. (1987) *The New China: Comparative Economic Development in Mainland China, Taiwan, and Hong Kong*, San Francisco, Westview Press.

Redding, G. and Richardson, S. (1972) "Job Satisfaction and Management Styles in South East Asia", *Asia Research Bulletin*, 1-31 July, pp.1066-1088.

Redding, G. and Whitley, R. (1990) "Beyond Bureaucracy: Towards a Comparative Analysis of Forms of Economic Resource Coordination and Control". In Clegg, S. and Redding, G. (eds.), *Capitalism in Contrasting Cultures*, Berlin, de Gruyter, pp.79-104.

Reid, D. and Lee Kam Hon (1989) "Strategic Planning Practices in Hong Kong: A Cultural Dimension". In Kaynak, E. and Lee Kam Hon (eds.), *Global Business: Asia-Pacific Dimensions*, London, Routledge, 238-257.

Republic of China (1990) *Yearbook of Labour Statistics 1989*, Taipai, Executive Yuan, Republic of China.

Rhee Yang Soo (1985) "A Cross-Cultural Comparison of Korean and American Managerial Styles: An Inventory of Propositions". In Kim Bun Woong, Bell, D. and Lee Chong Bum (eds.), *Administrative Dynamics and Development: The Korean Experience*, Seoul, Kyobo, pp.78-98.

Riddle, D. and Sours, M. (1984) "Service Industries as Growth Leaders on the Pacific Rim", *Asia-Pacific Journal of Management*, 3 (1), pp.190-199.

Rigg, J. (1991) *South East Asia: A Region in Transition*, London, Unwin Hyman.

Robison, R. (1989) "Structures of Power and the Industrialization Process in South East Asia", *Journal of Contemporary Asia*, 19 (4), pp.371-397.

Robbins, S. (1983) "Theory Z From a Power-control Perspective", *California Management Review*, 25 (2), pp.67-75.

Rodan, G. (1989) *The Political Economy of Singapore's Industrialization*, London, MacMillan.

Rosa, L. (1990) "The Singapore State and Trade Union Incorporation", *Journal of Contemporary Asia*, 20 (4), pp.487-508.

Sako, M. (1987) "Buyer-Supplier Relations in Britain: A Case of Japanization?", Paper presented to the Conference on The Japanization of British Industry, Cardiff Business School, Cardiff, 17-18 September.

Saravanamuttu, J. (1986) "Imperialism, Dependent Development and ASEAN Regionalism", *Journal of Contemporary Asia*, 16 (2), pp.204-222.

Saravanamuttu, J. (1988) "Japanese Economic Penetration in ASEAN in the Context of the International Division of Labour", *Journal of Contemporary Asia*, 18 (2), pp.139-164.

Selmer, J. (1987) "Swedish Managers' Perceptions of Singaporean Work Related Values", *Asia-Pacific Journal of Management*, 5 (1), pp.80-88.

Sethi, S., Namiki, N. and Swanson, C. (1984) *The False Promise of the Japanese Miracle*, London, Pitman.

Sewell, G. and Wilkinson, B. (1992) "'Someone to Watch over Me': Surveillance, Discipline and the Just-in-time Labour Process", *Sociology*, 26 (2), pp.271-289.

Shepard, J., Chung, C.H. and Dollinger, M. (1989) "Max Weber Revisited: Some Lessons from East Asian Capitalistic Development", *Asia-Pacific Journal of Management*, 6 (2), pp.307-322.

Shim Jae Hoon (1989a) "The Making of Lee", *Far Eastern Economic Review*, 16 March, pp.19-20.

Shim Jae Hoon (1989b) "To the Left, March!", *Far Eastern Economic Review*, 2 March, p.19.

Sit, V.F.S. and Wong, S.L. (1989) *Small and Medium Industries in an Export Oriented Economy: The Case of Hong Kong*, Hong Kong, Hong Kong University, Centre of Asian Studies.

So, A.Y. and Kwitko, L. (1990) "The New Middle Class and the Democratic Movement in Hong Kong", *Journal of Contemporary Asia*, 20 (3), pp.384-398.

Song Hui Sze (1992) The Transferability of Japanese Management Practices in Hong Based Subsidiaries, Unpublished MBA dissertation, Cardiff Business School, Cardiff.

Stahl, C. (1984) "Singapore's Foreign Workforce: Some Reflections on its Benefits and Costs", *International Migration Review*, 18 (1), pp.37-49.

Tabata, H. (1989) *Changes in Plant-Level Trade Union Organizations: A Case Study of the automobile Industry*, Occasional Papers in Labour Problem and Social Policy no. 3, Institue of Social Science, University of Tokyo, Tokyo.

Tam, S. (1990) "Centrifugal Versus Centripetal Growth Processes: Contrasting Ideal Types for Conceptualizing the Developmental Patterns of Chinese and Japanese Firms". In Clegg, S. and Redding, G. (eds.), *Capitalism in Contrasting Cultures*, Berlin, de Gruyter, pp.153-183.

Tan Chee Hwat (1984) "Human Resource Management in Singapore: Some Current Issues". In Anantaraman, V., Chong Li Choy, Richardson, S. and Tan Chee Hwat (eds.), *Human Resource Management: Concepts and Perspectives*, Singapore, Singapore University Press, pp.75-85.

Tang, Y.W. and Lin, T.M. (1984) "Uniform Accounting System for State Owned Enterprises in Taiwan", *Asia Pacific Journal of Management*, 2 (1), pp.10-21.

Tank, A. (1992) "The Quality Puzzle: How Has Korean Industry Mastered Technology So Fast?", *Papers of the British Association for Korean Studies*, 2, pp.51-64.

Ting Wen Lee (1988) "Technological and Investment Risks in East Asia: Protective Measures for Intellectual/Industrial Property Rights", Paper presented to the Conference of the Asia Pacific Researchers in Organization Studies on Firms, Management, the State and Economic Cultures, University of Hong Kong, Hong Kong, 6-8 April.

Tokunaga, S. (1992) "Japan's FDI Promoting Systems and Intra-Asia Networks: New Investment and Trade Systems Created by the Borderless Economy". In Tokunaga, S. (ed.), *Japan's Foreign Investment and Asian Economic Interdependence*, Tokyo, Tokyo University Press, pp.5-48.

Tricker, R. (1990) "Corporate Governance: A Ripple on the Cultural Reflection". In Clegg, S. and Redding, G. (eds.), *Capitalism in Contrasting Cultures*, Berlin, de Gruyter, pp.187-214.

Tsang Chiu Hok (1992) *The Japanization of Hong Kong Industry*, Unpublished MBA dissertation, University of Hong Kong Business School, Hong Kong.

Tu Wei Ming (1984) *Confucian Ethics Today: The Singapore Challenge*, Singapore, Federal Publications.

Turner, H., Fosh, P., Gardner, M., Hart, K., Morris, R., Ng Sek Hong, Quinlan, M. and Yerbury, D. (1980) *The Last Colony: But Whose?*, Cambridge, Cambridge University Press.

Turner, H., Fosh, P. and Ng Sek Hong (1991) *Between Two Societies: Hong Kong Labour in Transition*, Hong Kong, University of Hong Kong, Centre of Asian Studies.

Turpin, D. (1991) "'Gambare': Never Say Die! Why Japanese Companies Won't Give Up", *Perspectives for Managers*, (3), pp.1-4.

Wade, R. (1990) *Governing the Market: Economic Theory and the Role of Government in East Asian Industrialization*, Princeton, New Jersey, Princeton University Press.

Wang Yen Kyung (1990) "Education System for Technology Manpower in Korea", Paper presented to the International Conference on Technological Manpower, Korea Institute for Economics and Technology, Chung Ang University, Seoul, 20 February.

Weber, M. (1930) *The Protestant Ethic and the Spirit of Capitalism*, London, Allen and Unwin.

Weber, M. (1951) *The Religion of China: Confucianism and Taoism*, New York, Free Press.

Wee Chow Hou, Lee Seok Kuan and Farley, J. (1989) "Corporate Planning Practices of Companies in Singapore: A Comparison by Nationalities". In Kaynak, E. and Lee Kam Hon (eds.), *Global Business: Asia-Pacific Dimensions*, London, Routledge, pp.200-237.

Westphal, L., Kim Lin Su and Dahlman, C. (1984) *Reflections on Korea's Acqui-sition of Technological Capability*, Report no. DRD77, Development Research Department, World Bank, Washington DC.

Whitehill, A. and Takezawa, S. (1986) *The Other Worker*, Honolulu, East-West Centre Press.

Whitley, R. (1992) *Business Systems in East Asia: Firms, Markets and Societies*, London, Sage.

Wilkinson, B. (1986) "Human Resources in Singapore's Second Industrial Rev-olution", *Industrial Relations Journal*, 17 (2), pp.99-114.

Wilkinson, B. (1988) "Social Engineering in Singapore", *Journal of Contempo-rary Asia*, 18 (2), pp.165-188.

Wilkinson, B. and Leggett, C. (1985) "Human and Industrial Relations in Sin-gapore: The Management of Compliance", *Euro-Asia Business Review*, 4 (3), pp.9-15.

Williams, K., Haslam, C., Williams, J. Adcroft, A. and Sukhdev, J. (1992) *Fac-tories or Warehouses?: Japanese Manufacturing FDI in Britain and the US*, Occasional Papers on Business, Economy and Society no. 6, Polytechnic of East London, London.

Wimalasiri, J. (1984) "Correlates of Work Values of Singapore Employees", *Singapore Management Review*, 6 (1).

Wolf, M. (1985) *The Japanese Conspiracy: Their Plot to Dominate the World and How to Deal With It*, Sevenoaks, New English Library.

Wong, A. (1979) "The National Family Planning Programme and Changing Fam-ily Life". In Kuo, E. and Wong, A. (eds.), *The Contemporary Family in Singa-pore*, Singapore, Singapore University Press, pp.211-238.

Wong, C.F. (1990) "Labour Shortages in Hong Kong in the 1990s: Problems and Prospects", Unpublished MBA dissertation, Cardiff Business School, Cardiff.

Wong Yim Yu and Maher, T. (1992) "Textile and Apparel Industries: Technolog-ical Attempts of Pacific Rim Countries to Overcome Protectionism", *Manage-ment Research News*, 15 (9), pp.1-7.

Woronoff, J. (1983) *Korea's Economy: Man-made Miracle*, Oregon, Pace Inter-national Research.

Wu, F. (1991) "The ASEAN Economies in the 1990s and Singapore's Regional Role", *California Management Review*, Fall, pp.103-114.

Wu Rong I (1988) "The Distinctive Features of Taiwan's Development". In Berger, P. and Hsia Hsin Huang (eds.), *In Search of an East Asian Development Model*, New Jersey, Transaction Books, pp.179-196.

Yamamoto, K. (1990) *The 'Japanese Style Industrial Relations' and an 'Informal' Employee Organization: A Case Study of the Ohgi-kai at T Electric*, Occasional Papers in Labour Problem and Social Policy no. 3, Institue of Social Science, University of Tokyo, Tokyo.

Yeo Jeu Nam (1984) "Teambuilding for Higher Productivity: Improving Labour-Management Relations – A Framework for Action", *Productivity Digest* [Singapore], 2 (12), pp.64-70.

You Poh Seng and Lim Chong Yah (1984) "Introduction". In You Poh Seng and Lim Chong Yah, *Singapore: Twenty Five Years of Development*, Singapore, Nan Yang Xing Zhou Lianhe Zaobao, pp.1-10.

Zeile, W. (1990) *Industrial Policy and Organizational Efficiency: The Korean Chebol Examined*, Working Paper no. 30, Institute of Governmental Affairs, Research Program in East Asian Business and Development, University of California, Davis.

Newspapers, etc.

Business Week
China News (Taiwan)
China Post (Taiwan)
Far Eastern Economic Review
The Economist
Financial Times (UK)
The Free China Journal (Taiwan)
The Guardian (UK)
The Independent (UK)
Japan Times
Korea Economic Weekly
Korea Herald
Korea Times
New Straits Times (Malaysia)
The Observer (UK)
Straits Times (Singapore)
Sunday Times (Singapore)

Index

Walter de Gruyter
Berlin • New York

Management in Western Europe
Society, Culture and Organization in Twelve Nations
Ed. by Hickson, David J.
25,0 x 15,5 cm. XIV, 288 p. 3 fig. 1993. Bound. DM 118,- / öS 921,- / sFr 114,- ISBN 3110141744
Pb. DM 48,- / öS 375,- / sFr 49,.- ISBN 3110127105
(de Gruyter Studies in Organization, 47)

Eberwein, Wilhelm / Tholen, Jochen
Euro-Manager or Splendid Isolation?
International Management - an Anglo-German Comparison
23,0 x 15,5 cm. IX, 266 p. 4 tab. 1993. Bound. DM 110,- / öS 858,- / sFr 107,- ISBN 3110134810
(de Gruyter Studies in Organization, 48)

Bolle De Bal, Marcel
The Double Games of Participation
Pay, Performance and Culture
Transl. by Shayler, Irene.
23,5 x 16,0 cm. XIV, 265 p. 1993. Bound. DM 138,- / öS 1.077,- / sFr 133,- ISBN 3110129728
(de Gruyter Studies in Organization, 43)

International Management Research
Looking to the Future
Ed. by Wong-Rieger, Durhane / Rieger, Fritz.
23,0 x 15,5 cm. IX, 157 p. 2 fig. 7 tab. 1993. Bound. DM 98,- / öS 765,- / sFr 96,-
ISBN 3110133784
(de Gruyter Studies in Organization, 46)

Industrial Relations Around the World
Labor Relations for Multinational Companies
Ed. by Rothman, Miriam / Briscoe, Dennis R. / Nacamulli, Raoul C.
23,0 x 15,5 cm. XX, 419 p. 10 fig. 23 tab. 1993. Bound. DM 130,- / öS 1.014,- / sFr 126,-
ISBN 3110125447
Pb. DM 68,- / öS 531,- / sFr 67,- ISBN 3110125471
(de Gruyter Studies in Organization, 45)

Blunt, Peter / Jones, Merrick L.
Managing Organisations in Africa
23,0 x 15,5 cm. XIV, 356 p. 1992. DM 148,- / öS 1.155,- / sFr 143,- ISBN 311012646X
(de Gruyter Studies in Organization, 40)

Blunt, Peter / Jones, Merrick L. / Richards, David
Managing Organisations in Africa: Readings, Cases, and Exercises
23,0 x 15,5 cm. XII, 219 p. 6 figs and 4 tabs. 1993. Pb. DM 48,- / öS 375,- / sFr 49,-
ISBN 3110136716
(de Gruyter Studies in Organization, 49)

Bergmann, Jörg R.
Discreet Indiscretions
The Social Organization of Gossip
Transl. by Bednarz, John. In Collab. with Kafka Barron, Eva.
23,0 x 15,0 cm. XVI, 206 p. 1993. Bound. DM 84,- / öS 655,- / sFr 82,- ISBN 3110142058
Pb. DM 42,- / öS 328,- / sFr 43,- ISBN 3110142066
(Communication and Social Order)
Aldine de Gruyter

Walter de Gruyter & Co., Berlin • New York Postfach 30 34 21, D - 10728 Berlin
Tel.: (030) 2 60 05 - 0, Fax: (030) 2 60 05 - 2 51